The
FLORIDA
Quiz Book

How Much Do You Know about Florida?

Pineapple Press, Inc.
Sarasota, Florida

Dedicated to the pursuit of knowledge

Acknowledgments

The faculty, staff, and students of Hallandale High School have earned my gratitude for their interest and support, especially Dr. Fred Hartford, Mrs. Gibson, Ms. Margaret Kolodziej, Mr. Rivera, and Miss Jeanette Pablo. Kind appreciation goes to the faculty and staff at South Plantation High School, with special thanks going to the science chair, Mr. Molaka. I gratefully acknowledge the faculty, staff, and students of Lanier James Education Center, with special thanks going to Ms. Penny Nurnburg, Mrs. Anna Calderon, Mr. Walden, Ms. Steff, and D. I. Dinsey for their kindness and encouragement. Thanks also to Cypress Bay High School faculty, Marjory Stoneman Douglas High School faculty, and science teachers Ms. Ellen F. Cohen and Ms. Judy Marburger. The Broward County Art Guild merits special recognition for the drawings that appear in this book. Special thanks go to artists Julia Andrews, Elizabeth Jurado, and Deanna Brennen. Big thanks go to David and June Cussen and everyone at Pineapple Press for their appreciation of the fascinating state of Florida and for the great job they do putting it into books.

Inquiries should be addressed to:

Pineapple Press, Inc.
P.O. Box 3889
Sarasota, Florida 34230
www.pineapplepress.com

Library of Congress Cataloging-in-Publication Data

Temple, Hollee, 1956-
The Florida quiz book : how much do you know about Florida? / Hollee Temple.— 1st ed.
p. cm.
Includes bibliographical references and index.
ISBN-13: 978-1-56164-353-0 (pbk. : alk. paper)
ISBN-10: 1-56164-353-X (pbk. : alk. paper)
 1. Florida—Miscellanea. I. Title.
F311.5.T46 2006
975.9—dc22
2005033054

First Edition
10 9 8 7 6 5 4 3 2 1

Printed in the United States of America

Contents

Introduction

When I became a substitute teacher I faced the challenge of keeping students engaged in learning activities until the end of class. During the last ten minutes of class students tend to chat and stand by the door waiting for the bell to ring. So I began asking them questions that related to their lessons. The students loved this risk-free educational question-and-answer activity, which I successfully employed until the bell rang.

The first group of questions I wrote happened to be about the Everglades. I used these questions in many science classes in a south Florida school district where, in the recent past, the Everglades occupied the very land upon which many of the schools had been built. I became alarmed at how little high school students knew about the nearby Everglades, and I soon found this to be the case with other Florida environmental topics as well. Why was I anxious about students lack of knowledge about Florida's environment? As residents of Florida, we are all responsible for taking care of our state. In just a few years these same students will have the duties of protecting Florida and empowering their children and communities to do so as well.

Florida is one of the most bio-diverse states in the United States and has unique species and ecosystems that are not found anywhere else in the world. Tourists, who drive Florida's economy and make a state income tax unnecessary, are attracted by the states many natural wonders. The population in Florida is exploding such that natural resources are being strained and reduced to critical levels. Our future depends on the state of our state, and students must be prepared to take care of it—yet many are not. This book is a small contribution toward that goal.

Making Learning Fun

Today's teachers compete with a myriad of entertainments for students' attention. Videos, music, video games, food, e-mail, and talking are the chief interests of most students. In order to get their attention, we need to make learning fun, too. *The Florida Quiz Book* question-and-answer activity successfully engages students because it is both interactive and fun. Question-and-answer activities not only have the interactive appeal of a game show, they make students think and articulate. Students are often more motivated to learn if learning is fun.

Another appealing aspect of *The Florida Quiz Book* is that it stimulates discussions and prompts students to ask questions. In the classroom, when a student vocalized a related question, I seized the opportunity to make suggestions that might lead to further reading. For example, I might suggest that the subject of the question would make a great research topic. Sometimes I asked for a student volunteer to find the answer to the question and share it with the class. Curiosity motivates students to read.

Most teachers will agree that students need to read more. Teachers who use this book in their classrooms will find many opportunities to leverage student interest and suggest further reading on topics of interest to students and thereby encourage interdisciplinary reading, especially in English, science, and history classes. Math teachers might also find the statistics section useful in their classrooms.

Origins and Evolution of Facts

Many of the facts represented in this book were collected from the most currently available official state documents. Most sources of information were written within the last five to ten years. Older texts provided some historical facts.

Most historical facts are static, yet it is possible for facts about the past to change. For instance, future archaeological discoveries may change the name of the oldest shipwreck off Florida's coast. Future events will certainly change answers to some of the questions asked in this book; for example, the tonnage of solid waste recycled in Florida every year will likely change, museums and businesses may change their names, and endangered species may make a comeback or become extinct.

The most common answers are given for questions that have multiple answers. In some cases there may be alternative answers to a question, such as a regional moniker that could exist for, say, a hoary bat or a specific sea shell. The author hopes that such cases will give readers points of discussion and research.

How to Use This Book

Classroom teachers will find lesson planning support in the Sunshine State Standards Index, which cross references Sunshine State Standards Science and History benchmarks with the sections of the book that reinforce benchmark topics and concepts.

Please note that on the Pineapple Press website, www.pineapplepress.com, you can find a list of the questions in this book without the answers. You can use this for any activities—tests, for example—for which students should not see the answers.

There are many ways this book might be used to stimulate learning in classrooms, libraries, homes, and educational recreation programs. Listed below are some ways that question-and-answer (Q&A) activities might be employed to make learning fun.

1. *The Florida Quiz Book* could be used for family activities. Each family member could take a turn asking questions from their favorite categories, or play "Jeopardy" style (stating the answer first and then the players must give the corresponding question).

2. Teachers might declare that a Q&A game will be played on Fridays during the last half hour of class, since students are often restless and difficult to engage on Fridays. Naming the game something like "Fun Factual Fridays" suggests that the learning is for enjoyment. Keep score. Give one point for each correct answer and award a prize at the end of the day, month, or quarter. (Local merchants are often willing to donate small prizes.)

3. Families, librarians, activity planners, and teachers can encourage pre-game reading and research by distributing, announcing, or posting a list of Q&A game topics ahead of time. The bibliography and the section on further reading may be copied for educational purposes. Appendix A includes a topic list that can be freely copied as well.

4. Give students or teams lists of identical or unique questions and let them look up answers on the Internet. Then let them share what they found in a group discussion.

5. Encourage students to jot down keywords of interest for further discussion and research. Consider giving a prize or recognition to the best keyword lists.

6. Encourage students to improve their vocabulary by discussing words they might not know.

7. Parents and teachers might allow students to earn extra credit for:
• writing a short three-paragraph report on a Florida quiz question or topic that interests them. There is a lot of information on Florida science topics available on the Internet.
• joining or attending a conservation group
• giving an oral report on a Florida environmental issue or on the activities of a Florida conservation group

8. Suggest that students research topics that interest them.

9. Encourage students to listen carefully to all the questions and answers by telling them that some of the questions and answers give clues about the answers to other questions, and that questions might be repeated.

10. Some ideas for game playing:
    • Round-robin in which each student takes a turn row by row.
    • Small teams in which the group has one minute to agree on an answer.
    • Pair ESOL students with good English speakers.
    • For questions that have more than one answer, give one point for each correct answer.

11. Take *The Florida Quiz Book* on your next road trip. Question-and-answer games are fun, educational, and entertaining for the whole family.

1
Agriculture in Florida

1.   How many farmers grow commercial crops in Florida?
     44,000

2.   How many different commercial crops are grown in Florida every year?
     about 280

3.   How many dollars are generated by Florida's agricultural industry?
     over $50 billion in 2000

4.   What is the annual cash value of Florida's crops?
     over $6 billion

5.   Where does Florida rank nationally in the export of agricultural products?
     16th in 2004

6.   Where does Florida rank nationally in the production of fresh vegetables?
     2nd, with annual sales of $1.5 billion in 2000

7.   Where do Florida's ranchers and herdsmen rank nationally in the production of beef, poultry, and pork?
     among the top 26 in 2000

8.   How many farm workers are employed by Florida farmers?
     about 94,000 in 2000

9.   How many acres of citrus groves are cultivated in Florida?
     857,681 acres in 2000

10. In 2000, how many acres of land in Florida were involved in vegetable production?
     350,800 acres

11. In 2000 how many total farm acres were in Florida?
     10,545,217 acres

12. What type of fruit does Florida grow more of than any other state?
     citrus

13. In 2000 what citrus fruit did Florida produce more of than any other country in the world?

> *Grapefruit. In 2000 Florida produced 42.6% of the world's grapefruit crop.*

14. What country produces more oranges than Florida?

> *Brazil*

15. In 2000 how many citrus trees did Florida citrus growers cultivate?

> *106.7 million*

16. What percentage of oranges grown in Florida are processed into orange juice each year?

> *95%*

17. How many gallons of orange juice did Florida produce in the 1999–2000 season?

> *more than 1.4 billion gallons*

18. What county is Florida's leading agricultural producer?

> *Palm Beach County*

19. What county is Florida's second leading agricultural producer?

> *Miami-Dade County*

20. What Florida county produces the most seafood?

> *Monroe County*

21. On average, how many pounds of seafood are harvested annually in Florida?

> *over 90 million pounds*

22. True or False: Florida is the nation's number two producer of horticultural products.

> *True*

23. What is the annual worth of Florida's horticulture products?

> *over $1.4 billon*

24. Florida is the leading producer of what three floriculture products?

> • *ferns*
> • *gladioli*
> • *house plants*

25. In the year 2000, Florida was the leading U.S. producer of what six fruits and vegetables?

> • *cucumber*
> • *okra*
> • *radish*
> • *snap bean*
> • *tomato*
> • *watermelon*

26.   What five citrus crops does Florida produce more of than any other state in the U.S.?
- *grapefruit*
- *lime*
- *orange*
- *tangelo*
- *tangerine*

27.   What does the Florida Department of Agriculture do to protect Florida agriculture from biological and criminal threats?
- *inspects food products and livestock*
- *investigates and prosecutes agricultural thefts*
- *performs tests*
- *regulates pesticides*
- *eradicates pests and diseases*

28.   What does the Florida Department of Agriculture do to promote Florida agriculture?
- *markets Florida's products*
- *operates farmers markets*

29.   What does the Florida Department of Agriculture do to protect the environment?
- *conducts tree planting programs*
- *develops best management practices*
- *manages more than 800,000 acres of state owned forest lands*
- *tests water wells and groundwater for pesticides and nitrates*

30.   Name some of Florida's most valuable farm crops.

- *avocado*
- *cabbage*
- *cucumber*
- *eggplant*
- *eggs*
- *feed corn*
- *foliage and floriculture*
- *grapefruit*
- *green pepper*
- *hay*
- *honey*
- *milk*
- *orange*
- *potato*
- *snap bean*
- *strawberry*
- *sugar cane*
- *sweet corn*
- *tangelo*
- *tobacco*
- *tomato*

2
Architecture in Florida

Anne Pfeiffer Chapel

31. What local building materials are used in Florida's architecture?
- *cypress*
- *heart pine*
- *limestone*
- *oyster tabby—a mixture of shells, sand, and limestone*

32. What style of architecture was originated by Addison Mizner, one of Florida's most famous architects?
Mediterranean Revival

33. Which architectural styles did Mizner combine to create Mediterranean Revival architecture?
- *Gothic*
- *Italian*
- *Moorish*
- *Renaissance*
- *Spanish*
- *Venetian*

Central Florida

34. In what town is the world's largest collection of Frank Lloyd Wright buildings?
Lakeland, Florida

35. What Florida college campus was designed by Frank Lloyd Wright?
Florida Southern College in Lakeland, Florida

36. What was on the site of Florida Southern College before it became a college?
an orange grove

37. How many Frank Lloyd Wright structures are on the campus of Florida Southern College?
12

38.   What is the most expensive Frank Lloyd Wright structure on the campus of Florida Southern College?

> *The Polk County Science Building, which was completed in 1958 at a cost of $1 million.*

39.   What Florida Southern College buildings were built with student labor?
> * *Anne Pfeiffer Chapel*
> * *E.T. Roux Library*
> * *Three Seminar Buildings*

40.   When did construction of Florida Southern College begin?
> *May 24, 1938*

41.   How many people visit Florida Southern College each year to view the legacy of Frank Lloyd Wright?
> *15,000–20,000*

42.   What is the architectural style of the Ringling Museum of Art in Sarasota?
> *Italian Renaissance*

43.   What is the name of St. Petersburg's monumental vintage 1928 Art Deco hotel?
> *The Don CeSar Hotel*

44.   What architect, famous for designing the most elaborate movie palaces in the U.S., designed the Tampa Theatre?
> *John Eberson*

45.   What Florida university was built in the Moorish Revival architectural style?
> *University of Tampa*

46.   What is the name of south Florida's last remaining antebellum mansion? (Hint: It is located in Bradenton.)
> *the Gamble Mansion*

Northeast Florida

47.   What is the architectural style of St. Augustine's Ponce de Leon Hotel?
> *Spanish Renaissance Revival*

48.   What architectural styles have been preserved in St. Augustine's historic buildings?

> * *Carpenter Gothic*
> * *Chinese Chippendale*
> * *Colonial*
> * *Colonial Revival*
> * *Georgian Colonial*
> * *Gothic*
> * *Greek Revival*
> * *Mediterranean Revival*
> * *Moorish Revival*
> * *Neo-Classical*
> * *Neo-Classical Revival*
> * *Queen Anne*
> * *Romanesque*
> * *Romanesque Revival*
> * *Spanish Renaissance Revival*
> * *Venetian*
> * *Venetian Revival*
> * *Victorian*

Northwest Florida

49.   What is the architectural style of the old capitol building in Tallahassee?
        Classical Revival

50.   What is the name of the historic district near the port of Pensacola?
        Seville Square Historic District

51.   What is the oldest church in Florida still standing on its original site?
        The Old Christ Church

52.   Where is that church located?
        Pensacola's Seville Square District

53.   When was Pensacola's Old Christ Church built?
        1832

54.   What is the architectural style of Pensacola's Old Christ Church?
        Gothic Revival

55.   What is the name of the cemetery in Pensacola's Seville Square District that was established by the King of Spain in the late eighteenth century?
        St. Michael's Cemetery

56.   What is the name of the preservation district North of Pensacola's Seville Square, which contains more than five hundred homes built between 1870 and the late 1930s?
        The North Hill Preservation District

Southeast Florida

57.   What Florida city has the world's largest collection of Art Deco style buildings?
        Miami Beach

58.   When were hundreds of Art Deco style apartments and hotels built in South Beach?
        1930s and 1940s

59.   What historic Miami structure, inspired by the fifteenth-century Giralda Tower in Seville, Spain, was originally a newspaper office and is also known as Miami's Ellis Island?
        Freedom Tower

60.   What Miami city government Art Deco building was originally a base for seaplanes?
        Miami City Hall

61.   What South Florida town is the home of the opulent Biltmore Hotel?
        Coral Gables

62.   The architecture of what South Florida town was inspired by the book *1001 Tales of the Arabian Nights*?
        Opa-locka in north Miami-Dade County

63.   What is the Coral Gables water tower disguised to look like?
      a lighthouse

64.   What Coral Gables church is a replica of a baroque church in Costa Rica?
      the Coral Gables Congregational Church

65.   What spring-fed swimming pool in Coral Gables was formerly a rock quarry and is reminiscent of Venice, Italy, in design and architecture?
      the Venetian Pool

66.   In what year was the Biltmore Hotel in Coral Gables built? (Hint: It was built during Florida's original age of opulence.)
      1925

67.   What is the name of the oldest building in Miami-Dade County that is still in its original location? (Hint: The house, built in 1891, overlooks Biscayne Bay in Coconut Grove.)
      Barnacle House

68.   What building complex in north Miami contains the oldest buildings in North America?
      the Spanish Monastery of St. Bernard de Clairvaux

69.   When was the Spanish Monastery of St. Bernard de Clairvaux originally built?
      in the twelfth century, circa 1133–1141

70.   Where was the Monastery of St. Bernard de Clairvaux originally built?
      Sacramenia, in the Province of Segovia, Spain

71.   How did the Spanish Monastery of St. Bernard de Clairvaux get to South Florida?
      In 1925 William Randolph Hearst purchased the Cloisters and the monastery complex and then had the buildings dismantled and shipped to the United States, where they were reconstructed in the 1950s.

72.   Where in Palm Beach can you see the architecture of Addison Mizner?

      * *Cocoanut Row*
      * *Everglades Club at 356 Worth Avenue*
      * *Mizner Memorial Park*
      * *Mizner's Casa de Leoni at 450 Worth Avenue*
      * *Phipps Plaza*
      * *Town Hall at 360 S. County Road*
      * *Via Mizner at 337–339 Worth Avenue*
      * *Via Parigi*
      * *Other answers are possible, as many private homes in Palm Beach were designed by Mizner.*

73.   What are some of the historic buildings in Palm Beach?
      * *The Breakers Hotel at One S. County Road, built in 1925*
      * *The Gothic Revival Episcopal Church of Bethesda-by-the-Sea at 141 S. County Road, built in 1927*

• *Sea Gull Cottage, which was built in 1886, at 60 Cocoanut Row*
• *Society of the Four Arts*
• *Whitehall at One Whitehall Way, built in 1902*

3
Art in Florida

74.   What southeast Florida towns host the annual Art Fest by the Sea every March?
       Art Fest by the Sea is held on a one-mile stretch of oceanfront
       between Jupiter Beach and Juno Beach.

75.   What Florida museum has a world-class collection of works by Salvador Dali?
       the Salvador Dali Museum in St. Petersburg

76.   What is the artistic style of Salvador Dali?
       surrealist

77.   What Sarasota museum has one of the largest baroque art collections in the U.S.?
       John and Mable Ringling Museum of Art

78.   What Tampa museum houses a collection of European antiques?
       Henry B. Plant Museum

79.   The building that houses the Henry B. Plant Museum was formerly known as what?
       the Tampa Bay Hotel

80.   What DeLand museum displays only works created by African-American
       and Caribbean-American artists?
       African American Museum of the Arts

81.   What Daytona museum is home to a 130,000-year-old ground sloth?
       Museum of Arts and Sciences and Planetarium

82.   What Ormond Beach museum houses Florida's first World War II memorial?
       the Ormond Memorial Art Museum and Gardens

83.   What Ormond Beach museum is framed by the Halifax and Tomoka Rivers?
       Fred Dana Marsh Museum at Tomoka State Park

84.   What Ormond Beach museum is located on the site of Nocoroco, a former
       Timucuan Indian village?
       Fred Dana Marsh Museum at Tomoka State Park

85.   For what is the Lightner Museum in St. Augustine known?
       Nineteenth-century decorative arts and antiques

86.   What artist created the kinetic environmental sculpture entitled *Endangered,* which
       is displayed at entrance of The Art Gallery at the University of West Florida?
       William Jackson Maxwell

87. Where is the Indian Temple Mound Museum?
     Fort Walton Beach

88. The Morse Charles Hosmer Museum of American Art contains the world's largest collection of glass works by what famous artist?
     Louis Comfort Tiffany

89. What Palm Beach museum is housed in a 1930s Art Deco building that was originally built to be a movie theater?
     the Norton Museum of Art

90. For what is South Florida's Morikami Museum known?
     Its Japanese museum, Japanese garden, and Japanese cultural center

91. In what town is the Cuban Museum which houses the art collection of former Cuban President Fulgencio Batista?
     Daytona Beach

92. Bonnet House in Fort Lauderdale is the historic home and museum of what famous artist couple?
     Helen Birch and Fredrick Clay Bartlett

93. Why was Bonnet House so named?
     Bonnet House was named for a yellow lily that grows in the estates marshlands.

94. What Florida institution houses the world's largest collection of swimming art?
     Tripp Family Art Gallery in the International Swimming Hall of Fame

95. In what Florida town is the International Swimming Hall of Fame?
     Fort Lauderdale

96. Where is the Florida Museum of Hispanic and Latin American Art?
     Coral Gables

97. What is the name of the Miami museum that is dedicated to preserving and displaying Florida's Jewish history and culture?
     Sanford L. Ziff Jewish Museum of Florida

98. Which Miami Beach museum is known for its collection of old masters?
     Bass Museum of Art

99. What is the name of the sculpture garden at the Society of the Four Arts in Palm Beach?
     Philip Hulitar Sculpture Garden

100. What is the name of the museum of fine arts in Eatonville?
     Zora Neale Hurston National Museum of Fine Art

101. What sculptor/painter retired to Winter Park after thirty years as the head of the Department of Sculpture at the Art Institute of Chicago? (Hint: He was born in Poland.)
     Albin Polasek

102.   What awards were posthumously given to Albin Polasek?
>• *Great Floridian 2000*
>• *induction into the Florida Artists Hall of Fame in 2004*

103.   What Florida museum is the home of Albin Polasek's sculptures?
>*Albin Polasek Museum and Sculpture Gardens*

4
Economy of Florida

104.   What is the number one industry in Florida?
>*tourism*

105.   What is Florida's state sales tax rate?
>*State sales tax is 6%, but individual towns and counties may add their own sales tax.*

106.   What is Florida's corporate tax rate?
>*5.5%*

107.   What is Florida's state personal income tax rate?
>*There is no Florida state personal income tax.*

108.   Why doesn't Florida have a state income tax?
>*Taxes generated by tourist dollars make a state income tax unnecessary.*

109.   What are Florida's economic strengths?

• *agriculture*
• *construction*
• *health technology:*
  medical, biotech,laboratories
• *international trade*
• *tourism*

• *university research (more than $500 million per year in sponsored research at Florida universities)*

110.   What percentage of U.S. exports to Latin America pass through Florida?
>*40%*

111.   True or False: The Florida Documentary Stamp Tax is a tax on documents that transfer interest in real property.
>*True*

112.   What property and financial documents require Florida Documentary Stamp Tax?
>• *deeds*
>• *mortgages, liens, and other documents of indebtedness*
>• *notes and written obligations to pay money*
>• *stocks and bonds*

113.   What is Florida's tax on intangible personal property such as stocks, bonds, interest, and shares?
> *An annual tax based on the current market value, as of January 1, of intangible personal property owned, managed, or controlled by Florida residents or persons doing business in Florida*

114.   What substances are subject to Florida's pollutants tax?
- *ammonia*
- *chlorine*
- *perchloroethylene (also known as dry-cleaning fluid)*
- *pesticides*
- *production or importation of petroleum products*
- *solvents*

115.   What are the names of the trust funds that manage and collect the Florida pollutants tax?
- *Coastal Protection*
- *Hazardous Waste Management*
- *Inland Protection*
- *Water Quality Assurance*

116.   What articles of property are taxed by Florida's estate tax?

- *accounts receivable*
- *annuities*
- *artwork*
- *automobiles*
- *bonds*
- *equipment*
- *furniture*
- *jewelry*
- *life insurance*
- *money*
- *notes receivable*
- *real estate*

5
Ecosystems in Florida

117.   What is an ecosystem?
> *An ecosystem is an interdependent community of plants and animals in a specific physical environment.*

118.   True or False: Florida is one of the most biologically diverse states in the nation.
> *True*

119.   True or False: Florida has ecosystems not found in the other 49 states.
> *True*

120.   Name some wetlands that are considered critical ecosystems in Florida.
- *algae flats*
- *bogs*
- *marshes*

> • *mud flats*
> • *swamps*

121.   Name some of the forest ecosystems found in Florida.
> • *bottomland forests*   • *scrub*
> • *mangrove*   • *swamps*
> • *pine flatwoods*   • *tropical hammock*
> • *sandhills*   • *upland hardwoods*

122.   True or False: Coral reefs are not true ecosystems.
> *False. Coral reefs are ecosystems.*

123.   True or False: None of Florida's virgin forests remain, and old-growth forests in Florida are rare.
> *True*

124.   Where can old-growth forests be found in Florida today?
> • *Bald Cypress at Corkscrew Swamp Sanctuary*
> • *Big Gum Swamp in Osceola National Forest*
> • *Remote tropical hammocks in the Everglades, in Apalachicola National Forest, and a few other small isolated hammocks*
> • *Tosohatchee State Preserve*
> • *Woodyard Hammock at Tall Timbers Research Station*

125. True or False: The sandhill system is a forest ecosystem noted for dry, sandy soils that do not flood.
> *True*

126.   What trees dominate a sandhill ecosystem?
> • *longleaf pine*
> • *turkey oak*

127.   What non-dominant trees can be found in Florida's sandhill ecosystems?
> • *black cherry*   • *sand post oak*
> • *bluejack oak*   • *sassafras*
> • *persimmon*   • *southern red oak*

128.   True or False: Scrub is one of the youngest ecosystem types in Florida.
> *False. Scrub is one of the oldest ecosystem types in Florida.*

129.   Why is scrub habitat considered to be the most endangered major ecosystem type in Florida?
> *Because scrub land is high and dry, it is well-suited for homes and agricultural use, so these prime lands have been developed faster than any other ecosystem type in Florida.*

130.   True or False: Over two-thirds of the original scrub land in Florida has disappeared.
> *True*

131.   True or False: Only disconnected patches of scrub remain in Florida.
    True

132.   What is the dominant tree in Florida scrub ecosystems?
    sand pine

133.   True or False: Florida's upland hardwood forest ecosystems are the most diverse in the state because they cover a wide variety of climates, soils, and moisture conditions.
    True

134.   Where can bottomland forest ecosystems be found in Florida?
    • *along the edges of lakes and rivers*
    • *in sinkholes*

135.   What are the dominant trees in bottomland forest ecosystems?
    • *live oak*
    • *red maple*
    • *water oak*

136.   True or False: The tropical hammock ecosystem is confined to south Florida below the frost line and contains many plants and animals that live nowhere else.
    True

137.   True or False: Several plants and animal species that have special habitat requirements are becoming victims of habitat loss in Florida.
    True

138.   What animal species that require large territorial ranges are suffering from vanishing ecosystems in Florida?
    • *American black bear*
    • *Florida panther*
    • *Florida scrub-jay*

139.   True or False: Pine flatwoods represent the most extensive type of ecosystem in Florida, and cover fifty percent of the natural land area in the state.
    True

140.   How have humans altered flatwoods and dry prairie ecosystems?
    • *altered natural fire regimes*
    • *destroyed flatwoods and dry prairies for alternative land uses*

141.   What trees dominate pine flatwoods ecosystems?
    • *longleaf pine*
    • *slash pine*

142.   What are the major threats to conservation and ecosystem management in Florida?
    • *escalating water use*
    • *fire exclusion*
    • *land development*
    • *non-native invasive species*

The Everglades

Marjory Stoneman Douglas

143.   Is the water in the Everglades fresh water or salt water?
        fresh water

144.   What is brackish water?
        fresh and salt water mixed

145.   Where can brackish water be found?
        in coastal areas where ocean tides intrude into bodies of fresh water

146.   True or False: South Florida is the only place in the world where alligators and
        crocodiles exist side by side.
        True

147.   Do crocodiles live in fresh water, salt water, or brackish water?
        salt water and brackish water

148.   True or False: The Everglades is a river which flows slowly over and through porous
        limestone bedrock.
        True

149.   True or False: Only part of the Everglades is in the Everglades National Park.
        True

150.   What are the chief sources of the water that flows through the Everglades?
        • *Big Cypress Swamp*
        • *Lake Okeechobee*

151.   What is the speed of the water flowing through the Everglades?
        1/4–1/2 mile per day, or 400–800 meters per day

152.   The Everglades flows from Lake Okeechobee to where?
        Florida Bay, and then into the Gulf of Mexico

153.   How far is it from Lake Okeechobee to Florida Bay?
        about 100 miles

154.　On average, how wide is the Everglades?
　　　50 miles

155.　What is the average depth of the Everglades?
　　　6 inches

156.　In what direction does the Everglades slope?
　　　south

157.　What is the slope of the Everglades?
　　　2–3 inches per mile

158.　True or False: Everglades pine forests have a natural resistance to fire.
　　　True

159.　What fire-resistant quality is characteristic of Everglades pine trees?
　　　thick corklike bark

160.　True or False: Lightning strikes cause frequent fires in the Everglades.
　　　True

161.　How do fires help the Everglades pine lands survive?
　　　　• *Fires expose mineral soil that pine seedlings need.*
　　　　• *Fires prune back hardwoods that would crowd out pines if left unchecked.*

162.　True or False: There is no other landscape like the Everglades anywhere on Earth.
　　　True

163.　True or False: There are biking, hiking, and canoe trails in the Everglades.
　　　True

164.　What carnivorous mollusk that feeds on oysters lives in the Everglades?
　　　apple murex

165.　Why are there only a few giant cypress trees remaining in Florida?
　　　Most of the giant cypress tress were removed by heavy logging from 1930 to 1950. It takes five hundred years or more for a giant cypress tree to reach maturity.

166.　How many different color forms of tree snails live in the Everglades?
　　　52

167.　How many bird species make the Everglades their home for at least part of the year?
　　　347

168.　What are the cylindrical masses of yellowish-green algae that float on the water in the Everglades?
　　　periphyton

169.　How is periphyton important to the Everglades? (Hint: It is part of the food chain.)
　　　　• *It is the base of the food chain.*

     • *Periphyton is habitat and food for many kinds of larvae.*
     • *Periphyton removes calcium from the water and deposits it as marl in which sawgrass takes root.*

170.   How do alligators clear muck and vegetation out of alligator holes?
     They use their feet and snouts to scoop out the holes.

171.   True or False: Alligators are the only animals that live in alligator holes.
     False. During the dry season, many fish and turtles take refuge in alligator holes.

172.   True or False: If alligators did not clear the muck and vegetation out of alligator holes, the holes would fill in and become tree islands.
     True

173.   How many threatened or endangered species live in the Everglades?
     more than 36

174.   What endangered mammals live in the Everglades?
     • *Florida panther*
     • *Key Largo cotton mouse*
     • *Key Largo wood rat*
     • *West Indian manatee (Amid controversy, the manatee's state status changed from endangered to threatened in 2006. Federal status is under review at this time.)*

175.   What endangered reptiles live in the Everglades?
     • *American crocodile*
     • *Atlantic hawksbill turtle*
     • *Atlantic leatherback turtle*
     • *Atlantic ridley turtle*
     • *green turtle*

176.   What endangered birds live in the Everglades?
     • *Cape Sable seaside sparrow*
     • *Everglades kite (also known as the snail kite)*
     • *red-cockaded woodpecker*

177.   What endangered butterflies live in the Everglades?
     • *Garber's spurge*
     • *Schaus' swallowtail*

178.   What year did the Everglades become a national park?
     1947

179.   Who is known as the father of the Everglades?
     Ernest F. Coe

180.   Why is Ernest Coe known as the father of the Everglades?
     In 1925 Coe wrote the proposal to make the Everglades a national park.

181.   What did Marjory Stoneman Douglas do for the Everglades?
   • *She wrote* Everglades: River of Grass, *the first book on Everglades ecology, first published in 1947.*
   • *She raised public awareness and concern about issues concerning the Everglades.*
   • *She founded a conservation group called Friends of the Everglades, which is dedicated to preserving and restoring the Everglades.*

182.   True or False: The Everglades was the first U.S. national park preserved primarily for its abundance and variety of life, rather than for scenic or historic values.
   True

183.   What U.S. President formally dedicated the Everglades National Park on December 6, 1947, in a ceremony held at Everglades City?
   President Harry S. Truman

184.   True or False: The Everglades National Park contains a rich variety of temperate and tropical plant communitites, including sawgrass prairies, mangrove and cypress swamps, pinelands, and hardwood hammocks, in addition to marine and estuarine environments.
   True

185.   How many acres of federal land are in the Everglades National Park?
   1,398,617 acres, as of September 2000

186.   How many people visit the Everglades National Park every year?
   over 1 million

187.   How many orchid species are known to grow in the Everglades?
   25

188.   How many kinds of seed-bearing plants are known to live in the Everglades?
   over 1,000

189.   How many tree species grow in the Everglades?
   about 120

190.   True or False: The Everglades National Park's designation as an International Biosphere Reserve gives it protection and recognition as a major ecosystem type.
   True

191.   International Biosphere Reserves is a project of the Man and the Biosphere Program of what international organization?
   United Nations Educational Scientific and Cultural Organization (UNESCO)

192.   When was the Everglades National Park added to the International Biosphere Reserves list?
   October 26, 1976

193.   When was the Everglades designated a wetland of international importance?
   June 4, 1987

194.   What kinds of ecosystems are found within the Everglades?
- *lakes*
- *large hardwood hammocks*
- *mangrove swamps*
- *ponds*
- *rivers*
- *sawgrass marshes*
- *sloughs*
- *small tree islands of bald cypresses, willows, and slash pine*

195.   What is the Seminole word for the Everglades?
Pay-Hay-Okee, which means "grassy waters"

196.   What is the dominant plant in the Everglades?
sawgrass

197.   How tall does sawgrass grow?
over 6 feet high

198.   What species of wading birds live in the Everglades?
- *glossy ibis*
- *great blue heron*
- *great flamingo (rare)*
- *little blue heron*
- *roseate spoonbill*
- *scarlet ibis*
- *snowy egret*
- *white ibis*
- *wood stork*

199.   What species of pelicans live in the Everglades?
- *American white pelican*
- *brown pelican*

200.   What species of woodpeckers can be found in the Everglades?
- *downy woodpecker*
- *hairy woodpecker*
- *pileated woodpecker*
- *red-bellied woodpecker*
- *red-headed woodpecker*

201.   What eagle species live in the Everglades?
- *bald eagle*
- *golden eagle*

202.   What rare and endangered bird species lives in the Everglades and feeds exclusively on the apple snail?
the Everglades kite, also known as the snail kite

203.   How many reptile species live in the Everglades?
more than 50

204.   How many snake species live in the Everglades?
about 26

205.   How many turtle species live in the Everglades?
around 16

206.   How many amphibian species live in the Everglades?
          about 18

207.   What are the names of the two main channels of water that flow through the Everglades?
          • *Shark River Slough*
          • *Taylor Slough*

208.   What are the two families of epiphytes or air plants that live on the branches and trunks of trees in the Everglades?
          • *bromeliads*
          • *orchids*

209.   Name some bromeliads commonly found in the Everglades.

          • *ball moss*   • *soft-leaved wild pine*
          • *needle-leaved air plant*   • *Spanish moss*
          • *reflexed wild pine*   • *stiff-leaved wild pine*
          • *small catopsis*   • *twisted air plant*

210.   What is the most critical conservation issue for the Everglades?
          water management

211.   What is endangering the Everglades?

          • *declining water quality*   • *loss of species*
          • *explosive regional*   • *non-native invasive species*
            population growth   • *water supplies*

212.   What can Florida residents and visitors do to help save the Everglades?
          • *Avoid polluting the environment inside and outside the Everglades.*
          • *Conserve water.*
          • *Don't litter, and try to keep others from littering.*
          • *Learn more about the Everglades.*

213.   What can you do to conserve water?
          • *Don't let the water run when washing your hands, brushing your teeth, shaving, or washing dishes.*
          • *To get cold water, don't run the tap until the water is cold; keep water in the refrigerator instead.*
          • *Adjust your toilet tank float to use a minimum amount of water, or put a brick or a plastic bottle filled with water into the toilet tank to reduce water usage.*
          • *Use dishwashers only when full.*
          • *Take shorter showers and turn off the water while you apply soap.*
          • *Flush the toilet only when necessary, and don't use it as a trash can.*
          • *Water lawns in the cool of the morning or evening so less water will evaporate.*
          • *When washing a car, turn the hose off while you apply soap.*
          • *Use soap instead of detergent. Using soaps with low phosphates and nitrates keeps the water table cleaner.*
          • *Spread the word. Talk to your friends and family about the Everglades and water conservation.*
          • *Contact conservation organizations for more information. Many environmental groups are working on issues relating to Everglades protection and restoration.*

• Keep environmental issues in mind when voting.
• Join a conservation group.

214.   What conservation groups are concerned about the Everglades?
   • The Sierra Club
   • Friends of the Everglades
   • The Audubon Society
   • Other answers are possible.
   Note: These groups sponsor free or low-cost nature walks and lectures. They also wel-come guests and new members and have great family activities. See their websites for details.

215.   What pollutants are threatening the Everglades?
   • excess nutrients from agricultural runoff
   • mercury pollution
   • saltwater intrusion

Wetlands: Marshes and Swamps

216.   In terms of hydrologic movement, what are the two major swamp types found in Florida?
   • river
   • still water

217.   In terms of structure and ecosystem, how many distinct swamp types can be found in Florida?
   8

218.   What are the eight types of swamps found in Florida?
   • basin, bayhead, or depression swamp—large basin, seasonally inundated, still water
   • bottomland forest—flatland, occasionally inundated
   • dome swamp—rounded depression, seasonally inundated, still waters
   • floodplain forest—alluvial floodplain, seasonally inundated
   • floodplain swamp—floodplain with organic substrate, usually inundated
   • freshwater tidal swamp—river mouth wetland, organic soil, inundated
   • strand swamp—broad, shallow channel, seasonally inundated, flowing
   • tidal swamp—intertidal area, salt-tolerant trees

219.   True or False: Florida's swamps are ecosystems.
   True

220.   What are the functions of wetlands?
   • erosion control
   • flood control
   • habitat for rare and endangered species
   • habitat for waterfowl and other wildlife
   • pollution control
   • produce fish and shellfish
   • store water
   • trap and control sediments

221.   True or False: Most of the Okefenokee Swamp is in Florida.
        False. Most of the Okefenokee Swamp is in Georgia.

222.   Is the water in the Okefenokee Swamp fresh water or salt water?
        fresh water

223.   True or False: Peat deposits up to 15 feet thick cover most of the Okefenokee Swamp floor.
        True

224.   True or False: Peat deposits in the Okefenokee Swamp are so unstable that trees and bushes tremble when the ground surface is stomped upon.
        True

225.   True or False: The name Okefenokee comes from a Choctaw word meaning "land of the trembling earth."
        True

226.   How long ago did the Okefenokee basin form?
        around 250,000 years ago

227.   What is the largest swamp system in Florida?
        Green Swamp

228.   The Green Swamp is in what Florida counties?
        Pasco County, Lake County, Sumter County, and Polk County

229.   How many square miles does the Green Swamp encompass?
        870 square miles or 570 acres

230.   The headwaters of what five Florida rivers are in the Green Swamp?
        • *Hillsborough River*
        • *Little Withlacoochee River*
        • *Oklawaha River*
        • *Peace River*
        • *Withlacoochee River*

231.   What southwest Florida swamp is home to the oldest remaining cypress stand in the state?
        Corkscrew Swamp

232.   What river swamp is home to the largest cypress stand in the United States?
        the Fakahatchee Strand

233.   True or False: The Fakahatchee Strand is home to a wide variety and abundance of air plants, or epiphytes.
        True

234.   What river feeds the Big Cypress Swamp?
        None. The Big Cypress Swamp depends on rain for its water.

235.   What is a palustrine wetland?
       a freshwater wetland

236.   What is a estuarine wetland?
       a saltwater or brackish water wetland

237.   What types of wetlands make up Florida's freshwater wetlands?
       • *cypress swamps*
       • *freshwater marshes*
       • *mixed hardwood swamps*
       • *shrub swamps*
       • *wet prairies*

238.   What is a wetland hydroperiod?
       the amount of time during the year that the area is inundated or flooded by water

239.   What is the hydroperiod of a mixed hardwood swamp?
       300 days per year

240.   True or False: Some plants only grow in a specific type of wetland.
       True

241.   Why are ecosystems important to the survival of species?
       Many plants and animals live only in the specific growing conditions found in the ecosystems in which they live.

242.   What are the dominant trees found in a mixed hardwood swamp?
       • *bald cypress*   • *red bay*
       • *black gum*   • *red maple*
       • *dahoon holly*   • *sweet bay*
       • *Florida elm*   • *tupelo*
       • *loblolly bay*   • *water hickory*
       • *pond cypress*   • *water locust*
       • *pop ash*

243.   What common shrubs are found in Florida mixed hardwood swamps?
       • *cocoplum*
       • *shiny lyonia*
       • *Virginia willow*
       • *wax myrtle*

244.   What typical understory vegetation is found in Florida's mixed hardwood swamps?
       • *cinnamon fern*   • *royal fern*
       • *lizard's tail*   • *swamp fern*
       • *marsh fern*   • *swamp lily*

245.   What wildlife is typically found in Florida's mixed hardwood swamps?
       • *alligators*   • *green tree frogs*
       • *barred owls*   • *gray squirrels*
       • *cottonmouths (water moccasins)*   • *nonpoisonous water snakes*
       • *great crested flycatchers*   • *opossums*

- *pileated and red-bellied woodpeckers*
- *raccoons*
- *river otters*

- *striped mud turtles*
- *warblers*
- *wood ducks*

246.   Where are pop ash and pond apple sloughs found?
> *These sloughs are found in the wettest parts of freshwater swamps. The best examples of pop ash and pond apple sloughs are found in the Fakahatchee Strand.*

247.   Where is the Fakahatchee Strand?
> *southwest Florida in the Big Cypress Swamp*

248.   What is the hydroperiod (see question 238) of a slough?
> *300–360 days per year*

249.   If a bayhead does not experience a fire for many years, what type of ecosystem does it become?
> *a hammock*

250.   Where in Florida are bayheads found?
> *Bayheads are found throughout the state.*

251.   What is the hydroperiod (see question 238) of a freshwater marsh?
> *225–275 days per year*

252.   How do humans destroy swamps by draining water into canals?
> *Draining a swamp shortens its hydroperiod.*

253.   Where in Florida are freshwater marshes found?
> *Freshwater marshes occur throughout Florida as floodplain marshes and basin marshes.*

254.   How often does a freshwater marsh naturally burn?
> *every 1–5 years*

255.   How do periodic fires help maintain marshes and swamps?
> *Periodic wetland fires*
> - *destroy invasive woody plants.*
> - *recycle nutrients.*
> - *reduce amount of fire fuel.*
> - *stimulate fresh growth.*

256.   How does moisture in a wetland control fire?
> - *When soils are moist, fires remain small and burn only the surface litter.*
> - *When soils are dry, fires have more fuel and burn indiscriminately.*

257.   What plants are found in Florida's freshwater marshes?
> - *American lotus*
> - *arrowhead*
> - *bulrush*
> - *buttonbush*
> - *cattail*
> - *fire flag*
> - *grasses*

> - *pickerelweed*
> - *rushes*
> - *sawgrass*
> - *white water lily*
> - *willow*
> - *other answers are possible*

258.   What is the hydroperiod (see question 238) for a wet prairie?
        50–150 days a year

259.   What plants are commonly found on Florida's wet prairies?
        - *beakrush*
        - *bladderworts*
        - *coreopsis*
        - *floating hearts*
        - *grasses*
        - *guardian*
        - *maidencane*
        - *marsh pinks*
        - *sand cordgrass*
        - *St. John's wort*
        - *terrestrial orchids*
        - *yellow-eyed grass*

260.   Where do salt marshes form?
        Salt marshes form on tidal flats along shores with little wave activity.

261.   Where are salt marshes found in Florida?
        Salt marshes are primarily found in three parts of Florida:
        - *Cordgrass salt marshes are found behind the barrier islands along the northeast coast of Florida.*
        - *Needlerush-dominated marshes are found north of Tampa along Florida's west coast.*
        - *Isolated mixed marshes are scattered along Florida Bay.*

262.   What kinds of plants are commonly found in Florida's salt marshes?
        - *cordgrass*
        - *golden leather fern*
        - *marsh elder*
        - *marsh lavender*
        - *saltbush*
        - *sea oxeye*
        - *seashore saltgrass*

263.   What is an impounded marsh?
        Impounded marshes are enclosed by dikes.

264.   Where are algae flats likely to be found?
        Algae flats are found on rock or mud in areas flooded by the highest tides.

265.   True or False: Algae flats survive only when an area is salty enough to eliminate most of the snails and other animals that eat algae.
        True

266.   Where are Florida's algae flats located?
        Well-developed algal mats are found in the Keys. Sugarloaf Key and Crane Key have the best examples of algae flat habitat.

267.   What kinds of plants grow in algae flats?
        - *bacteria*
        - *blue-green algae*
        - *diatoms*
        - *flagellates*
        - *scrubby red and black mangroves*
        - *one-celled green algae*
        - *saltwort*

268. What are the environmental characteristics of Florida's swamps? (Hint: The answers to this question are covered in previous questions and answers.)
    - *hydroperiod*
    - *fire frequency*
    - *soil characteristics*
    - *water source*

269. What environmental factors affect Florida's wetlands? (Hint: Think about necessary growing conditions of wetlands.)
    - *climate*
    - *fire frequency*
    - *gradients*
    - *hydrology*
    - *invasion by non-native plants and animals*
    - *nutrient level*
    - *salinity*
    - *soil content*
    - *soil depth*
    - *temperature*

Mangrove Marshes

270. Why are mangrove marshes important to the coastline?
    Mangroves
    - *supply food for animals at the bottom of the food chain.*
    - *provide habitat for many animals.*
    - *clean the water.*
    - *keep shorelines from eroding.*

271. True or False: Mangrove trees form the base of the mangrove marsh food chain.
    True

272. How do mangrove trees form the base of the mangrove marsh food chain?
    Mangrove leaves fall into the water and decompose, creating a dark, smelly substance called detritus, which is eaten by bacteria and fungi, which are eaten by fish and shellfish, which are eaten by other animals.

273. What animals that live in mangrove marshes eat fish and shellfish?
    - *birds*
    - *mammals*
    - *reptiles*

274. True or False: Thousands of years ago mangrove trees lived inland.
    True

275. What adaptations did mangrove trees make to live on the coastline?
    They developed aerial and salt-filtering roots; the leaves developed glands to excrete salt; seeds germinate on the tree before dispersal into a harsh saline environment; and the seeds of some species developed the ability to float for long distances.

276. True or False: Mangrove seeds start to germinate, or grow, while they are still on the tree.
    True

277.   What are mangrove seeds called?
propagules

278.   What are the three types of mangrove trees that live in Florida?
• *red mangrove*
• *black mangrove*
• *white mangrove*

279.   Which type of mangrove tree is the most common in Florida?
red mangrove

280.   Which kind of mangrove tree lives on the water line?
red mangrove

281.   True or False: Red mangrove trees have roots that drop down out of the branches, called prop roots that help hold the tree up in soft mud.
True

282.   Why is the red mangrove sometimes called "the walking tree"?
Because the prop roots make the tree look like it is walking on water.

283.   True or False: Red mangroves remove the salt from the water with their roots.
True

284.   True or False: The red mangroves propagules are green, shaped like pencils, and they plant themselves as they fall off the tree.
True

285.   True or False: Black mangroves grow farther away from the shoreline than red mangroves.
True

286.   True or False: Black mangroves have lots of fingerlike roots that stick out of the mud around their trunks.
True

287.   True or False: Black mangrove trees breathe with their roots.
True

288.   What happens to a black mangrove tree if its roots stay under water too long?
The tree drowns.

289.   What color are the leaves of a black mangrove tree?
Black mangrove leaves are dark green on top and silver on bottom.

290.   How do black mangroves remove salt from their systems?
They remove salt with their leaves. On hot days, salt may be visible on top of the leaves.

291.   True or False: The propagules of black mangroves look like large lima beans.
True

292. True or False: White mangroves cannot live in water and therefore they grow farther away from the water than red and black mangroves.
     True

293. What shape and color are the leaves of a white mangrove tree?
     The leaves are light green and oval-shaped.

294. How do white mangrove trees remove salt from their systems?
     White mangroves have two bumps on their leaf stems; these are salt glands, which pump out the salt that is taken in by the roots.

295. What do the propagules of the white mangrove look like?
     They are small, wrinkled, and teardrop-shaped.

Cypress Swamps

296. What is the hydroperiod (see question 238) of a cypress swamp?
     240–290 days each year

297. What prevents hardwoods from invading cypress swamps?
     periodic fires

298. What type of soil is characteristic of a cypress swamp?
     peat deposits overlying sand or rock

299. Why are some cypress swamps circular and dome-shaped?
     Cypress domes develop around sinkholes.

300. Where can cypress domes be found?
     throughout Florida

301. What is a cypress strand?
     Cypress strands are slow moving, forested rivers. The Fakahatchee Strand is the best example of a major cypress strand in Florida.

302. Where are dwarf cypress savannahs and forests found?
     They are found in southern Florida; the most extensive dwarf cypress savannahs are found in the Big Cypress National Preserve.

303. How tall are dwarf cypress trees?
     about 10 meters or 30 feet tall

304. What causes the gnarled appearance of dwarf cypress trees?
     Scarce nutrients cause dwarf cypresses to grow very slowly and develop huge gnarled crowns and buttresses.

6
Environment

Air Quality

305.   What Florida governmental agency is charged with enforcing air quality standards?
the Florida Department of Environmental Protection (FDEP)

306.   True or False: Vehicle emissions are a major source of Florida's air pollution.
True

307.   True or False: Ground-level ozone is the primary pollutant of concern in southeast Florida.
True

308.   True or False: Ozone is found at the earth's surface and is the main ingredient in smog.
True

309.   True or False: Ozone is emitted directly from vehicle exhaust systems.
False

310.   True or False: Emissions from motor vehicles, lawn equipment, and power plants react and combine in the presence of strong sunlight to form ozone.
True

311.   True or False: Ground-level ozone damages the foliage of Florida's trees and plants, and also has a negative impact on the landscape of Florida's cities, national parks, forests, and recreation areas.
True

312.   How many pounds of pollution does an average car produce in one year?
15,725 pounds

313.   True or False: Air pollution can shorten your lifespan.
True

314.   What toxic pollutants are directly emitted by vehicle exhaust systems?
   • *benzene*
   • *carbon dioxide*
   • *carbon monoxide*
   • *hydrocarbons*
   • *nitrogen oxides*

315.   What health problems are known to be caused by chemicals in polluted air?
        • *birth defects*
        • *cancer*
        • *long- and short-term respiratory illnesses*
        • *nerve damage*

316.   What can vehicle owners do to be sure their vehicle exhaust systems are working
        correctly?
        inspect and maintain vehicle emission systems

317.   True or False: Motor vehicles do not pollute in equal amounts; in fact, half of
        Florida's motor vehicle air pollution is generated by 10 percent of the motor
        vehicles operating in Florida.
        True

318.   How many pounds of carbon dioxide (CO_2) does the average gasoline-fueled car
        produce in one year?
        about 15,200 pounds

319.   How many pounds of carbon dioxide (CO_2) does the average gasoline-fueled light
        truck produce in one year?
        almost 22,000 pounds

320.   How many pounds of carbon monoxide (CO) does the average gasoline-fueled car
        produce in one year?
        about 420 pounds

321.   How many pounds of hydrocarbons (HC) does the average gasoline-fueled car
        produce in one year?
        about 55 pounds

322.   How many pounds of nitrogen oxide (NOx) does the average gasoline-fueled car
        produce in one year?
        about 50 pounds

323.   What can vehicle owners do to reduce motor vehicle air pollution?
        • *Avoid driving at high speeds.*   • *Conserve energy.*
        • *Avoid spilling fuel when refueling.*   • *Properly inflate vehicle tires.*
        • *Avoid stop-and-go driving.*   • *Properly maintain vehicles.*
        • *Avoid unnecessary driving.*   • *Use public transportation or walk.*
        • *Buy cars that use alternative
        energy sources.*

324.   True or False: Motor vehicles that produce visible smoke are subject to law
        enforcement citation in Florida.
        True

325.   What should you do if you see a smoking vehicle in Florida?

Note the following:
- *the smoking vehicle's license number*
- *the make, model, and color of the vehicle*
- *the date and time the vehicle was seen*
- *location and city where you saw the vehicle*
  and report the smoking vehicle to the county Environmental Complaint Hotline.

326.   What health problems can be caused by inhaling low levels of ozone?
- *chest pains*
- *congestion*
- *coughing*
- *nausea*
- *throat irritation*

327.   What long-term health problems can be caused by inhaling ozone?
- *asthma*
- *emphysema*
- *heart disease*
- *reduced lung capacity*

328.   True or False: In Florida, industrial air polluters must obtain a permit to pollute the air and must also comply with monitoring requirements.
True

Non-native Species in Florida

329.   There is only one state that has more non-native species than Florida. What state is it?
Hawaii

330.   True or False: Florida has no laws to protect itself from non-native species.
False. There are state, federal, and local laws that protect Florida from the importation of non-native species.

331.   True or False: Non-native species can damage ecosystems.
True

332.   What is a non-native species called when it becomes a threat to the survival of an ecosystems native species?
invasive species

Non-native Plants

333.   What makes Florida vulnerable to the unchecked growth of exotic plants?
its plant-friendly subtropical climate

334.   What percentage of the 3,834 plant species found in Florida have arrived here in the past 300 years?
30%, or 1,180 species

335. How many acres of Florida's remaining natural areas have become infested with non-native plant species?
    approximately 1.5 million acres

336. True or False: Fifty percent of the worst invasive plant species are still commercially available for sale in Florida.
    False. Thirty-nine percent of the worst invasive plant species are commercially available for sale in Florida.

337. True or False: Forty-five percent of the invasive plant species found in Florida were imported for ornamental or agricultural purposes.
    True

338. How many invasive aquatic plant species are growing in Florida?
    over 600

339. What non-native plant was brought from Australia to Florida to drain the Everglades?
    the melaleuca tree, also known as the Australian cajeput

340. How many acres in south Florida contain melaleuca trees?
    several million acres

341. True or False: Sites with severe melaleuca infestations may contain as many as 31,000 trees and saplings per acre.
    True

342. True or False: Compared to freshwater marsh fires, melaleuca forest fires burn at higher temperatures, which can dry out and ignite the soil.
    True

343. How much does it cost to control melaleuca trees in Florida?
    over $2.2 million annually

344. When was the aquatic pest plant hydrilla brought to Florida ?
    in the 1950s

345. How long did it take hydrilla to infest forty percent of Florida's public lakes and rivers?
    about 40 years

346. What are some of the functions and benefits of native aquatic plant species?
    - *buffering banks from wake and wave erosion*
    - *food sources for wildlife*
    - *nesting and nursery habitat*
    - *water purification*

347. What non-native aquatic plants are currently the most destructive to Florida's aquatic systems?
    - *alligator weed*
    - *hydrilla*

> • *torpedo grass*
> • *water hyacinth*
> • *wild taro*

348. True or False: Water hyacinth grows extremely fast and is capable of doubling in area in two weeks.
>> *True*

349. How can non-native plant species jeopardize plant-dependent wildlife and their ecosystems?
>> *Plants are at the bottom of the food chain, so disrupting them affects the entire food chain.*

350. What are some of the problems that are caused by the invasion of non-native plant species?
>> *Non-native plants*
>> • *alter hydrology.*
>> • *change fire regimes.*
>> • *displace native species.*
>> • *modify soil resources.*
>> • *reduce wildlife habitat.*

351. What does Florida do to control invasive pest plants?
>> • *applies herbicides*
>> • *destroys pest plants with fire*
>> • *fights plants with pathogens such as fungal plant-eaters*
>> • *removes plants manually and mechanically*
>> • *uses species-specific natural enemies to fight pests*

352. What can you do to help stop the spread of non-native aquatic plants in Florida?
>> • *Before you leave a boat ramp, inspect and remove any plant material from your boat and trailer.*
>> • *Consult a Department of Environmental Protection biologist before controlling any aquatic plants.*
>> • *Never empty the contents of your aquarium into the environment.*
>> • *Never transplant aquatic plants without consulting a Department of Environmental Protection aquatic biologist.*
>> • *Report new non-native plant infestations to the Department of Environmental Protection.*

353.   Name some of the invasive plants that are currently displacing native species in Florida.

- *air potato*
- *aquatic soda apple*
- *Asian sword fern*
- *asparagus fern*
- *Australian pine*
- *beach naupaka*
- *bischofia*
- *Brazilian jasmine*
- *Brazilian pepper*
- *Burma reed*
- *camphor tree*
- *cane grass*
- *carrotwood*
- *cat claw mimosa*
- *cat's claw vine*
- *chinaberry*
- *Chinese privet*
- *Chinese tallow tree*
- *Christmas cassia*
- *Christmas senna*
- *climbing cassia*
- *cogon grass*
- *coral ardisia*
- *downy rose myrtle*
- *earleaf acacia*
- *glossy privet*
- *gold coast jasmine*
- *green hygro*
- *guava*
- *hedge privet*
- *hydrilla*
- *Japanese climbing fern*
- *Japanese honeysuckle*
- *kudzu*
- *lantana*
- *lather leaf*
- *laurel fig*
- *melaleuca*
- *Mexican petunia*
- *mimosa*
- *nandina*
- *napier grass*
- *Old World climbing fern*
- *onion vine*
- *orchid tree*
- *popcorn tree*
- *rosary pea*
- *Santa Maria*
- *sapodilla*
- *scaevola*
- *schefflera*
- *sewer vine*
- *shoe button ardisia*
- *skunk vine*
- *strawberry guava*
- *suckering Australian pine*
- *Surinam cherry*
- *sword fern*
- *torpedo grass*
- *water hyacinth*
- *water lettuce*
- *water spinach*
- *West Indian marsh grass*
- *wetland night shade*
- *wild taro*
- *winged yam*

Non-native Aquatic Animals

354.   How many non-native freshwater fish species live in Florida?
         at least 73

355.   How many non-native species have been introduced to Florida coastal waters in the Gulf of Mexico?
         about 225

356.   What non-native fish can survive outside of water for extended periods of time and can sometimes be seen crossing roads in south Florida as they move between water bodies?
         walking catfish

357.   How are most of the non-native microbes and organisms introduced to Florida's Gulf waters?
> *discharge of ship ballast water*

358.   How is the problem of non-native species in ship ballast discharge in the Gulf of Mexico being solved?
> • *Ballast water is sometimes sterilized before release.*
> • *Ballast water is sometimes treated with chemicals.*
> • *Ballast water release is prohibited in some places.*

359.   How are non-native fish species introduced into Florida's Gulf coast waters?
> • *fish released from aquariums*
> • *fish stocked for sport*
> • *live bait released*

360.   True or False: Most of the non-native fish in Florida's Gulf coast waters are from other parts of the United States.
> *False. Most of the non-native fish in Florida's Gulf waters are from foreign waters.*

361.   True or False: Of the five states that border the Gulf of Mexico, Florida has the least number of non-native aquatic vertebrates in the Gulf region.
> *False. Of the five Gulf states, Florida has the highest number of non-native aquatic vertebrates in the Gulf region.*

362.   How many non-native aquatic vertebrate species live in the Gulf of Mexico off the coast of each of the five Gulf states?
> • *Alabama has about 53.*
> • *Florida has about 149.*
> • *Louisiana has about 30.*
> • *Mississippi has about 23.*
> • *Texas has about 106.*

363.   True or False: Several non-native shrimp viruses are a concern in the Gulf of Mexico.
> *True*

364.   True or False: It may take many years for an established non-native aquatic species to become an invasive pest that threatens the diversity or abundance of native species.
> *True*

365.   What marine vertebrate species are prohibited in Florida?
> • *sea snakes*
> • *stonefish*
> • *weaverfish*

366.   How much did Florida state agencies spend managing terrestrial and aquatic non-native species in 1999 and 2000?
> • *$94.5 million in 1999*
> • *$127.6 million in 2000*

Non-native Insects

367. How much damage is caused by non-native insects in Florida every year?
    about $1 billion

368. How many non-native insect species become established in Florida every year?
    12–18

369. What non-native poisonous spider can be found in almost any place that has remained undisturbed for a lengthy period of time?
    brown recluse spider

370. What stinging ant was imported to Florida from South America?
    red fire ant

371. When was Florida invaded by red fire ants?
    in the mid-1930s

372. What non-native insect is considered a pest because it eats old books?
    book lice

373. How many book lice and bark lice species live in Florida?
    over 80

374. What non-native insects attack Florida's potato crops?
    - *The Colorado potato beetle from the western United States, which entered Florida in 1920*
    - *The sweet potato whitefly from Asia, which entered Florida in 1890*
    - *The sweet potato weevil from Asia, which entered Florida in 1878*

375. What dangerous mosquito species have invaded Florida?
    - *Yellow fever mosquito from Africa, a carrier of yellow fever and dengue, entered Florida before 1850.*
    - *Asian tiger mosquito from Asia, a carrier of dengue, entered Florida in 1986.*

376. What non-native fruit fly has been fought by Florida at great expense?
    Mediterranean fruit fly

377. What non-native caterpillars damage Florida's crops?

Pest Caterpillar	Crop Food
banana moth	many ornamental plants
cabbageworm	cole crops
cactus moth	cactus
citrus leafminer	citrus
corn earworm	corn, soybeans, cotton
cotton leafworm	cotton
diamondback moth	cabbage and cole crops
soybean looper	soybeans
sugarcane borer	sugarcane
velvetbean caterpillar	soybeans, legumes

378. How do non-native insects arrive in Florida?
     - *flying*
     - *on cargo ships (usually on infested plants that are commercially imported)*
     - *rafting*
     - *swimming*
     - *walking*

Non-native Birds and Mammals

379. What negative environmental impacts do invasive animal species have in Florida?
     - *competition with native species*
     - *disease*
     - *habitat destruction*
     - *hybridization*
     - *parasites*
     - *predation*

380. Name some of the non-native bird species which are considered pests in Florida.
     - *muscovy ducks*
     - *rock doves*
     - *European starlings*
     - *house sparrows*
     - *monk parakeets*

     For a complete list of Florida's non-native birds visit this website:
     http://myfwc.com/critters/exotics/resultsClass.asp?taxclass=B

381. Name some of Florida's non-native rodent pests.
     - *house mouse*
     - *Norway rat*
     - *roof rat*

382. What cat, native to Central America, has been introduced to Florida?
     The jaguarundi, which has a weasel-like body and an otterlike head, and has been sighted in Florida's Gulf coast and northeastern Atlantic counties.

Waste Management

383. What are "superfund sites"?
     Superfund sites contain dangerous toxic wastes and qualify for special federal clean-up funding.

384. How many superfund sites are within Florida?
     51 in Florida as of 2004

385. What Florida counties have the most superfund sites?
     Miami-Dade and Hillsborough Counties have 14 sites each.

Hazardous Household Waste

386. True or False: Many cleaning products used in homes contain toxic chemicals and pollute Florida's water and air.
     True

387.   Why is it important to properly dispose of hazardous household waste in Florida?
        *Because hazardous household waste can be a threat to health and to the
        environment. Mismanagement can result in hazardous household waste
        entering the foodchain, where it may cause birth defects and cancer, and kill
        fish and wildlife.*

388.   True or False: Proper disposal of hazardous waste protects Florida's water quality.
        True

389.   What percentage of Florida's hazardous household waste is properly collected?
        about 1%

390.   What household products are considered hazardous household waste?

        • *batteries*   • *fluorescent bulbs*
        • *chemicals*   • *furniture polish*
        • *cleaning products*   • *herbicides*
        • *corrosives*   • *leather polish*
        • *electronics*   • *mercury-containing devices*
        • *fertilizers*   • *motor oil*
        • *flammables*   • *paint*
        • *floor wax*   • *pesticides*

391.   What should you do with hazardous waste in Florida?
        *Some Florida counties will pick up hazardous waste from your site. In other
        Florida counties you must take your hazardous waste to a hazardous waste
        collection site.*

392.   What should you do if you are not sure your household waste is hazardous?
        *Before you dispose of it, call your county's department of waste management
        and ask about the proper method of disposal.*

393.   True or False: There are more than 1,000 used motor oil collection centers in
        Florida and they are free to households.
        True

394.   True or False: There are many nontoxic alternatives to household products that
        contain toxic chemicals.
        True. You can find lists of alternatives on the Web or at your library.

Landfills

395.   How many tons of municipal solid waste does Florida generate every year?
        about 25 million tons

396.   How many total pounds of waste, including industrial and construction waste,
        does Florida generate every year?
        about 48.6 billion pounds

397.   On average, how many pounds of solid waste is generated by each person in
        Florida every day?
        about 9.6 pounds

398.   How many tons of municipal solid waste per capita was disposed of in Florida in 1997?
       about 0.99 tons

399.   What was the percentage of municipal solid waste reduction per capita in Florida due to recycling in 1997?
       10%

400.   How many tons of solid waste are recycled in Florida ever year?
       over 7 million tons

401.   What happens to municipal solid waste in Florida?
       • *combusted in waste-to-energy facilities or industrial boilers*
       • *composted*
       • *deposited in landfills*
       • *recycled*

402.   True or False: Because of Florida's high water table, Florida's solid wastes are not buried in holes; instead Florida landfills are mounds that begin at ground level and rise up.
       True

403.   What material is found in the highest percentages in Florida's landfills?
       paper

404.   What percentage of Florida landfill waste is paper?
       20%

405.   What percentage of Florida landfill waste is plastic?
       6%

406.   How many acres of land are needed for a landfill?
       1,000–4,000 acres

407.   True or False: In Florida, landfills are classified according to the amount and types of waste they receive.
       True

408.   True or False: A tipping fee is the cost per ton to dump municipal solid waste in a landfill.
       True

409.   What is the average tipping fee in Florida's landfills?
       average cost is $42.47 per ton (the range is $23.00 per ton to $92 per ton)

410.   True or False: Florida landfills that accept biodegradable waste are required to have a gas control monitoring system designed to prevent explosions and fires.
       True

411.   What happens to waste when it is buried a landfill?
       It decomposes.

412.   Why are landfills vulnerable to explosions and fires? (Hint: It is the same reason that landfills emit a bad smell.)
Decomposing wastes produce flammable gases.

Methane Recovery

413.   How many cubic feet of gas does one pound of landfill garbage make in one year?
approximately 0.10 cubic feet

414.   What percentage of landfill gas is methane?
about 50%

415.   For how many years does landfill garbage produce gas?
20–30 years, decreasing over time

416.   How much methane gas did the 26.8 billion pounds of garbage buried in 1990 in Florida generate in 1991?
1.3 billion cubic feet of methane gas

417.   True or False: Yard waste and paper products in a landfill increase methane production.
True

418.   How many Florida landfills recovered methane in 1998?
9

419.   What are some of the benefits to landfill methane recovery?
• *Greenhouse gases that damage the atmosphere are reduced.*
• *Local odors are reduced.*
• *Methane is a reliable renewable energy source.*

Recycling

420.   True or False: The Solid Waste Management Act requires each county to create a recycling program.
True

421.   What year did Florida enact the Solid Waste Management Act?
1988

422.   What is the waste reduction/recycling goal for Florida counties with populations greater than 750,000?
30%

423.   What are the "minimum five" materials targeted for recycling in Florida?
• *aluminum cans*
• *glass*
• *newspaper*
• *plastic*
• *steel*

424. How much newspaper waste is collected and how much of it is recycled every year in Florida?

    approximately 1,350,000 tons collected and about 578,000 tons recycled

425. How much glass waste is collected and how much of it is recycled every year in Florida?

    around 750,000 tons collected and about 180,000 tons recycled

426. How many tons of aluminum can waste is collected and how much of it is recycled in Florida every year?

    about 170,000 tons collected and about 32,000 tons recycled

427. How many tons of plastic bottle waste is collected and how much of it is recycled every year in Florida?

    around 280,000 tons collected and about 40,100 tons recycled

428. How many tons of steel can waste is collected and how much of it is recycled in Florida every year?

    around 310,000 tons collected and about 95,000 tons recycled

429. How much construction waste is collected and how much of it is recycled every year in Florida?

    around 5,500,000 tons collected and about 412,000 tons recycled

430. How many tons of tire waste is collected and how much of it is recycled every year in Florida?

    around 170,000 tons collected and about 54,000 tons recycled

431. How much office paper waste is collected and how much of it is recycled in Florida every year?

    around 900,000 tons collected and about 150,000 tons recycled

432. How much yard waste is collected and how much of it is recycled in Florida every year?

    around 3,700,000 tons collected and about 1,875,000 tons recycled

433. True or False: It is not a violation of hazardous waste regulations to dispose of a used oil filter in a landfill.

    False. It is a violation of hazardous waste regulations to dispose of a used oil filter in a landfill.

434. True or False: By law, used oil filters must be recycled by an oil filter processor or municipal refuse incinerator.

    True

435. What products result from recycled yard waste in Florida?

    • *compost, which is used to cover landfills*
    • *fuel, which is used for energy generators and fireplaces*
    • *mulch, which is used for erosion control*

436.   One hundred square yards of yard waste is reduced to how many square yards of post recycled yard waste?
          25 square yards, for a reduction of 75%

437.   How many operating waste-to-energy plants does Florida have?
          13

438.   How many tons of municipal solid waste are burned in Florida's waste-to-energy facilities every day?
          around 15,500 tons

439.   How many watt-hours of electricity can one pound of unprocessed garbage generate when it is burned at a waste-to-energy plant?
          250 watt-hours

440.   How many megawatts of electricity are generated by burning municipal solid waste in Florida's waste-to-energy facilities every day?
          around 534 megawatts

441.   How much energy is saved from recycling one ton of plastic bottles? Answer in BTUs (British Thermal Units)
          about 65.8 million BTUs

442.   How much energy is saved from recycling one ton of glass?
          about 4.4 million BTUs

443.   How much energy is saved from recycling one ton of aluminum?
          about 219 million BTUs

444.   What should you do if you want to start a recycling program in your school or office?
          Contact your county recycling coordinator.

445.   How much do Florida's recycling programs cost per capita annually?
          about $7.50

446.   How many people are employed in the recycling sector in Florida?
          about 32,000

447.   How many recycling centers are in Florida?
          58

448.   How much revenue was generated by state agencies and universities that recycled nearly 1,903 tons of paper in 1998?
          over $43,000

449.   What is the price range per ton for recyclable corrugated cardboard in Miami?
          $22–$62 per ton

450.   What is the price range per ton for recyclable steel cans in Miami?
          $15–$52 per ton

Underground Injection Wells

451.   True or False: Florida injects hazardous waste, non-hazardous waste, and municipal waste into wells below the lowermost underground drinking water sources.
True

452.   What prevents waste injection wells from contaminating underground drinking water sources?
An impermeable layer of rock lies between the upper drinking water aquifer and the lower waste injection aquifer.

453.   How often is testing conducted on waste injection wells in order to determine that injection well waste has not leaked into the drinking water supply?
at least every 5 years

454.   How many waste injection wells are in Florida?
over 125

455.   How many gallons of waste is injected into Florida's waste injection wells every day?
around 361 million gallons per day

456.   What three counties inject the most waste into Florida's waste injection wells?
   • *Broward County*
   • *Miami-Dade County*
   • *Palm Beach County*

457.   True or False: In Florida some groundwater is stored in underground injection storage wells to be withdrawn as needed.
True

458.   True or False: Water storage injection wells are separated from waste injection wells by an impermeable layer of rock.
True

459.   True or False: Water injected into storage wells must meet Florida's drinking water quality standards.
True

Water Quality

460.   What is the main reason Florida faces major water management problems now and in the future?
Population growth will strain the limited supply of fresh water and place greater demands on Florida's waste water management systems.

461.   How many people move to Florida every day?
about 800

462.   On average, how many gallons of water does each person in Florida use every day?
>*190 gallons*

463.   What is Florida's projected population in the year 2020?
>*20.7 million people*

464.   How much fresh water was used in Florida every day in the year 2000?
>*about 8 billion gallons*

465.   What is the projected daily fresh water usage in Florida for the year 2020?
>*9.3 billion gallons per day*

466.   How much water will be required every day for Florida agriculture in the year 2020?
>*4.4 billion gallons per day, or 47% of Florida's total daily water usage*

467.   How much water will be required every day for public domestic water usage in Florida in the year 2020?
>*2.8 billion gallons per day, or 30% of total daily water usage*

468.   True or False: Water withdrawals to meet human needs are causing harm to Florida's ecosystems.
>*True*

469.   What is the total daily capacity for Florida's domestic wastewater treatment plants?
>*2,220 million gallons per day*

470.   What state department has the primary role of regulating public water systems in Florida?
>*the Department of Environmental Protection*

471.   How many public water systems are in Florida?
>*approximately 6,500*

472.   How many water management districts are there in Florida?
>*5*

473.   What happens to Florida's treated effluent waste?
>* *discharged into the Gulf of Mexico or the Atlantic Ocean*
>* *injected into deep wells*
>* *reused*

474.   What is reclaimed water used for in Florida?
>* *agriculture 19%*
>* *groundwater recharge 16%*
>* *industry 15%*
>* *landscape irrigation 44%*
>* *wetlands and other usages 6%*

475.   What Florida county uses the most reclaimed water?
>*Indian River County*

476.   How many wastewater treatment facilities are in Florida?
        4,130

477.   How many of Florida's wastewater facilities are authorized to discharge treated wastewater to surface water?
        560; the remainder discharge to groundwater.

478.   True or False: Chlorine and UV irradiation are used in Florida to disinfect water.
        True

479.   True or False: Nitrate contamination threatens many of Florida's major spring systems.
        True

480.   What is runoff?
        Runoff is rainwater that runs over or through and out of an area.

481.   True or False: Runoff can carry contaminants out of an area to other places.
        True

482.   What is the source of most of the surface water pollution in Florida's lakes and streams?
        agricultural runoff

483.   What is the leading cause of surface water pollution in Florida's estuaries?
        land development and construction

484.   True or False: Most fish kills in Florida waters are the result of too little oxygen in the water.
        True

485.   Why are lakes, ponds, and canals located in residential areas the most vulnerable to fish kills related to dissolved oxygen? (Hint: What pollutants are in the rainwater runoff of residential areas?)
        Rainwater runoff in residential areas contains high amounts of oxygen-dissolving nutrients from septic tanks, lawns, and golf courses.

486.   How many fish kills are reported in Florida every year?
        150–200

487.   True or False: Fish kills can only be prevented by maintaining good water quality.
        True

7
Florida Fauna

Amphibians

Frogs and Toads

488.   What is Florida's largest native frog?
bullfrog

489.   What is Florida's second largest native frog?
pig frog

490.   How long is an adult bullfrog?
8 inches

491.   How long is an adult pig frog?
6 inches

492.   What toad dines exclusively on ants and termites?
eastern narrowmouth toad

493.   What is the third largest frog species in Florida?
river frog

494.   What is the rarest native frog in Florida?
bog frog

495.   Where in Florida can the bog frog be found?
the Panhandle

496.   What is the largest non-native tree frog in Florida?
Cuban tree frog

497.   How do tree frogs climb trees?
Their large toe pads secrete mucous that enables them to stick to dry surfaces.

498.   True or False: The gray tree frog can be identified by the orange coloration on the undersurfaces of its legs and groin.
True

499.   True or False: Most tree frog species can quickly turn from green to brown.
True

500.   What is the largest native tree frog in Florida?
barking tree frog

501.   Which Florida frog species' legs are most likely to be part of a human dinner?
bullfrogs and pig frogs

502. What are juvenile frogs and toads called? (Hint: This stage of life occurs after they emerge from their eggs and before they become adults.)
      tadpoles

503. What do tadpoles eat?
      algae

504. Are tadpoles above or below algae in the food chain?
      Tadpoles are above algae in the food chain.

505. Name an animal that is above frogs in the food chain.
      Answers may vary. A correct answer would be naming any animal that eats frogs, or any animal that eats an animal that eats frogs, and so on.

506. What is the difference between frogs and toads?
(Hint: The most obvious differences are in their skin and legs.)

	Frogs	**Toads**
habitat	*ground and trees*	*ground only*
legs	*long*	*short*
movement	*leap*	*hop*
skin	*smooth and moist*	*warty and dry*

507. Name some of Florida's frog and toad families.
      • *narrowmouth toads*
      • *spadefoot toads*
      • *tree frogs*
      • *tropical frogs*
      • *true frogs*
      • *true toads*

508. What do frogs and toads eat?
      insects

509. What do spadefoot toads do with their spaded hind feet?
      They dig in soil as deep as 8 inches.

510. Where do spadefoot toads spend most of their lives?
      underground

511. True or False: The skin secretions of many of Florida's toads can be irritating to humans.
      True

512. What Florida toad species is the smallest toad in the United States?
      oak toad

513. How long is the oak toad?
      barely over 1 inch long

514.   What non-native toad species found in Florida can be lethal to pets?
       marine toad, also called the giant toad or cane toad

515.   How long is an adult marine toad?
       up to 9 inches

516.   How much does a full grown marine toad weigh?
       up to 2 pounds

517.   Where are a marine toad's poison glands located?
       behind the head

518.   Is the marine toad an omnivore, carnivore, or herbivore?
       omnivore

519.   What are the favorite foods of a marine toad?
       - *cat and dog food*
       - *insects*
       - *lizards*
       - *mice*
       - *small frogs*
       - *worms*

520.   What is the life span of a marine toad?
       up to 10 years

521.   What toad species are native to Florida?
       - *eastern narrowmouth toad*
       - *eastern spadefoot toad*
       - *Fowler's toad*
       - *oak toad*
       - *southern toad*

522.   True or False: Frogs and toads feed on mosquitoes.
       True

523.   How do toads and frogs capture prey?
       They lunge forward and shoot out their sticky tongues to catch insects.

524.   True or False: Toads and frogs chew their prey.
       False. Toads and frogs do have not teeth. They swallow their prey whole.

525.   What is the rarest tree frog in Florida?
       pine barrens tree frog

526.   True or False: In Florida, a permit is required to capture frogs intended for sale.
       True

527.   What frog species are native to Florida?

- *barking tree frog*
- *bird-voiced tree frog*
- *bronze frog*
- *bullfrog*
- *carpenter frog*
- *Cope's gray tree frog*
- *dusky gopher frog*
- *Florida bog frog*
- *Florida chorus frog*
- *Florida cricket frog*
- *Florida gopher frog*
- *green tree frog*
- *little grass frog*
- *northern cricket frog*
- *northern spring peeper*
- *ornate chorus frog*
- *pig frog*
- *pine barrens tree frog*
- *pinewoods tree frog*
- *river frog*
- *southern chorus frog*
- *southern cricket frog*
- *southern leopard frog*
- *southern spring peeper*
- *squirrel tree frog*
- *upland chorus frog*
- *Other answers may be possible.*

528.   What frog species are protected by law in Florida?
- *bog frog*
- *gopher frog*
- *pine barrens tree frog*

Salamanders

529.   How many legs do salamanders have?
2 or 4

530.   What body parts can salamanders regenerate?
- *legs*
- *optic nerves*
- *retinas*
- *tails*

531.   What do salamanders eat?
- *insects*
- *worms*

532.   True or False: The slimy salamander secretes a slimy gluelike substance that can glue together the jaws of its predators.
True

533.   Name some of Florida's salamander families.
- *lungless salamanders*
- *mole salamanders*
- *mudpuppies*
- *newts*
- *sirens*

534.   How do lungless salamanders breathe?
through their skin

535. How many lungless salamander species live in Florida?
      12

536. True or False: All salamanders live in the same habitat.
      False

537. What are the species, habitats, descriptions, and protected status of the lungless
      salamanders that live in Florida?
      a. southern dusky salamander
         Habitat: wet areas in north and central Florida
         Description: dark brown or black with flecks of white on its sides, belly,
               and tail, 2–5 inches long
         Status: Unprotected
      b. spotted dusky salamander
         Habitat: near small streams in the Panhandle
         Description: brown gold spotted body and mottled underside, up to 3.5 inches
               long
         Status: Unprotected
      c. Appalachian seal salamander
         Habitat: Canoe Creek in Escambia County
         Description: dark mottled, brown to gray brown above and a cream belly, up to
               6.3 inches long
         Status: Unprotected
      d. southern two-lined salamander
         Habitat: small streams in the Panhandle
         Description: gray to yellowish body with two black lines, up to 4 inches long,
               orange-yellow belly, hind feet have five toes
         Status: Unprotected
      e. three-lined salamander
         Habitat: swamps and small streams in north Florida
         Description: tan with a black stripe down the back and along each side, up to
               5.5 inches long
         Status: Unprotected
      f. dwarf salamander
         Habitat: wet areas in north and north-central Florida, around Lake
               Okeechobee, and in Pinellas, Sarasota, and Miami-Dade Counties
         Description: thin with a gray or yellowish back, a yellowish belly, and a thin
               black stripe down each side, four toes on each of its four legs, up to
               3.5 inches long.
         Status: Unprotected
      g. Georgia blind salamander or southeastern blind cave Salamander
         Habitat: clear water in caves near the Georgia border
         Description: albino, no eyes, red feathery external gills, long, thin legs, and a
               finned tail, up to 3 inches long
         Status: Protected
      h. four-toed salamander
         Habitat: under logs and rocks in damp areas in Leon, Jefferson, and Walton
               Counties
         Description: back is coppery red or brown, sides are gray, and the belly is
               white with black spots, round head and tail, four legs with four toes
               on each leg, up to 2.75 inches long
         Status: Protected

i. slimy salamander
> *Habitat: moist hammocks in north and central Florida*
> *Description: shiny black body with white flecks on its back and sides, up to 7 inches long.*
> *Status: Protected*

j. rusty mud salamander
> *Habitat: small hammock streams and springs in northern Florida and in Orange and Seminole Counties*
> *Description: rusty red with a yellowish, red-flecked underside, up to 7.5 inches long*
> *Status: Protected*

k. southern red salamander
> *Habitat: clear streams in the Panhandle*
> *Description: white-flecked bright red to purplish brown, up to 6.5 inches long*
> *Status: Protected*

l. many-lined salamander
> *Habitat: black water streams, ponds, and ditches along the southern edge of the Okefenokee Swamp*
> *Description: brown or dark tan with a yellowish, black-flecked belly, up to 3.75 inches long*
> *Status: Protected*

Birds

anhinga

538.   Approximately how many bird species live in Florida for some part of the year?
> *about 467 year-round, but this number depends on the season*

539.   What bird inserts its bill into partially open shellfish and then pulls out the soft parts?
> *American oystercatcher*

540.   Why do cowbirds lay their eggs in the nests of other birds?
> *Because they do not incubate their own eggs; instead they rely on other birds to do so. Thus, they are called nest parasites.*

541. What large water bird found in Florida cannot waterproof its feathers because it does not have oil glands?
    anhinga

542. What habitat does the anhinga prefer?
    shallow freshwater ponds, streams, and swamps

543. How does the anhinga catch its prey?
    Anhingas swim and dive after fish, which they spear with their sharp, pointed beaks.

544. What is the most common cormorant found in Florida?
    double-crested cormorant

545. True or False: Double-crested cormorants have tufts of feathers that appear on their heads only during breeding season.
    True

546. How do cormorants catch fish?
    Cormorants dive after fish and catch them with their hooked beaks.

547. How many varieties of ducks visit Florida every year?
    20–30

548. What bird is sometimes called a man-o-war bird?
    Magnificent frigatebirds earned this nickname because they sometimes attack other birds to steal food and nesting materials.

549. How do magnificent frigatebirds usually get food?
    They swoop low over water and scoop up fish in their beaks.

550. What color is the throat of a magnificent frigatebird?
    Females are white, while males are red.

551. How many gull species (of the family Laridae) are found in Florida?
    24

552. What gulls are commonly found in Florida?
    - *Bonaparte's gull*
    - *great black-backed gull*
    - *herring gull*
    - *laughing gull*
    - *lesser black-backed gull*
    - *ring-billed gull*

553. How many gull species breed in Florida?
    1

554. What is the only gull species that breeds in Florida?
    laughing gull

555. What slow-moving bird walks as if it is crippled and is known for making terrifying screams?
    limpkin

556.   What pelican species live in Florida?
  • *brown pelican*
  • *American white pelican*

557.   What pelican species breed in Florida?
  brown pelican

558.   How do brown pelicans hunt?
  They dive into water and scoop fish into their mouths.

559.   True or False: Brown pelicans are born featherless.
  True

560.   True or False: Brown pelicans often fly in formations.
  True

561.   How do white pelicans catch their food?
  Many birds gather offshore to form a large group, then they herd schools of fish toward shore as they scoop them up in their mouths.

562.   Where does the rare and secretive mangrove cuckoo live?
  south central Florida and south Florida mangrove habitats, and in the Florida Keys

563.   What are Florida's four native species of goatsuckers (nightjars)?
  • *Antillean nighthawk*
  • *chuck-will's-widow*
  • *common nighthawk*
  • *whip-poor-will*

564.   When do birds in the goatsucker family feed?
  at dusk and at night

565.   What do goatsuckers eat?
  insects

566.   Where do goatsuckers lay their eggs?
  Goatsuckers lay their eggs on open ground. The nighthawk sometimes lays eggs on stumps and rooftops.

567.   What oriole species are found in Florida?
  • *Baltimore oriole*
  • *Bullock's oriole*
  • *orchard oriole*
  • *spot-breasted oriole*

568.   What do orioles eat?
  insects and fruit

569.   In what area of Florida does the spot-breasted oriole live?
  the southeastern coast

570. What kinds of trees does the red-cockaded woodpecker usually require for its nest?
   - *living longleaf pine*
   - *loblolly pine*
   - *pond pine*
   - *slash pine*
   - *Other answers are possible.*

571. How long does it take the red-cockaded woodpecker to excavate a nest?
   1–3 years

572. What environmental factors put the red-cockaded woodpecker on the endangered species list?
   - *fire suppression*
   - *overcutting of mature pine forests*

573. What organizations can you contact to find out more about bird watching in Florida?
   - *American Birding Association*
   - *Audubon Society*
   - *Other answers may be possible.*

Wading Birds

574. What are some characteristics of wading birds?
   - *long beaks for fishing*
   - *long legs for wading in water*

575. True or False: Florida's egrets and herons were almost driven to extinction by plume hunters at the beginning of the twentieth century.
   True

576. What is Florida's largest wading bird?
   great blue heron

577. How many ibis species are known to live in Florida? Name them.
   There are 4 ibis species known to live in Florida. They are
   - *glossy ibis*
   - *scarlet ibis (rare)*
   - *white ibis*
   - *white-faced ibis (rare)*

578. How do roseate spoonbills catch their food?
   They wade in shallow water sweeping their open bills back and forth in the water. Their beaks snap shut when food touches it.

Cranes

579. How many crane species are known to live in Florida? Name them.
   There are 2 crane species known to live in Florida. They are
   - *sandhill crane*
   - *whooping crane*

580.   Where in Florida are sandhill cranes found?
- *farmlands*
- *inland shallow freshwater marshes*
- *lawns*
- *pastures*
- *prairies*

581.   True or False: Florida has both resident and migratory crane populations.
True

582.   At what state park in north central Florida do a large number of migratory cranes winter?
Paynes Prairie State Park

583.   Where do cranes build their nests?
Cranes normally build their large, bulky nests in shallow wetlands surrounded by vegetation.

584.   How many eggs do cranes usually lay?
2

585.   How long is the incubation period of a crane's eggs?
about 30 days

586.   What do cranes eat?

- *acorns*
- *aquatic invertebrates*
- *berries*
- *insects*
- *seeds*
- *shoots*
- *tubers*

587.   In 1993 where in Florida were fourteen young captive-reared whooping cranes released in an attempt to establish a non-migratory population?
Three Lakes Wildlife Management Area in Osceola County

Egrets

588.   What color are a great egret's feathers?
white

589.   What color are a great egret's legs and feet?
black

590.   What color is a great egret's beak?
yellow

591.   Does a great egret have long or short legs?
long legs

592.   How do a great egret's legs help it find prey?
Egrets wade in shallow water to hunt for fish.

593.　What egret species can be found in Florida?
　　　　• *cattle egret*
　　　　• *great egret*
　　　　• *reddish egret*
　　　　• *snowy egret*

594.　What color are a reddish egrets feathers?
　　　　The dark phase has a rust-colored neck and slate gray body, while the white phase is all white.

595.　What color is a reddish egret's beak?
　　　　pink with a dark tip

596.　What color are a snowy egret's feathers?
　　　　white

597.　What color are a snowy egret's legs?
　　　　black legs with bright yellow feet

598.　What color is a snowy egret's beak?
　　　　black

Storks

599.　How many stork species live in Florida? Name them.
　　　　Only 1 stork species lives in Florida—the wood stork.

600.　How tall are wood storks?
　　　　3 feet tall

601.　What is the wingspan of a wood stork?
　　　　5 feet

602.　Wood storks do not feed by sight. How to they feed?
　　　　By touch reflex called tacto-location. Walking slowly forward the stork sweeps its submerged bill from side to side in the water. When the bill touches prey, it snaps shut.

603.　True or False: The closing of a wood stork's beak is one of the fastest movements in the animal kingdom.
　　　　True

Herons

604.　How tall is an adult great blue heron?
　　　　about 4 feet

605.　What color is the beak of a great blue heron?
　　　　yellow

606.　What is the wingspan of a great blue heron?
　　　　about 6 feet

607.   True or False: Great blue herons often return to the same nesting site every year.
       True

608.   What is the name of the heron wildlife refuge in the Florida Keys?
       the Great White Heron National Refuge

609.   True or False: The great white heron is a color phase of the great blue heron.
       True

610.   What are the two kinds of night-herons that live in Florida?
       • *black-crowned night-heron*
       • *yellow-crowned night-heron*

Birds of Prey

611.   What is the population of bald eagles in Florida?
       about 3,000

612.   True or False: Bald eagles do not have any feathers on their heads.
       False. They have white feathers on their heads.

613.   How much does an adult bald eagle weigh?
       up to 9 pounds

614.   What is the diet of the bald eagle?
       Bald eagles prefer fish, but will eat snakes, small mammals, and carrion.

615.   How many hawk species live in Florida?
       5

616.   What hawk species can be found in Florida?
       • *broad-winged hawk*
       • *Cooper's hawk*
       • *red-shouldered hawk*
       • *red-tailed hawk*
       • *sharp-shinned hawk*
       • *short-tailed hawk*

617.   What owl species live in Florida?
       • *barn owl*
       • *barred owl*
       • *burrowing owl*
       • *eastern screech-owl*
       • *great horned owl*

618.   How long is the burrowing owl?
       about 9 inches

619.   What is the wingspan of a burrowing owl?
       22 inches

620. True or False: Burrowing owls build their nests in hollow logs.

False. Burrowing owls dig holes in the ground where they build nests and raise their young.

621. How deep is the burrowing owl's burrow?

8–10 feet

622. What is the incubation period for a burrowing owl's eggs?

about 4 weeks

623. At what age do burrowing owls learn to fly?

6 weeks

624. Are burrowing owls nocturnal (active at night) or diurnal (active during the day)?

Burrowing owls are diurnal; most owls, however, are nocturnal.

625. How much does an adult great horned owl weigh?

3 pounds

626. What is the wingspan of a great horned owl?

30–60 inches

627. How many vulture species are known to live in Florida? Name them.

There are 2 vulture species known to live in Florida. They are
  - *turkey vulture*
  - *black vulture*

628. Where do vultures make their nests?

Vultures don't build nests; they lay their eggs in a sheltered location on the ground.

629. Do vultures scavenge or hunt for their prey?

scavenge

630. What do vultures eat?

carrion (dead animals)

631. True or False: Vultures do not have feathers on their heads or necks.

True

632. What do ospreys eat?

fish

633. How do ospreys catch their prey?

They swoop down and grab prey with their feet, sometimes going under water in the process.

Endangered Species in Florida

634.   How many species are on the Florida Fish and Wildlife Commission's list of endangered species?

41

635.   How many species are considered threatened in Florida?

26

636.   How many species of special concern live in Florida?

51

637.   How many bats are on Florida's endangered species list? Name them.

There are 3 bats on Florida's endangered species list. They are
   • gray bat
   • Indiana bat
   • Wagner's mastiff bat

638.   What deer species is on Florida's endangered species list?

Key deer

639.   How many mouse species are on Florida's endangered species list?

5

640.   What freshwater fish are on Florida's endangered species list?

   • blackmouth shiner
   • Lake Eustis pupfish
   • Okaloosa darter

641.   True or False: The river otter is not on Florida's endangered species list.

False. The river otter is an endangered species in Florida.

642.   How many reptile species are considered endangered in Florida?

There are 6.

643.   What Florida reptiles are endangered species?

   • American crocodile
   • Atlantic green turtle
   • Kemp's ridley turtle
   • leatherback turtle
   • striped mud turtle

644.   What animal family has the highest combined total species on the endangered, threatened, and species of special concern list? (choices: amphibians, reptiles, fish, birds, mammals, invertebrates)

Birds. There are 36 total: 8 endangered species, 10 threatened species, and 18 species of special concern.

645.   What animal family has the most endangered species in Florida?

mammals

646.   How many mammals are on Florida's endangered species list?
> *21*

647.   How many tree snail species are on Florida's endangered species list?
> *2*

648.   How many crayfish are species of special concern in Florida?
> *3*

649.   How many frog species are endangered in Florida?
> *none*

650.   How many of Florida's frog species are listed as species of special concern?
> *4*

651.   How many animal species have become extinct in Florida since the mid-1800s?
> *at least 19*

652.   How many plant species have become extinct in Florida since the mid-1800s?
> *at least 12*

653.   True or False: Extinction of a species occurs quickly.
> *False. Extinction is gradual.*

654.   How does a species become extinct?
> *When an essential habitat component is reduced to a level inadequate for a species survival, that species becomes extinct.*

655.   What land mammals are on Florida's endangered species list?
> • *Anistasia Island beach mouse*
> • *Choctawhatchee beach mouse*
> • *Florida mastiff bat*
> • *Florida panther*
> • *Florida salt marsh vole*
> • *gray bat*
> • *Indiana bat*
> • *Key deer*
> • *Key Largo cotton mouse*
> • *Key Largo wood rat*
> • *Lower Keys marsh rabbit*
> • *Perdido Key beach mouse*
> • *red wolf*
> • *silver rice rat*
> • *St. Andrews beach mouse*

Freshwater Fish

656.   How many freshwater fish species are native to Florida?
> *over 250*

657.   How many non-native freshwater fish live in Florida?
> *73*

658.   How many of Florida's native fish spawn in fresh water but mature in the ocean?
> *4*

659.   What are the four native Florida fish that spawn in fresh water but mature in the ocean?
> • *Alabama shad*
> • *American shad*
> • *blueback herring*
> • *hickory shad*

660.   How many of Florida's native fish spawn in salt water but mature in rivers or lakes? Name them.
> *There are 2: the American eel and the hogchoker.*

661.   How many of Florida's native fish species live only in brackish estuarine water? Name them.
> *There are 4. They are:*
> • *darter goby*
> • *rainwater killifish*
> • *spinycheek sleeper*
> • *violet goby*

662.   How many of Florida's native fish species live in both fresh and brackish water? Name them.
> *There are 3. They are:*
> • *fat sleeper*
> • *inland silverside*
> • *naked goby*

663.   How many of Florida's native fish species live in salt water, brackish water, and fresh water? Name them.
> *There are 6. They are:*
> • *Atlantic needlefish*
> • *freshwater goby*
> • *Gulf pipefish*
> • *ladyfish*
> • *marsh killifish*
> • *striped mullet*

664.   How many of Florida's native fish species live in both salt water and brackish water?
> *around 50*

665.   The Florida Department of Health has recommended a statewide limited consumption of what fish caught in Florida?
> • *bass*
> • *bowfin*
> • *gar*

666.   Why does the Florida Department of Health recommend limited consumption of some species of fish caught in Florida?
> *Some fish species contain toxic levels of mercury and pesticides.*

667. The Florida Department of Health has issued consumption warnings for fish in how many bodies of water?
11 bodies of water in 12 counties

668. How many freshwater fish species are affected by limited consumption warnings issued by the Florida Department of Health?
at least 11 species

669. What types of fish contain the highest levels of mercury?
Fish at the top of the food chain—mainly long-lived predatory fish such as largemouth bass, tuna, and swordfish—contain the highest levels of mercury.

670. What are the sources of the mercury contaminating Florida's fish?
Mercury enters the food chain in several ways, including
- *chemical production byproducts*
- *emissions from coal-burning power plants*
- *emissions from incinerators that burn waste containing mercury*
- *small amounts of mercury that occur naturally in soils*

Insects and Spiders

671. Where does Florida rank nationally in terms of insect population?
Third

672. What two states have higher insect populations than Florida?
California ranks first and Arizona second.

673. How many insect species have been identified in Florida?
tens of thousands

674. How many insect species are found only in Florida?
About 500 have been identified so far.

675. How many mosquito species live in Florida?
68

676. Where do mosquitoes lay their eggs?
in wet or damp places

677. How many silverfish species live in Florida?
6

678. Why are silverfish considered pests?
They eat paper.

679. How long are centipedes?
1–6 inches

680. What is the life span of a centipede?
up to 6 years

681.   True or False: Millipedes are wormlike, cylindrical animals with many body segments.
        True

682.   How many pairs of legs do millipedes have on each body segment?
        2

683.   True or False: Some millipede species secrete a foul-smelling fluid to repel predators.
        True

684.   True or False: Earwigs enter peoples' ears and infest their brains.
        False. Earwigs are harmless to humans.

685.   How many water strider species live in Florida?
        27

686.   How do water striders walk on water?
        They have tiny water-repellent hairs on their feet.

687.   How many fly species live in Florida?
        Nobody knows for sure, because only a few fly species have been studied in Florida.

688.   True or False: Terrestrial amphipods, also known as lawn shrimp, are native to Florida and live on the ground surface or in the top half-inch of mulch and moist ground.
        True

689.   How many leaf-cutter bee species can be found in Florida?
        65

690.   What shapes do leaf-cutter bees cut out of leaves?
        circles or ovals

691.   Where do carpenter bees build their nests?
        dead trees or other wood

Ants

692.   How many ant species live in Florida?
        about 207

693.   How many of Florida's ant species are considered major pests?
        5 or 6

694.   True or False: Every ant builds its own nest.
        False. All ants are social insects and live in family units.

695. True or False: Carpenter ants repel their attackers by spraying a tiny amount of formic acid.
     True

696. What Florida ant species build a volcano-shaped nest?
     cone ants

697. How many fire ant species live in Florida? Name them.
     There are 2:
       • *red fire ant*
       • *tropical or native fire ant*

698. Why are fire ants considered pests?
       • *They damage plants and crops.*
       • *They can interfere with harvesting.*
       • *Their stings can kill people and animals.*

Beetles

699. How many beetle species live in Florida?
     Over 5,000, and more are being discovered all the time.

700. True or False: Some beetles eat only one thing.
     True

701. What are some of the foods beetles eat?
       • *dung*
       • *insects*
       • *plants*
       • *tree bark*

702. How many ground beetle species live in Florida?
     about 370

703. True or False: Some beetles squirt hot corrosive fluids when attacked.
     True

704. True or False: All beetles can fly.
     False

705. To what beetle family do dung beetles belong?
     scarab beetles

706. Where do dung beetles lay their eggs?
     in balls of dung

707. What is Florida's largest beetle?
     Hercules beetle

708. Where does the Hercules beetle lay its eggs?
     rotting wood

709.   True or False: Some plants depend on beetles to pollinate them.
>   *True*

710.   True or False: Some beetles have legs with teeth and blades for digging.
>   *True*

711.   Why does a click beetle make a clicking sound?
>   *They click to startle predators and to flip themselves away from danger.*

712.   How many luminescent click beetle species live in Florida?
>   *3*

713.   True or False: The bright coloring of some insects warns predators that they contain toxic chemicals.
>   *True*

714.   True or False: Fireflies are beetles.
>   *True*

715.   How many firefly species live in Florida?
>   *more than 50*

716.   How do fireflies use their flashers to attract mates of their own firefly species?
>   *The color and length of the flashes are species-specific.*

717.   How many ladybug beetle species live in Florida?
>   *about 100*

718.   What beetle family whirls on the surface of water and can fly and swim equally well?
>   *whirligig beetles*

719.   How many whirligig beetle species live in Florida?
>   *17*

720.   What unusual defensive behavior is displayed by tortoise beetle larvae?
>   *They collect skin and fecal matter on their backs and throw it at intruders.*

721.   What do tortoise beetles eat?
>   *plants*

722.   How many leaf beetle species live in Florida?
>   *around 375*

723.   Why are many leaf beetle species considered pests?
>   *Because they eat the leaves of crops and garden plants.*

724.   How many longhorn beetle species live in Florida?
>   *about 225*

725.   What does the longhorn beetle do with its horns?
>   *It uses them for smelling and fighting.*

726.   True or False: Weevils are a small family of beetles that live in Florida.
        False. Weevils are the largest family of beetles that live in Florida.

727.   How many weevil species live in Florida?
        around 575

728.   True or False: Weevils eat only plants.
        True

Butterflies and Moths

729.   How many butterfly species live in Florida?
        around 160

730.   What state has the most butterfly species?
        Arizona, which has at least 320 butterfly species

731.   True or False: Butterflies are the second most populous insect family in the world.
        True

732.   True or False: Butterflies have the same pattern on the top and bottom sides of their wings.
        False. Butterflies have different patterns on the top and bottom sides of their wings.

733.   What is the name of the long tongue or feeding tube that most butterflies and moths use to suck up liquid food?
        proboscis

734.   True or False: A butterfly's proboscis may be as much as three times the length of its body.
        True

735.   True or False: Butterflies are cold-blooded and must bask in sunlight to warm their bodies for flight.
        True

736.   What is the common name given to butterfly and moth larvae? (Hint: The larval stage occurs just after emerging from the egg.)
        caterpillars

737.   True or False: A caterpillar sheds its skin only once before turning into a butterfly.
        False. Caterpillars shed their skins several times.

738.   Where do butterflies and moths lay their eggs?
        on plant leaves

739.   True or False: Caterpillars will eat almost any plant.
        False. The larvae of many butterfly species eat only one specific plant.

740.   What animals prey upon caterpillars and butterflies?
> • *birds*
> • *insects*
> • *toads*

741.   How do butterflies and moths become poisonous to their predators?
> *While they are caterpillars, they feed on plants that are poisonous to their predators.*

742.   True or False: Adult butterflies are harmless.
> *True*

743.   What endangered butterfly species is found today only on the northernmost Florida Keys?
> *Schaus's swallowtail butterfly*

744.   How many butterfly species have suffered drastic population reductions due to loss of habitat in Florida?
> *at least 60*

745.   What is the name of the butterfly research and education aviary in Coconut Creek, Florida?
> *Butterfly World*

746.   What kind of feet does the zebra longwing butterfly have?
> *The zebra longwing is brush-footed.*

747.   What color are zebra longwing butterflies?
> *black with narrow yellow stripes*

748.   Where in Florida can the zebra longwing butterfly be found?
> *statewide in gardens, woods, and fields*

749.   What is the lifespan of a zebra longwing butterfly?
> *4–6 months*

750.   True or False: Zebra longwing caterpillars are covered with barbed spines that they use to sting predators.
> *False. Zebra longwing caterpillars have barbed spines but they do not sting.*

751.   How long are a zebra longwing butterflies' wings?
> *2.8–4 inches*

752.   What unusual roosting characteristic do zebra longwing butterflies have?
> *They roost at night in groups of up to 60 butterflies.*

753.   True or False: Many swallowtail butterfly species emit a noxious-smelling substance when threatened by predators.
> *True*

754. True or False: Many butterfly species migrate hundreds of miles northward in the spring and southward in the fall.
     True

755. What families of butterflies are the most common in Florida and worldwide?
     whites and sulphurs

756. True or False: Some wasps and flies lay their eggs on caterpillars and when the eggs hatch, the larvae eat the caterpillar.
     True

757. Why do some caterpillars have spines on their skin?
     The spines are used to discourage and dislodge predators.

758. What are the differences between moths and butterflies? (Note: There are exceptions to these general rules.)

	Butterflies	**Moths**
Antennae	*slender, knobbed*	*feathery*
Body shape	*slender*	*stout*
Nocturnal/Diurnal	*diurnal*	*most are nocturnal*
Population	*fewer than moths*	*numerous*
Scales	*flat, smooth*	*furry*
Smelling method	*feet and antennae*	*antennae only*
Warm-up method	*bask in sunlight*	*shiver muscles*
Wing attachment	*no frenulum*	*frenulum*
Wing fold	*vertical*	*horizontal*

Dragonflies and Damselflies

759. How many dragonfly species live in Florida?
     over 150

760. Where do dragonflies lay their eggs?
     in water or on aquatic plants

761. What animals prey upon dragonflies?
     • *birds*
     • *dragonflies*
     • *frogs*

762. What are dragonflies called just after they hatch?
     dragonfly larvae

763. Where do dragonfly and damselfly larvae live?
     underwater in ponds, streams, pools, and ditches

764. What do damselflies and dragonflies eat?
     • *mosquito larvae*
     • *small fish*

765.   What are the black lines visible in a dragonfly's wings?
veins

766.   How fast can a dragonfly fly?
up to 35 miles per hour

767.   What do dragonflies eat?
insects, especially mosquitoes

768.   How many individual facets are on a dragonfly's eye?
over 25,000

769.   How many families of dragonflies live in Florida?
7

770.   What are the patterns of dark spots visible in a dragonfly's wings?
blisters of blood called stigmata

771.   How many damselfly and dragonfly species live in Florida?
over 150

772.   How many damselfly families live in Florida?
3

773.   True or False: Dragonflies sometimes form swarms.
True. They are most likely to swarm where there is a mass emergence of prey.

774.   True or False: A dragonfly can lift twice its own weight.
True

775.   How many wings do dragonflies have?
4

776.   True or False: The eyes of many dragonfly species are so close together that they touch at the top of the head.
True

777.   True or False: The eyes of damselflies are widely separated.
True

Grasshoppers and Crickets

778.   How many grasshopper and cricket species live in Florida?
over 250

779.   What two grasshopper species are considered major pests in Florida?
the lubber grasshopper and the bird grasshopper, which damage small trees

780.   How many grasshopper species are unique to Florida?
at least 20

781. How many mole cricket species live in Florida?
     4

782. How many mole cricket species are native to Florida?
     1

783. Of the four mole cricket species in Florida, how many are pests?
     3; all of them are non-native species.

784. Why are non-native mole crickets considered pests?
     They create brown spots on lawns and golf courses.

785. How much money has been spent fighting the mole cricket in Florida?
     at least $11.7 million

786. What Florida grasshopper species can raise its wings and produce poisonous bubbles when threatened by a predator?
     the lubber grasshopper

Cockroaches

787. True or False: The term "palmetto bug" is often used as a euphemism for cockroach.
     True

788. How many cockroach species live in Florida?
     at least 38

789. Where do most cockroach species live in Florida?
     outdoors under rotten logs, in grasses, or in leaf litter

790. How many native and exotic cockroach species live in Florida homes? Name them.
     There are at least 8. They are
     - *American cockroach*
     - *Asian cockroach*
     - *Australian cockroach*
     - *brown cockroach*
     - *brown-banded cockroach*
     - *Florida woods roach*
     - *German cockroach*
     - *smoky-brown cockroach*

Spiders

791. How many spider species live in Florida?
     around 2,000

792. Spiders are insects.
     False. They are arachnids.

793.   All spider venom is harmful to humans.
       False. Spider venom is almost always harmless to humans—with a few exceptions like the black widow and brown recluse.

794.   True or False: The nephila spider is known as the golden silk spider because it constructs an amber-tinted web.
       True

795.   Where can golden silk spiders be found in Florida?
       hammocks and swamps

796.   True or False: Female golden silk spiders are much larger than male golden silk spiders.
       True

797.   True or False: A golden silk spider builds a new web every day.
       False

798.   What is the typical diameter of a golden silk spider's web?
       6 feet

799.   What spider commonly found in swamps and hammocks decorates its web with a series of whitish tufts?
       spiny stomach spider (also known as the spiny orb-weaver)

800.   True or False: Fishing spiders are commonly found in Florida's swamps.
       True. Fishing spiders can also be found in Florida's rivers.

801.   How large is Florida's largest fishing spider?
       4 inches long

802.   What is the name of Florida's largest fishing spider?
       Okefenokee dolomedes

803.   True or False: Fishing spiders walk on water but cannot dive down into water.
       False. Some fishing spiders can dive down into water while clutching an air bubble that supplies oxygen while they are submerged.

804.   What do fishing spiders eat?
       crawfish and minnows

805.   How do bolus spiders capture prey?
       They lasso prey with a ball of sticky silk.

Ticks

806.   True or False: Ticks are parasites.
       True

807.   True or False: Ticks are insects.
       False. Ticks are closely related to spiders.

808.   How many legs does an adult tick have?
           8

809.   How many legs does a tick larva have?
           6

810.   What do ticks eat?
           They suck blood from animals.

811.   True or False: Ticks can live for a long period of time without feeding.
           True

812.   What is the lifespan of a tick?
           It ranges from 3 months to 3 years.

813.   What tick species found in Florida is known to cause Lyme disease?
           deer tick

814.   True or False: Ticks can be found in Florida year-round.
           True

Wasps

815.   How many wasp species live in Florida?
           estimated 3,000–6,000

816.   True or False: Many of Florida's wasps are parasitic.
           True

817.   What do parasitic wasps eat?
           • *caterpillars*
           • *insects*
           • *larvae*
           • *spiders*

818.   True or False: Gall wasps create and live in small blisters on trees.
           True

819.   ·What wasp species create nests out of mud?
           • *folded-wing hunter wasps*
           • *mud daubers*
           • *potter wasps*

820.   How many tiny parasitic wasp species live in Florida?
           1,000–2,000

821.   How do paper wasps make paper?
           They scrape pulp fibers from tall weeds.

822.   In 1997 Florida scientists released tiny parasitic wasps in an attempt control what insect?
           a giant breed of whitefly

823.   What wingless wasp is sometimes called "cow killer" because of its painful sting?
         velvet ant

Other Invertebrates

Slugs

824.   True or False: Most Florida slugs are not considered pests.
         False. Most Florida slugs are considered pests because they feed on plants.

825.   How many slug species are native to Florida?
         3

826.   When do slugs feed?
         at night

827.   Why do slugs feed at night?
         They feed at night to avoid the sun. Since they have no shell to protect them, the sun can dry them out.

828.   What is the best way to catch a slug?
         Place a board on the ground. Slugs will take shelter under it in the daytime.

829.   What do snails and slugs do with their two pairs of tentacles?
         Their eyes are on the ends of the long pair; the others are used for smelling.

830.   Why do snails and slugs secrete mucus?
         to aid in movement

831.   True or False: Slugs are snails that have lost their shells through evolution.
         True

Snails

832.   How many snail species are native to Florida?
         about 97

833.   How many non-native snail species live in Florida?
         about 34

834.   How long is the largest of Florida's snails?
         A south Florida tree snail can reach three inches in length.

835.   True or False: Most of Florida's snails are not considered pests and are beneficial to the environment.
         True

836.   How are Florida's snails beneficial to the environment?
         • *They feed on algae and fungi.*
         • *A few snail species eat slugs.*

837.   What color is the manatee snail?
  The shell is transparent. The snail is gray.

838.   What does the manatee snail do to conserve water during droughts?
  It secretes a protective plug to cover its shell opening.

839.   Why do citrus growers consider the manatee snail beneficial?
  It clears algae and mold from the leaves of citrus trees.

840.   How far out of the shell does the manatee snail extend?
  2 inches

841.   How much did it cost to eradicate the giant African snails, which were introduced into south Florida in 1969, and what year were they eradicated?
  They were eradicated in 1975 at a cost of over $300,000.

842.   What Florida snail preys on slugs and other snails?
  the euglandina snail

843.   What is the lifespan of a euglandina snail?
  1–2 years

844.   How many slugs and snails will a euglandina snail eat during its lifetime?
  over 300

845.   How does the euglandina snail capture its prey?
  • *It swallows small mollusks whole.*
  • *It eats larger snails by sticking its mouth into an opening in the snail's shell and sucking out the live snail.*

846.   True or False: The apple snail is one of Florida's largest snails.
  True

847.   True or False: Apple snails are the size of a baseball.
  False. Apple snails are the size of a golf ball.

848.   How does an apple snail survive when its pond dries out?
  It burrows into the slime and mud to protect itself from drying out.

849.   True or False: Some tree snails are endangered and it is illegal to collect or harm them.
  True

Mammals

850.   How many mammal species live in Florida?
  around 80

851.   How many of Florida's mammals are endangered or threatened?
  28

852.   How many of Florida's mammals are considered species of special concern?
          6

Bats

853.   How many bat species live in Florida?
          17

854.   True or False: Bats are the only mammals that can fly.
          True

855.   When do bats eat?
          at night

856.   True or False: Bat wings are much like human hands, but they have longer fingers
          and a thin, tough membrane between the fingers.
          True

857.   True or False: Bats are blind but they "see" with radarlike hearing.
          *False. Bats have eyes and can see. Many bat species have highly developed
          ultrasonic bio-sonar capabilities, called echolocation, which they use to
          navigate in the darkness.*

858.   Are Florida's bat species omnivores, herbivores, or insectivores?
          insectivores

859.   How many insects can a bat eat in one night?
          about 3,000

860.   True or False: Most insectivorous bats eat their body weight in insects each night.
          True

861.   Where do bats roost in Florida?
          • *abandoned buildings*
          • *attics*
          • *caves*
          • *hollow trees*

862.   True or False: Bats frequently attack people.
          False

863.   True or False: Most of the world's bat species live in the tropics.
          True

864.   True or False: Most bats are rabid.
          *False. Less than one percent of bats contract rabies, and when they do they
          generally die within three or four days.*

865.   True or False: Some bat species hibernate in winter.
          True

866.　How many teeth do Florida's bats have?
　　　26–38, depending on the species

867.　What is the favorite food of the big brown bat?
　　　beetles

868.　What is the lifespan of a big brown bat?
　　　about 19 years

869.　How big are the big-eared bat's ears?
　　　1 inch

870.　What is the lifespan of a big-eared bat?
　　　2–5 years

871.　Why is the hoary bat so called?
　　　The hoary bat's fur is a brown-gray color with heavy white fringe that gives it a frosted appearance.

872.　To where does the hoary bat migrate during the winter months?
　　　California, Mexico, and South America

873.　What is Florida's largest bat?
　　　Wagner's mastiff bat

874.　What is the wingspan of a Wagner's mastiff bat?
　　　19.5–22 inches

Bears

875.　How many bear species live in Florida? Name them.
　　　One—the American black bear

876.　Where in Florida can the black bear be found?
　　　in large heavily wooded areas throughout Florida

877.　How big is an adult black bear?
　　　4–7 feet long (nose to tail) and 2–3 feet tall at the withers

878.　What is the average weight range of an adult male black bear?
　　　250–450 pounds

879.　What is the average weight range of an adult female black bear?
　　　125–250 pounds

880.　What is the territorial range of a black bear in Florida?
　　　• females: 10–25 square miles
　　　• males: 50–120 square miles

881.　What is the lifespan of a wild black bear?
　　　about 15 years

882.   What is the population of black bears in Florida?
        1,500 in 2004

883.   How many toes are on the foot of a black bear?
        5

884.   How fast can a black bear run?
        up to 30 mph

885.   Where do black bears make their dens?
        • *caves*
        • *hollow logs*
        • *hollow trees*
        • *thickets*

886.   Is the black bear an herbivore, carnivore, or omnivore?
        omnivore

887.   Do black bears hibernate in winter?
        Florida's black bears do not hibernate; however, during the colder months they enter a dormant period when their body temperature, metabolism, movement, and heart rate decrease.

888.   How many cubs are in a black bear's litter?
        1–4 cubs

889.   What percentage of black bear cubs die before they are 1 year old?
        approximately 25–50%

890.   How long do black bear cubs stay with their mother?
        2 years

891.   True or False: The American black bear is an endangered species.
        False. The American black bear is not endangered; it is, however, a threatened species and is therefore protected by law.

892.   What are the greatest threats to the Florida's black bears?
        habitat loss and fragmentation

Beavers

893.   Where can beavers be found in Florida?
        in streams, swamps, and lakes in the Panhandle and the Suwannee River

894.   Are beavers nocturnal or diurnal?
        nocturnal

895.   How much do beavers weigh?
        30–60 pounds

896.   How tall is an adult beaver?
        40–50 inches

897.   True or False: Beavers can swim the day they are born.
        True

Foxes and Coyotes

898.   Where in Florida can the gray fox be found?
        in wooded areas throughout Florida, except for the Keys

899.   True or False: Both red and gray foxes can be found in Florida.
        True

900.   What fox species is native to Florida?
        the gray fox

901.   True or False: The gray fox is primarily nocturnal, spending the daylight hours in an underground den or hollow log.
        True

902.   How fast can a gray fox run?
        33 miles per hour

903.   True or False: Gray foxes climb high up into trees for protection.
        True

904.   True or False: The gray fox is the only American canid that can climb trees.
        True

905.   True or False: Foxes cannot swim.
        False. Foxes are excellent swimmers.

906.   True or False: In Florida it is illegal to keep a wild fox without a permit.
        True

907.   What is in the diet of a gray fox?
        - *acorns*
        - *berries*
        - *cottontail and marsh rabbits*
        - *deer mice*
        - *grapes*
        - *insects*
        - *paw paws*
        - *rice and cotton rats*
        - *songbirds*

908.   What are the predators of foxes?
        man, dogs, and bobcats

909.   Where is the red fox found?
        in abandoned citrus groves and woodlands statewide, except for the Keys

910.   Where in Florida do coyotes make their homes?
        Coyotes dig large dens throughout the state, primarily in fields, pastures, and open areas.

911.   What do coyotes eat?
>   *Coyotes eat animals, including rodents, cats, dogs, and livestock, as well as some plants.*

Key Deer

912.   What is the Key deer population in Florida?
>   *In 2000 it was estimated to be 600–800.*

913.   What was the Key deer population in the 1940s?
>   *fewer than 50*

914.   Where do Key deer live?
>   *Key deer live in the Florida Keys—their range extends from Johnson Key to Sugarloaf Key.*

915.   What Florida Keys have the highest Key deer population?
>   *75% of the Key deer population live on Big Pine Key and No Name Key.*

916.   Are Key deer omnivores, herbivores, or carnivores?
>   *herbivores*

917.   True or False: Key deer are the smallest species in the White Tail Deer family.
>   *True*

918.   How tall are Key deer?
>   *24–36 inches*

919.   How much do mature Key deer weigh?
>   *65–100 pounds*

920.   How much do Key deer weigh at birth?
>   *2–4 pounds*

921.   True or False: It is illegal for people to feed Key deer.
>   *True*

Panthers and Bobcats

922.   What two feline species are native to Florida?
>   • *bobcat*
>   • *Florida panther*

923.   What native Florida cat is an endangered species?
>   *Florida panther*

924.   Where do Florida panthers live?
>   *They live in south Florida, mostly in the Everglades and Big Cypress Swamp.*

925.   True or False: In the past, Florida panthers lived all over Florida and in parts of Georgia, Alabama, and Mississippi.
>   *True*

926.   Are Florida panthers omnivores, herbivores, or carnivores?
        carnivores

927.   How much does a mature Florida panther weigh?
        70–160 pounds

928.   How long is a mature Florida panther?
        6–8 feet long from tip of nose to tip of tail

929.   What color are the eyes of an adult Florida panther?
        shades of brown to pale gold

930.   How fast can an adult Florida panther run?
        up to 35 miles per hour for short distances

931.   True or False: Florida panthers can swim and often cross wide rivers.
        True

932.   What is the primary food of the Florida panther?
        wild hogs and white-tailed deer, but they will eat smaller mammals

933.   At what time of day are Florida panthers most likely to hunt?
        dusk and dawn

934.   How many Florida panther kittens are in a litter?
        1–4

935.   How much does a panther kitten weigh at birth?
        about 1 pound

936.   True or False: Florida panther kittens are blind at birth.
        True

937.   What color are a Florida panther kitten's eyes?
        blue

938.   How long does a Florida panther kitten remain with its mother?
        12–18 months

939.   How old are Florida panther kittens when they begin to hunt with their mother?
        about 2 months old

940.   How old are panther kittens when they begin hunting alone?
        • *At 9–12 months they hunt small prey.*
        • *At 18 months they begin to hunt large prey such as deer and hogs.*

941.   How does a Florida panther mark the boundaries of its hunting territory?
        • *clawing tree trunks*
        • *making scent markings*
        • *scraping soil, leaves, and pine needles*

942.   What is the range of an adult male panther?
           about 250 square miles

943.   What is the range of an adult female panther?
           70–200 square miles

944.   True or False: Panthers live most of their lives alone.
           True

945.   How many years do panthers live in the wild?
           Females live 10–15 years, while males often die before the age of 6.

946.   In what year was the Florida panther declared an endangered species?
           1958

947.   How many Florida panthers remain in the wild?
           about 80 adults and sub-adults

948.   What is threatening the survival of Florida panthers?
           • *disease*
           • *dwindling supply of large prey*
           • *inbreeding*
           • *loss, fragmentation, and degradation of habitat*
           • *mercury and other pollution*

949.   What has caused the inbreeding of Florida panthers?
           *Land development has isolated the Florida panther from other populations of
           its species, so panthers have inbred with others that are too closely related.*

950.   What are the effects of inbreeding on the Florida panther?
           • *congenital heart defects*
           • *high incidence of birth defects*
           • *infertility*
           • *poor sperm quality*

951.   True or False: Biologists are attempting to revitalize panther populations in Florida.
           True

952.   What animal has been introduced to Florida in an attempt to genetically restore the
       Florida panther?
           Texas cougars, a close relative of the Florida panther

953.   What diseases plague Florida panthers?
           • *calcivirus (a respiratory disorder)*
           • *feline leukemia (FeLV)*
           • *FIV (feline AIDS virus)*
           • *panleukopenia (feline distemper)*
           • *pseudorabies virus (PRV, which is carried by wild hogs)*

954.   True or False: Because the Florida panther sits at the top of the food chain, its
       health is an indicator of the health of everything in the chain below it.
           True

955.   What are the predators of Florida panthers?
        humans and dogs

956.   When and how did the Florida panther become the state mammal?
        in 1982, by a vote of school children

957.   True or False: Killing a Florida panther is a criminal misdemeanor.
        False. Killing a Florida panther is a felony.

958.   True or False: There has never been a verified report of a panther attacking a human in Florida.
        True

959.   What should you do if you see a panther?
        • *Appear to be as tall as possible.*
        • *Back away from the cat.*
        • *Do not turn your back to the animal.*
        • *Make noise.*
        • *Remain calm.*

960.   What should you do if you see an injured panther in Florida?
        Report it immediately to the Florida Fish and Wildlife Commission.

961.   What has Collier County done to protect the endangered Florida panther from highway traffic?
        Collier County placed fences along Interstate 75 and constructed tunnels every few miles. The panthers are using these tunnels instead of crossing the road.

962.   What were the three leading causes of radio-collared Florida panther deaths from 1978 to 1997? (Bonus: see if you can rank them)
        1. Fighting
        2. Highway mortality
        3. Non-infectious diseases

963.   What organizations could you contact to find out more about protecting Florida panthers?
        • *Defenders of Wildlife*
        • *The Florida Panther Society*
        • *The National Wildlife Federation*
        • *U.S. Fish and Wildlife Service*
        • *Other correct answers are possible.*

964.   Where can bobcats be found in Florida?
        throughout Florida

965.   How long is a bobcat's tail?
        4–6 inches

966.   How much does a mature bobcat weigh?
        15–30 pounds

967.   How tall is a mature bobcat?
         about 2 feet

968.   How long is mature bobcat?
         30–50 inches

969.   Are bobcats nocturnal or diurnal?
         nocturnal

970.   What does a bobcat eat?
         • *domestic cats*   • *rodents and rabbits*
         • *game birds and songbirds*   • *small mammals*
         • *lizards*   • *snakes*

971.   What animals prey upon bobcats?
         Dogs and humans. Great horned owls, panthers, coyotes, and foxes sometimes prey on bobcat kittens.

Reptiles

972.   How many reptile species live in Florida?
         about 140

Crocodilians

973.   Does Florida's American alligator live in fresh water, salt water, or brackish water?
         Alligators prefer fresh water, although they do inhabit brackish water as well.

974.   How long is an adult American alligator?
         Females are 8–10 feet long, and males are up to 15 feet long.

975.   What color is an American alligator?
         black

976.   What is the lifespan of an American alligator?
         35–50 years

977.   How many teeth does an American alligator have?
         70–80

978.   True or False: When an alligator loses a tooth it does not grow back.
         False. Alligators regrow teeth.

979.   Are alligators cold-blooded or warm-blooded?
         cold

980.   When is alligator mating season?
         March through May

981.   How many eggs does the average alligator clutch contain?
         30–40

982.   How long does a mother alligator tend her young?
        2 years

983.   How long is a 2-year-old alligator?
        about 2 feet

984.   How many people were killed by alligators in Florida from1948 to 2001?
        11

985.   True or False: Harassing an alligator is against the law.
        True

986.   How many alligators live in Florida?
        over 1 million

987.   True or False: It is against the law to feed an alligator.
        True

988.   What do American alligators eat?

• *fish*	• *snakes*
• *frogs*	• *turtles*
• *small mammals*	• *water birds*

989.   Where is the American crocodile found in Florida?
        Most of Florida's crocodiles live in the southern and southeastern regions of the Everglades.

990.   What color is the American crocodile?
        gray

991.   How long is a full-grown American crocodile?
        about 15 feet

992.   What are the differences between the American Alligator and the American Crocodile?

	Alligator	**Crocodile**
color	*black*	*gray*
eating method	*swallow food whole*	*break food apart*
jaw strength	*more powerful than crocodiles*	*less powerful than alligators*
jumping skill	*cannot jump*	*can jump about 5 feet straight up*
snout	*wide and shorter*	*long and narrow*

993.   How many crocodiles live in Florida?
        500–1,000 (not including hatchlings)

994.   Is the brown caiman a native or non-native Florida crocodilian species?
        non-native

995.   Where in Florida is the brown caiman found?
        in canals in the Miami area

996.   How long is an adult brown caiman?
about 6 feet

Lizards

997.   True or False: There are no venomous lizards in Florida.
True

998.   How many glass lizard species live in Florida?
4

999.   How many legs do glass lizards have?
None. Glass lizards are legless lizards.

1000.   True or False: Glass lizards look like snakes.
True

1001.   What are some of the differences between glass lizards and snakes?
• Glass lizards have ears; snakes do not.
• Glass lizards have eyelids; snakes do not.

1002.   How long are glass lizards?
8–45 inches long

1003.   How many gecko species live in Florida?
8

1004.   What is the only gecko species native to Florida?
reef gecko

1005.   True or False: Ringed lizards look like worms with square scales arranged in rings around their bodies.
True

1006.   True or False: The Florida worm lizard has no legs, eyes, or ears, and its mouth is recessed under its jaw.
True

1007.   What color is the Florida worm lizard?
pink

1008.   How many native skink species can be found in Florida?
11

1009.   How many skink species are protected by law in Florida?
3 as of 2004

1010.   How many mole skink species live in Florida? Name them.
There are 5. They are
   • *bluetail mole skink*
   • *Cedar Key mole skink*
   • *Florida Keys mole skink*

- *northern mole skink*
- *peninsula mole skink*

1011. True or False: Some mole skinks lay their eggs as deep as 6 feet underground.
True

1012. Name some families of Florida lizards.
- *anoles*
- *skinks*
- *geckos*
- *worm lizards*

1013. What do lizards eat?
- *insects*
- *frogs*
- *vegetation*

1014. What color changes is a green anole able to make?
- *brown or tan*
- *gray*
- *green*

1015. What makes green anoles change color?
- *Breeding displays: males turn bright green to attract females, and when two males fight, the winner turns green while the loser turns brown.*
- *Camouflage: they turn green when moving onto something green, and brown when moving onto something brown.*
- *Temperature: they turn green in warm weather and brown in cold weather.*

1016. Where in Florida can the green anole be found?
throughout the state

1017. True or False: The green anole is the only anole that is native to Florida.
True

1018. How many anole species can be found in Florida?
6

Snakes

1019. How many pit viper species live in Florida?
5

1020. What pit viper species live in Florida?
- *cottonmouth (Florida cottonmouth and eastern cottonmouth), also known as water moccasin*
- *dusky pygmy rattlesnake*
- *eastern diamondback rattlesnake*
- *southern copperhead*
- *timber rattlesnake*

1021.   How do pit vipers detect their prey?
       • *They have heat-detecting pits near their nostrils.*
       • *They smell with their tongues.*

1022.   True or False: It is illegal to keep a venomous snake in Florida without a license from the Florida Game and Wildlife Commission.
       True

1023.   What should you do if you are bitten by a poisonous snake?
       • *Remain calm.*
       • *Lie down.*
       • *Get emergency assistance.*

1024.   How many nonpoisonous snake species live in Florida?
       37

1025.   True or False: Florida has more snake species than any other state east of Texas.
       True

1026.   What three nonvenomous snake species are found only in Florida?
       • *Florida crowned snake*
       • *rim rock crowned snake*
       • *short-tailed snake*

1027.   What three colors could be found on the belly of a red-bellied snake?
       brown, red, or yellow

1028.   Where can the Florida brown snake be found?
       • *cypress heads*
       • *ditches*
       • *edges of freshwater ponds*

1029.   What does the Florida brown snake eat?
       • *earthworms*
       • *slugs*
       • *snails*

1030.   What is the common feature among the different species of ribbon snakes?
       lengthwise stripes

1031.   What are the colors of an eastern mud snake?
       shiny black on top with red and black blotches underneath

1032.   What Florida snake tries to poke its captors with its tail?
       eastern mud snake

1033.   What colors and patterns are on the skin of rainbow snakes?
       red, black, and yellow stripes

1034.   What ribbon snake species live in Florida?
       • *bluestripe ribbon snake*
       • *southern ribbon snake*

1035.   What snake found in Florida is turquoise or blue-green, with light stripes and black spots arranged in rows?
> *eastern garter snake*

1036.   True or False: All garter snakes bear live young.
> *True*

1037.   True or False: Snakes have either flat smooth shiny scales or rough scales with ridges.
> *True*

1038.   True or False: Snakes usually eat their prey tail-first.
> *False. Snakes usually eat their prey head-first.*

1039.   Why do snakes usually swallow their prey head-first?
> *It is easier to swallow prey head-first because legs and hair fold backwards more easily.*

1040.   How can snakes swallow prey that is bigger than their mouth?
> *Their jaws unhinge allowing them to swallow prey.*

1041.   What is Florida largest native snake?
> *eastern indigo snake*

1042.   How long is a mature eastern indigo snake?
> *about 6–8 feet*

1043.   What is the prey of an eastern indigo snake?
> • *frogs*
> • *other snakes*
> • *rodents*
> • *toads*

1044.   What is the name of the only slender bright green snake found in Florida?
> *green snake*

1045.   What habitat does a green snake prefer?
> *They prefer to climb in trees and shrubs.*

1046.   True or False: A snake with a cloudy eye is about to shed its skin.
> *True*

1047.   True or False: Snakes can flick their tongues with their mouths closed because they have a notch in a scale in their upper lip through which they flick their tongue.
> *True*

1048.   How does a hognose snake react when threatened?
> *It flares its neck like cobra and/or plays dead.*

1049.   What do hognose snakes eat?
> *toads*

1050.   How many rat snake species are native to Florida? Name them.
   There are 2 rat snake species native to Florida—the red rat snake or corn snake and the Everglades rat snake.

1051.   How do rat snakes kill their prey?
   strangulation by constriction

1052.   What do rat snakes eat?
   rats and mice

1053.   What non-native rat snakes live in Florida?
   • *gray rat snake or oak snake*
   • *gulf hammock rat snake*
   • *yellow rat snake*

1054.   True or False: Crowned snakes are venomous but are not a danger to humans.
   True

1055.   How long is a mature crowned snake?
   about 10 inches

1056.   True or False: Crowned snakes are the smallest snakes native to Florida.
   True

1057.   What do king snakes eat?
   snakes and turtle eggs

1058.   True or False: King snakes give birth to live young.
   False. King snakes lay eggs.

1059.   True or False: King snakes are constrictors.
   True

Copperheads

1060.   What color and pattern is characteristic of a southern copperhead?
   shades of light brown and brown in hourglass patterns

1061.   What habitat do southern copperheads prefer?
   • *under logs*
   • *woodpiles*

1062.   True or False: A southern copperhead keeps the same color and patterning all its life.
   True

1063.   True or False: Copperheads are aggressive and easily provoked.
   True

1064.   True or False: Newborn copperheads look a lot like worms.
   True

1065.   True or False: The bite of a newborn copperhead can be deadly.
True

1066.   How can you tell a baby copperhead from a worm?
You often can't because baby copperheads look a lot like worms, but sometimes a tiny triangular head is visible and they also move in a serpentine fashion.

1067.   True or False: Copperheads are nocturnal.
True

1068.   How long is a mature southern copperhead?
Adults average 22–36 inches.

1069.   What part of Florida has a high concentration of southern copperheads?
the Panhandle, especially Liberty and Gadsden Counties

Coral Snakes

1070.   What colors and patterns are on a coral snake's skin?
wide black bands, narrow yellow bands, and wide red bands

1071.   In what part of Florida can coral snakes be found?
throughout Florida

1072.   Where can coral snakes be found?
The coral snake likes to burrow under leaves, trash piles, or in rotten logs.

1073.   What do coral snakes eat?
lizards and small snakes

1074.   True or False: Coral snakes give birth to live young.
False. Coral snakes lay eggs.

1075.   How long is an adult coral snake?
less than 30 inches long

1076.   True or False: Coral snakes are related to sea snakes, cobras, and mambas.
True

1077.   What two non-poisonous snakes mimic the coloring of the coral snake?
• *scarlet snake*
• *scarlet king snake*

1078.   True or False: A few rare specimens of coral snake found in Florida are all black.
True

1079.   True or False: Coral snakes are the most lethally venomous snakes in North America.
True

1080.   True or False: Coral snake venom attacks the nervous system and causes paralysis.
>*True*

1081.   True or False: Coral snakes have long curved fangs.
>*False. Coral snakes have short straight fangs.*

1082.   True or False: Coral snakes strike in a manner similar to rattlesnakes.
>*False. Coral snakes use their fangs to bite and chew on their victims.*

Cottonmouths

1083.   The cottonmouth is also known by what other names?
>• *cottonmouth water moccasin*
>• *water moccasin*

1084.   What characteristic gives cottonmouths their name?
>*When cottonmouths feel threatened they open their mouths and reveal a white frothy cottonlike lining.*

1085.   What color are adult cottonmouths?
>*black*

1086.   What color are baby cottonmouths?
>*They have reddish-brown cross bands and bright yellow tails.*

1087.   Where can cottonmouths be found in Florida?
>• *flooded woodlands*
>• *forests*
>• *on the water's edge*
>• *pine woods*
>• *ponds*
>• *rivers*
>• *streams*

1088.   True or False: A bite from a cottonmouth may be deadly.
>*True*

1089.   True or False: Cottonmouths are aggressive and easily provoked.
>*True*

1090.   Can a cottonmouth bite underwater?
>*Yes*

1091.   How long is a mature cottonmouth?
>*An average adult can be up to 5 feet long.*

1092.   True or False: Baby cottonmouths are born with full poison sacs and a bite from one can kill.
>*True*

1093.   True or False: Cottonmouths like rivers and lakes with clear water.
>*False. Cottonmouths prefer murky water.*

Rattlesnakes

1094. How many rattlesnake species live in Florida?
       3

1095. What rattlesnake species live in Florida?
       * canebrake or timber rattlesnake
       * dusky pygmy rattlesnake
       * eastern diamondback rattlesnake*

1096. True or False: A dead rattlesnake cannot bite.
       False. Reflex muscle actions may cause a bite for up to an hour after death.

1097. True or False: A bite from a baby rattlesnake can be deadly.
       True

1098. True or False: Baby rattlesnakes look like worms.
       True. Baby rattlesnakes do look like worms, but if you look very closely you might be able to see a triangular head and a small bulge at the tail that is the beginning of a rattle.

1099. True or False: The fangs of a rattlesnake are hollow and filled with venom.
       True

1100. True or False: A rattlesnake can regrow lost fangs.
       True

1101. When provoked how many times does an eastern diamondback rattlesnake strike?
       Eastern diamondback rattlesnakes usually strike multiple times once they are provoked.

1102. How many times does a rattlesnake shed its skin in one year?
       1–5 times

1103. True or False: The age of a rattlesnake can be determined by the number of rattles on its tail.
       False. Rattles often break off so the number of rattles will not correspond to the snake's age.

1104. What area of Florida is known for its high population of albino rattlesnakes?
       Gainesville area

1105. How long is a mature canebrake rattlesnake?
       up to 5 feet long

1106. How long is a mature diamondback rattlesnake?
       up to 7 feet long

1107. How long is a mature dusky pygmy rattlesnake?
       about 20 inches

1108.   How are the rattles on a dusky pygmy rattlesnake different from the rattles of the canebrake or diamondback rattlesnakes?

Dusky pygmy rattlesnakes rattles are tiny, barely audible, and sound like a buzzing insect.

1109.   True or False: The dusky pygmy rattlesnake will strike at the slightest threat.

True

1110.   True or False: A rattlesnake's fangs are long and curved.

True

1111.   True or False: Rattlesnake venom destroys red blood cells and the walls of the victims blood vessels.

True

1112.   What is in the diet of a dusky pygmy rattlesnake?

• *frogs*
• *lizards*
• *mice*
• *snakes*

1113.   What do diamondback rattlesnakes eat?

• *birds*
• *mice*
• *rabbits*
• *rats*
• *shrews*
• *squirrels*

1114.   What areas of Florida are home to diamondback rattlesnakes?

all of Florida

1115.   Where in Florida can the canebrake rattlesnake be found?

mostly in northern Florida

1116.   Where in Florida can the pygmy rattlesnake be found?

throughout Florida

1117.   True or False: Rattlesnakes lay eggs.

False. Rattlesnakes give birth to live young.

1118.   True or False: A rattlesnake can only strike from a coiled position.

False. A rattlesnake can strike from any position.

Water Snakes

1119.   What colors and patterns are on the skin of the Florida water snake (also known as the Florida banded water snake)?

reddish, black and white banded, or mostly black

1120.   What Florida water snakes emit a foul-smelling musk?

• *Florida green water snake*
• *red-bellied water snake*

1121.   What are the color variations of the Florida green water snake?
dark olive green to brown

1122.   What Florida water snakes have a reputation for biting aggressively when handled?
- *brown water snake*
- *Florida green water snake*
- *red-bellied water snake*

1123.   What do water snakes eat?
- *crayfish*
- *dragonflies*
- *frogs*
- *small fish*

1124.   What is the color range of the mangrove water snake?
orange to straw-colored, gray, or pale olive

Turtles and Tortoises

1125.   How many snapping turtle species live in Florida?
3

1126.   How many of Florida's three snapping turtle species are protected by law?
only 1—the alligator snapping turtle

1127.   Do Florida's snapping turtles live in salt water or fresh water?
fresh water

1128.   When are snapping turtles most active?
at night

1129.   True or False: When snapping turtles are threatened they release a foul-smelling musk.
True

1130.   True or False: The alligator snapping turtle is one of the largest freshwater turtles in the world.
True

1131.   How much does a mature alligator snapping turtle weigh?
over 200 pounds

1132.   True or False: The alligator snapping turtle can sever human fingers with one bite.
True

1133.   What is the only tortoise species found in Florida?
the gopher tortoise

1134.   True or False: The gopher tortoise lives on land.
True

1135.   How long is the burrow of a gopher tortoise?
   10–35 feet

1136.   How many animal species use gopher tortoise burrows?
   over 300

1137.   True or False: The gopher tortoise is protected by law in Florida.
   True

1138.   How many eggs does a gopher tortoise lay?
   4–7

1139.   What is the incubation period of gopher tortoise eggs?
   about 80 days

1140.   What is the average length of a mature gopher tortoise?
   10–12 inches

1141.   What is the lifespan of a gopher tortoise?
   about 50 years

1142.   How many kinds of box turtles are known to live in Florida? Name them.
   4—they are
   - *eastern box turtle*
   - *Florida box turtle*
   - *Gulf coast box turtle*
   - *three-toed box turtle*

1143.   What is lifespan of a box turtle?
   50–150 years

1144.   True or False: Hard-shelled turtles periodically shed the outer layers of their skin.
   True

1145.   True or False: Soft-shell turtles have soft leathery skin.
   True

1146.   True or False: Soft-shell turtles have short snouts.
   False. Soft-shell turtles have long snouts.

1147.   How many soft-shell turtle species can be found in Florida?
   There are 4. They are
   - *Florida soft-shell turtle*
   - *Gulf coast smooth soft-shell turtle*
   - *Gulf coast spiny soft-shell turtle*
   - *spiny soft-shell turtle*

1148.   True or False: Soft-shell turtles are fast swimmers and can run on land.
   True

1149.   True or False: The Florida soft-shell turtle can bite and claw ferociously.
        True

1150.   Diamondback terrapins, cooters, and box turtles all belong to what turtle family?
        pond and marsh turtle family

1151.   True or False: The pond and marsh turtle family is the largest living family of turtles in the world.
        True

1152.   In what habitats do Florida's diamondback terrapins live?
        • *mangrove thickets*
        • *mudflats*
        • *saltwater marshes*

1153.   True or False: Diamondback terrapins excrete excess salt through glands in the corner of their eyes.
        True

1154.   Name some of Florida's diamondback terrapin species.
        • *Carolina diamondback terrapin*
        • *diamondback terrapin*
        • *Florida east coast diamondback terrapin*
        • *mangrove diamondback terrapin*
        • *Mississippi diamondback terrapin*
        • *ornate diamondback terrapin*

jellyfish

Poisonous Wildlife

1155.   How many poisonous spider species live in Florida? Name them.
        There are 2—the brown recluse and the black widow.

1156.   How many alleged cases of brown recluse spider bites does the Florida Poison Control Network record each year?
        around 300

1157.   How many venomous snake species live in Florida?
        6

1158.   What jellyfish-like creature found in Florida waters can inflict lethal stings?
Portuguese man-of-war

1159.   What color is the Portuguese man-of-war?
blue or pink-violet with a rainbow-colored, gas-inflated sail

1160.   How does the Portuguese man-of-war sting?
Free-floating tentacles feel for prey and attach themselves to release their venom.

1161.   True or False: Detached tentacles of the Portuguese man-of-war, which are often found washed ashore in fragments on the beach, can sting for months.
True

1162.   What is the peak season for the Portuguese man-of-war in Florida waters?
July through September

1163.   What should you do if you are stung by a Portuguese man-of-war?
Seek medical attention.

1164.   True or False: Sea nettles are smaller and less dangerous than other types of jellyfish.
True

1165.   What does a sea nettle sting look like?
Stung areas resemble an itchy, red, raised rash.

1166.   When should medical attention be sought for a sea nettle sting?
Medical attention should be sought if symptoms include nausea, aching muscles, or drowsiness, or if allergic reaction occurs.

1167.   True or False: Stingrays are aggressive and sting at the slightest provocation.
False. Stingrays are non-aggressive bottom feeders and only attack defensively.

1168.   Where is the stingray's stinger located?
The stinger is located midway along the whiplike tail.

1169.   How do most stingray stings occur?
Stings usually occur when a person walking in shallow water steps on the animal.

1170.   What are the symptoms of a stingray sting?
Any of the following:

• *bleeding*	• *nausea*
• *diarrhea*	• *redness and swelling*
• *immediate sharp pain*	• *vomiting*
• *increased heart rate*	• *welts*

1171.   True or False: Medical attention should be sought for stingray stings.
True

1172.   What does a catfish look like?
          slimy skin with facial catlike whiskers

1173.   True or False: A catfish's poison is in its whiskers.
          *False. The poison is in the skin and in glands located under the fins at the base
          of the fin spines.*

1174.   How do catfish stings usually occur?
          Catfish stings usually occur when the fish is handled.

1175.   True or False: Saltwater catfish stings are usually not severe.
          True

1176.   What is the best treatment for a catfish sting?
          *Immerse wound immediately in hot but not scalding water for 30 to
          90 minutes.*

1177.   What are the symptoms of a saltwater catfish sting?
          Any of the following:
               • *decreased heart rate*   • *scalding pain*
               • *fainting*   • *slowed breathing*
               • *intense throbbing*   • *swelling*
               • *muscle spasms*

1178.   True or False: In Florida there are thousands of insects species capable of stinging,
          but most of them are not dangerous.
          True

1179.   What ant found in Florida delivers a sting that feels like a hot match on skin?
          fire ant

1180.   What does a fire ant look like?
          reddish-brown or black in color, 1/8 to 1/4 of an inch long

1181.   What is the height and diameter of a fire ant hill?
          3 to 6 inches high, 1 to 3 feet in diameter

1182.   True or False: Fire ants are not aggressive, even when provoked.
          False. Fire ants are very aggressive when disturbed.

1183.   What are the symptoms of a fire ant sting?
          extreme pain and blisters

1184.   True or False: It is possible to die from multiple fire ant stings.
          True

1185.   True or False: Vinegaroons resemble scorpions in size and color, but they do not
          have stingers on thier tails.
          True

1186.   True or False: When provoked the vinegaroon sprays a vinegar-like substance that can be irritating to the eyes.
>   *True*

1187.   What is the best thing to do if sprayed by a vinegaroon?
>   *Flush the site of the sting with water for 15 minutes to relieve pain.*

1188.   True or False: The Florida scorpion is venomous.
>   *True. Florida scorpion stings are generally not lethal, but their stings can be very painful, and deadly allergic reactions may occur.*

1189.   What does a Florida scorpion look like?
>   *2–3 inches long with a tail that curves over its head or to the side*

1190.   Where can Florida scorpions be found?
>   *• closets*
>   *• dark corners of garages*
>   *• decayed wood*
>   *• under rocks*

1191.   True or False: Some assassin bug species, also known as kissing bugs, are native to Florida.
>   *True*

1192.   What does an assassin bug look like?
>   *black and white or orange and black coloring*

1193.   How many assassin bugs species live in Florida?
>   *about 65*

1194.   Do assassin bug stings require medical attention?
>   *Medical attention should be sought if extreme pain occurs, followed by swelling and redness.*

1195.   What insect found in Florida is known as "the toe biter"?
>   *giant water bug*

1196.   True or False: The giant water bug injects a tissue-dissolving venom that causes extreme pain and inflammation at the site of the bite.
>   *True*

1197.   True or False: The giant water bug swims but does not fly.
>   *False. The giant water bug both swims and flies.*

1198.   What color is the giant water bug?
>   *brownish-black*

1199.   How long is the giant water bug?
>   *up to 4 inches long*

1200. True or False: The blister beetle sucks the blood of its prey, which causes a blister to form at the feeding wound.
>*False. The blister beetle excretes juices that cause skin to blister.*

1201. True or False: A centipede sting causes pain and sensitivity similar to that of a bee.
>*True. And like bee stings, centipede stings may cause dangerous and deadly allergic reactions.*

1202. What does a centipede look like?
>*• 6–8 inches long*
>*• a pair of legs attached to each body segment*
>*• flat, elongated, segmented body*

1203. True or False: Handling some caterpillars may cause an intense burning pain due to the insect's spines becoming lodged in the skin.
>*True*

1204. What are the symptoms of a caterpillar sting?
>*• itching*
>*• localized pain*
>*• rash*
>*• redness*
>*• swelling*

1205. What is the best way to remove caterpillar spines from the skin?
>*Apply adhesive tape to the affected area and quickly pull it off.*

1206. What is the most common poisonous caterpillar in Florida?
>*puss caterpillar*

1207. What does a puss caterpillar look like?
>*The puss caterpillar is about 1 inch long, is a whitish-tan color, and has pine needle-like hairs covering its body.*

1208. True or False: The Io caterpillar is a stinging caterpillar with hollow spinelike hairs connected to venom cells.
>*True*

1209. What does the Io caterpillar look like?
>*The Io caterpillar has a pale green body with a red-yellow stripe and tufts of yellow spines, and can be up to 2 inches long.*

1210. True or False: The stinging saddleback caterpillar is brown with a light green back, a brown "saddle" spot, and groups of spines on its body.
>*True*

1211. True or False: Hornets, yellow jackets, and bees can deliver life-threatening stings.
>*True*

1212. Why is it important to carefully and quickly remove the stingers of honey bees after being stung?
>*Stingers should be removed promptly so the attached poison sac is not crushed.*

1213.   What is the best way to remove bee stingers after being stung?
A piece of cardboard or other blunt-edged object should be used to gently scrape the stinger away.

1214.   True or False: A honey bee can sting multiple times.
False. A honey bee can sting only once.

1215.   True or False: A wasp can sting only once.
False. A wasp is capable of stinging multiple times.

1216.   Where can hornets and yellow jacket nests be found?
• *attached to tree limbs or house eaves*
• *in the ground*

8
Florida Flora

1217.   How many tree species grow in Florida?
over 300

1218.   How many vascular plants species (plants with veins) live in Florida?
about 3,500

1219.   True or False: Ferns have no seeds, they reproduce by releasing tiny spores.
True

1220.   What poisonous plants live in Florida?

• *allamanda*	• *pencil tree*
• *angel's trumpet*	• *philodendron*
• *balsam pear*	• *physic nut*
• *Brazilian pepper*	• *poinsettia*
• *castor bean*	• *poison ivy*
• *coral plant*	• *poison sumac*
• *dieffenbachia*	• *rosary pea*
• *oleander*	

Botanic Gardens in Florida

1221.   What south Florida University campus is the home of the John C. Gifford Arboretum?
University of Miami's Coral Gables campus

1222.   What is the name of Miami's world-renowned botanical garden?
Fairchild Tropical Botanic Garden

1223.   For whom is Miami's Fairchild Tropical Botanic Garden named?
        David Fairchild (1869–1954)

1224.   What renowned landscape architect designed the Fairchild Tropical Botanic
        Garden? (Hint: He was the leading landscape designer in Florida in the 1930s.)
        William Lyman Phillips

1225.   What unique annual international festival is hosted by the Fairchild Tropical Botanic
        Garden in July?
        the International Mango Festival

1226.   What Florida city boasts a sunken botanical garden?
        St. Petersburg

1227.   What state garden is located between the Atlantic Ocean and the Matanzas River?
        Washington Oaks State Gardens

1228.   What historic North Miami Beach park was designed by William Lyman Phillips?
        Greynolds Park

1229.   Where is The Mountain Lake Sanctuary historic garden located?
        Lake Wales

1230.   True or False: The Fruit and Nut Park is a unique Florida garden that hosts over
        500 varieties of fruits, vegetables, spices, herbs, and nuts, and allows visitors to
        eat some of the edible exhibits.
        True

1231.   Where is the Fruit and Nut Park?
        Homestead, in Miami-Dade County

1232.   What is the name of Palm Beach's oldest and largest botanical garden?
        Mounts Botanical Garden

1233.   What world famous garden is in Winter Haven?
        Cypress Gardens

1234.   What Florida city is home to Alfred B. Maclay State Gardens?
        Tallahassee

1235.   The Montgomery Foundation Botanical Center in Coral Gables is dedicated to the
        establishment and research of scientifically valuable collections of what two plant
        families?
        cycads and palms

1236.   What Florida city is home to the American Orchid Society's International Orchid
        Center?
        Delray Beach

Pitcher Plant

Carnivorous Plants

1237.   How many carnivorous plant families live in Florida?
  4

1238.   What carnivorous plants are native to Florida?
  • *bladderworts*
  • *butterworts*
  • *pitcher plants*
  • *sundews*

1239.   Where can these carnivorous plants be found?
  • *peat bogs*
  • *swamps*
  • *wetlands*

1240.   How do carnivorous plants attract prey?
  • *Their bright colors attract insects.*
  • *They secrete a sweet and sticky substance to lure prey.*

1241.   How do pitcher plants trap prey?
  Once insects are lured inside the pitcher, backward-pointing hairs block their escape.

1242.   How do bladderworts capture prey?
  When insects touch the plant's "trap" hairs, they are sucked inside tiny saclike chambers and digested alive.

1243.   How do sundews and butterworts capture prey?
  They secrete a sticky substance that traps and digests insects that touch it.

Orchid blooming at
Corkscrew Swamp

Florida's Orchids

1244.   How many Florida counties have abundant orchids?
  all 67

1245.   How many orchid species are found only in Florida? Name them.
  There are 3 orchid species found only in Florida. They are
    • *Craighead's noddingcaps*
    • *Florida govenia*
    • *Rickett's noddingcaps*

1246.   How many endangered orchid species live in Florida?
  17

1247.   True or False: The orchid family is the largest family of flowering plants on earth.
  True

1248.   True or False: Orchids grow on every continent.
  False. Antarctica is the only continent on earth where orchids do not grow.

1249.   In what do the roots of epiphytic orchids grow?
  Roots of epiphytic plants grow in the air, usually supported on tree bark.

1250.   In what kinds of trees are Florida's epiphyte orchids usually found?
    • *buttonwoods*
    • *cypress*
    • *mangroves*

1251.   In what do the roots of terrestrial orchids grow?
  Terrestrial orchid roots grow in the ground.

1252.   True or False: Both epiphytic and terrestrial orchids can be found in Florida's hardwood hammocks.
  True

1253.   On what do the roots of lithophytic orchids grow?
        rocks

1254.   Are orchids annuals (plants with a life span of one year or one growing season) or perennials (plants that return every year)?
        perennials

1255.   What kinds of roots do terrestrial orchids have?
        corms, rhizomes, and tubers

1256.   True or False: About fifty orchid species grew in Miami-Dade and Broward Counties before the population and land development explosion but only a few species have survived the habitat destruction.
        True

1257.   True or False: Many of Florida's most rare orchid species can only be found deep in the interior parts of the Everglades.
        True

1258.   True or False: The Fakahatchee Strand contains many orchid species not found anywhere else in Florida.
        True

1259.   True or False: Central and northern Florida are extremely rich in terrestrial orchid species.
        True

1260.   True or False: The majority of northern and central Florida's terrestrial orchids are underground for most of the year.
        True

1261.   In what seasons do northern and central Florida's terrestrial orchids bloom?
        spring or late summer

1262.   How many epiphytic orchid species grow in central and northern Florida?
        2

9
Florida State Facts

1263.   What is Florida's state bird?
        northern mockingbird

1264.   What is Florida's state butterfly?
        zebra longwing

1265.   What is Florida's state marine mammal?
        manatee

1266.   What is Florida's state sea mammal?
        porpoise

1267.   What is Florida's state saltwater fish?
        sailfish

1268.   What is Florida's state freshwater fish?
        largemouth bass

1269.   What is Florida's state land mammal?
        Florida panther

1270.   What is Florida's state wildflower?
        coreopsis

1271.   What is Florida's state tree?
        sabal palm

1272.   What is Florida's state beverage?
        orange juice

1273.   What is Florida's state shell?
        horse conch

1274.   What is Florida's state song?
        "Swanee River"

1275.   What is Florida's state play?
        The Sword and the Cross

1276.   What is Florida's state stone?
        agatized coral

1277.   What is Florida's state gem?
        moonstone

1278.   What is Florida's state flower?
        orange blossom

1279.   What is Florida's state motto?
        "In God We Trust"

1280.   When were oranges first grown in Florida?
        The Spaniards grew oranges in St. Augustine in 1579.

1281.   What is Florida's official nickname?
        Florida's official nickname is "The Sunshine State." This nickname was adopted by the 1970 Florida Legislature.

1282.   Why is Florida named Florida?
        Explorer Juan Ponce de León chose to name the land Florida because of all the flowers he saw when he landed in 1513. Florida means "full of flowers."

10
Geology of Florida

1283.   About 700 million years ago, during the Precambrian geologic era, Florida was part of an ancient supercontinent called what?
Pangaea

1284.   How many years ago did the supercontinent Pangaea begin to break apart into separate continents?
600 million years ago, in the Paleozoic Era

1285.   By examining well cores geologists determined that Florida was once connected to what distant continent?
Africa

1286.   When were Florida's vast phosphate beds deposited?
65 million years ago during the Cenozoic Era

1287.   Most of the landforms characterizing Florida's modern topography—including the springs, lakes, and rivers—were formed during what geologic period?
during the last 1.8 million years, in the Quaternary Period

1288.   What kind of rock underlies Florida?
limestone

1289.   True or False: The Florida peninsula has been built outward and upward over time by the deposition of shells, mud, sand bars, and coral reefs.
True

1290.   How old are the oldest deposits on Florida's surface?
less than 6 million years old

1291.   How much higher was sea level in Florida 120,000 years ago?
about 25 feet higher than it is today

1292.   What types of limestone can be found in Florida?
   - *coquina limestone, which is composed of shells and quartz sand cemented together, found along the east coast of Florida*
   - *Key Largo limestone, which is hard, white to light gray, and contains coral fossils; found in the Keys*
   - *Marianna limestone is fossiliferous and white to cream in color; found Marianna, Jackson County*
   - *Miami limestone, or Miami oolite, which is soft white limestone composed of small rounded sand and quartz particles found at land surface in southern Florida*
   - *Ocala limestone, which is soft to hard calcium carbonate and fossils of small sea creatures; underlies almost all of Florida but is found at the sur face in only a few northern counties*
   - *Suwannee limestone, which is hard, compact calcium carbonate; found in central Florida*

• *Tamiami limestone can be light gray to tan, white, or green, and contains fos*
siliferous sands and sandy clays
• *Tampa limestone, which is hard, massive crystalline rock; found in central*
Florida on the Gulf coast
• *Other answers are possible, as there are many rock formations in Florida*
that are partially limestone.

1293.   True or False: Limestone is easily dissolved by groundwater.
     True

1294.   True or False: Sedimentary rocks are made of consolidated fragments of other
rocks or organic remains, or by the precipitates of minerals from solution.
     True

1295.   True or False: Igneous rocks are made from molten (melted) or partly molten material that has cooled and solidified.
     True

1296.   What is a metamorphic rock?
     A rock that has undergone chemical or structural changes. Heat, pressure, or a
     chemical reaction may cause such changes

1297.   True or False: The Florida peninsula is the emerging portion of a tectonic platform
called the Florida Plateau.
     True

1298.   What causes the formation of caves, drainage basins, sinkholes, and other geologic features that characterize Florida's topography?
     Florida's limestone bedrock is continuously dissolved by moving water on the
     surface and underground.

1299.   When and where did Florida's largest earthquakes occur?
     • *February 6, 1780, in northwest Florida*
     • *January 13, 1879, near St. Augustine*
     • *September 10, 2006, Gulf of Mexico*

1300.   True or False: Florida's Karst topography is characterized by irregular limestone in
which erosion has produced fissures, sinkholes, underground streams, and caverns.
     True

1301.   What rocks and minerals are mined in Florida?
     • *clay*
     • *heavy minerals*
     • *limestone*
     • *phosphate*
     • *sand and gravel*

1302.   In comparison with other states, where does Florida rank in terms of sand and
gravel production?
     approximately 15th

1303.   What percentage of the U.S. phosphate supply was mined in Florida in the year 2000?

75%

1304.   Where are the phosphate mines in Florida?

• *central Florida in Polk, Hillsborough, Manatee, and Hardee Counties*
• *northern Florida in Hamilton and Columbia Counties*

1305.   What minerals are potential by-products of phosphate production?

• *fluorine*
• *uranium*

1306.   True or False: Mining in Florida is done in deep mine shafts.

False. All mining in Florida is open pit or dredge mining.

1307.   Where can igneous rocks be found in Florida?

Igneous rocks have been found several thousand feet below Florida's surface in wells.

1308.   True or False: There are no metamorphic rocks exposed at the surface in Florida.

True. Some metamorphic rocks have been found in Florida wells several thousand feet below the surface.

1309.   How are the heavy minerals in Florida's sands separated from quartz sand?

After dredging sand, heavy minerals are separated by processing sand through a series of centrifugal, magnetic, and electrostatic separators.

1310.   How is peat formed?

Peat is formed when dead plant materials accumulate faster than they decay.

1311.   What fossil fuels are deposited beneath Florida?

oil

1312.   Where are the fossil fuel deposits in Florida?

• *South Florida oil fields are in Lee County, Hendry County, Collier County, and Miami-Dade County.*
• *The western Panhandle oil fields are in Escambia County and Santa Rosa County.*

1313.   How are oil deposits formed?

Layers of energy-rich organic materials built up and were covered and compressed by overlying sediments. Over millions of years the compressed organic matter gradually turned into oil pools.

1314.   Is oil a renewable or non-renewable natural resource?

non-renewable

1315.   When was oil discovered in south Florida?

1943

1316.   When was oil discovered in the western Panhandle?

1970

1317.   How many barrels of oil was produced in Florida from 1943 through 1991?
     529,517,000 barrels

1318.   What parts of Florida are most susceptible to flooding?
     • *barrier islands*
     • *estuarine areas*
     • *inland lakes*
     • *inland rivers*
     • *low-lying coastal areas*

1319.   True or False: Florida is considered a stable geological area.
     True

1320.   What rocks and minerals can be found in Florida at land surface?
     • *flint and chert—a mostly gray rock found in northwest Florida*
     • *ilmenite—a mineral that occurs in beach sand*
     • *limonite—a yellow or brown mineral*
     • *pyrite—a mineral found in well cores that have been dumped on the surface*
     • *rutile—a red, brown, or black mineral that occurs in beach sand*
     • *sandstone—a yellow, orange, red, brown rock*
     • *staurolite—a reddish-brown, brown, or black mineral found in beach sand*
     • *zircon—a red, blue, or lavender mineral that occurs in beach sand*

1321.   What are the most common mineral deposits found in Florida below the land surface?
     • *anhydrite*
     • *calcite*
     • *dolomite*
     • *gypsum*
     • *peat*
     • *phosphate*

Caves

1322.   True or False: There are hundreds of caves under Florida.
     True

1323.   What are most of Florida's caves filled with?
     water

1324.   When were Florida's caves formed?
     during recent ice ages

1325.   What is the name of the only Florida cave system that is not filled with water?
     Florida Caverns in Florida Caverns State Park

1326.   What year were the Florida Caverns in Florida Caverns State Park opened to the public?
     1942

1327.   True or False: There are more freshwater caves and caverns in Florida than anywhere else in the world.
     True

1328.   What can be seen in Florida's cave walls?
        fossils of sea creatures

1329.   What are the three biological classifications of Florida's cave life? (Hint: These three classes all have the prefix "troglo.")
        • *troglobites (cave dwellers)*
        • *troglophiles (cave lovers)*
        • *trogloxenes (cave visitors)*

1330.   True or False: Troglobites are true cave dwellers that cannot survive outside caves.
        True

1331.   How many aquatic troglobite species live in Florida's caves?
        27

1332.   True or False: Twenty-six of the twenty-seven aquatic troglobite species living in Florida are arthropods.
        True

1333.   What are characteristics of arthropods?
        • *exoskeletons*
        • *jointed legs*
        • *segmented bodies*

1334.   Cave dwelling animals usually lack what features?
        eyes and skin pigmentation

1335.   What name is given to animals that lack skin pigmentation?
        albino

1336.   Name some of the troglobites that are commonly found in Florida caves.
        • *blind cave snail*
        • *cave shrimp*
        • *Georgia blind salamander*

1337.   How do creatures that have no eyes sense their enemies and their prey?
        They detect odors, chemical changes, and movement in their environment.

1338.   What environmental factors are threatening many of Florida's troglobite species?
        • *contaminants in groundwater*
        • *decreased water flow*

1339.   True or False: Troglophiles reside both inside and outside caves.
        True

1340.   Name some troglophiles found in Florida.
        • *American eel*
        • *bull catfish*
        • *red eye or spring chub*

1341.   True or False: Trogloxenes visit caves, but must leave the cave to breed and feed.
True

1342.   Name some trogloxenes commonly found in Florida.
- *crayfish*
- *fish*
- *humans*
- *minnows*
- *salamanders*

1343.   True or False: Cave diving is dangerous and many people have lost their lives while diving in Florida's aquatic caves.
True

1344.   True or False: Skilled cave diving teams are currently exploring and mapping the maze of Florida's underground cave systems.
True

Fossils

1345.   What kinds of fossils can be found in Florida?
- *alligator*
- *birds*
- *bison*
- *camel*
- *coprolite (fossilized dung)*
- *coral*
- *deer*
- *diatomite (rock composed of tiny diatom skeletons)*
- *fish*
- *giant armadillo*
- *giant beaver*
- *giant ground sloth*
- *horse*
- *mammoth*
- *manatee*
- *mastodon*
- *petrified wood*
- *saber tooth tiger*
- *sand dollars*
- *shark's teeth*
- *shells of animals that lived in the shallow seas*
- *tapir*
- *turtles and tortoises*

1346.   Why are no dinosaur fossils found in Florida?
During the age of dinosaurs the Florida peninsula was under water and did not exist as a land mass. Therefore no dinosaur remains were deposited in Florida.

1347.   Is a permit required to collect fossils in Florida?
- *A permit is required to collect most vertebrate fossils, including bones, teeth, natural casts, molds, impressions, and other remains of prehistoric animals. No permit is required to collect fossilized sharks teeth, which are abundant in Florida.*
- *No permit is required to collect invertebrate fossils including: fossil plants, invertebrates, and shells.*

1348.   Where are the best places to look for fossils in Florida?
          • *edges of bays or gulfs*
          • *stream banks*
          • *stream beds*
          • *places where dirt has been dug up and overturned*

1349.   How can you learn to hunt fossils in Florida?
          • *Consult* Florida's Fossils *by Robin C. Brown.*
          • *Join one of Florida's fossil or archaeology clubs. These clubs sponsor trips, projects, and fun family activities. (For more information search the web for "Florida fossil clubs.")*

Hydrology

1350.   What can you do to protect Florida's aquatic systems?
          • *Always remove plant matter from boats before going to another body of water.*
          • *Always use designated entry areas to avoid bank erosion.*
          • *Avoid chopping aquatic plants with boat propellers.*
          • *Avoid disturbing the river bottom when paddling or tubing.*
          • *Inspect your yard, woods, garden, school, and boat for invasive plants.*
          • *Learn which plants are desirable natives and which are invasive non-natives.*
          • *Never buy plants you suspect may be non-native.*
          • *Never disturb wildlife.*
          • *Never empty the contents of your aquarium into a body of water.*
          • *Never remove, collect, or transport Florida's aquatic or wetland plants.*
          • *Promote, plant, and cultivate native species.*
          • *Report invasive plant occurrences to your district office of the Florida Department of Environmental Protection.*

1351.   What organizations can you contact to learn more about protecting Florida's aquatic systems?
          • *Florida Defenders of the Environment*
          • *Florida Fish and Wildlife Conservation Commission volunteer programs*
          • *Florida Keys National Marine Sanctuary volunteer programs*
          • *Florida Lake Management Society*
          • *League of Environmental Educators in Florida*
          • *Other answers are possible.*

Aquifers

1352.   True or False: Florida primarily relies on aquifers for drinking water.
          True

1353.   What aquifer supplies south Florida's drinking water?
          Biscayne Aquifer

1354.   How much of south Florida lies above the Biscayne Aquifer?
          around 3,000 square miles

1355.   In what part of the state is Florida's sand and gravel aquifer?
          the western Panhandle

1356.   What is the name of Florida's largest drinking water aquifer?
> *the Floridan Aquifer*

1357.   True or False: Florida has a high water table.
> *True*

1358.   The Floridan Aquifer underlies what states?
> • *all of Florida*
> • *southeastern Georgia*
> • *southern Alabama*
> • *southern South Carolina*

1359.   How many square miles above the Floridan Aquifer?
> *around 100,000 square miles*

1360.   The Floridan Aquifer system can be divided into what three units?
> • *upper Floridan Aquifer*
> • *middle confining layer*
> • *lower Floridan Aquifer*

1361.   What is the function of the middle confining unit of the Floridan Aquifer?
> *The middle confining unit restricts the movement of groundwater between the upper and lower Floridan Aquifers.*

1362.   What type of material composes the middle confining layer of the Floridan Aquifer?
> • *clay*
> • *dolomite with anhydrite-filled pores*
> • *fine-grained limestone*

1363.   Why is the middle confining layer of the Floridan Aquifer considered an aquifer?
> *In some places it yields several hundred gallons per minute to wells.*

1364.   Why is the water in the lower Floridan Aquifer not useful as a water supply?
> *The Lower Floridan Aquifer contains highly mineralized, saline water.*

1365.   Why is the Floridan Aquifer unusable from Lake Okeechobee southward?
> *South of Lake Okeechobee the Floridan Aquifer contains saltwater.*

1366.   How thick is the ground layer overlying the upper Floridan Aquifer?
> *In some places only a few feet of ground separate the surface and the aquifer. In other places the ground between the surface and the aquifer is several hundred feet thick.*

Springs

1367.   How many springs are in Florida?
> *more than 300*

1368.   True or False: Springs are classified into categories based on the volume of water they produce.
> *True—there are 3 spring classifications, 1st magnitude, 2nd magnitude, and 3rd magnitude.*

1369.   What is the magnitude classification given to springs that produce the largest volume of water?
     1st magnitude

1370.   How many 1st magnitude springs are in Florida?
     27

1371.   How much water does a 1st magnitude spring discharge per day?
     A 1st magnitude spring discharges more than 64 million gallons of water every day.

1372.   What is the combined flow rate of Florida's twenty-seven 1st magnitude springs?
     over 6 billion gallons per day

1373.   How many 2nd magnitude springs are in Florida?
     about 70

1374.   How much water does a 2nd magnitude spring discharge per day?
     A 2nd magnitude spring discharges from 7 million to 64 million gallons of water every day.

1375.   How many 3rd magnitude springs are in Florida?
     about 180

1376.   True or False: Florida has more springs than any other state.
     True

1377.   True or False: Florida's springs discharge more water than the springs in any country in the world.
     True

1378.   What is the source of the water in Florida's springs?
     the Floridan Aquifer

1379.   What is the temperature range for northern Florida's springs?
     $66–75^{o}$ F

1380.   What is the temperature range for Florida's southern springs?
     $75–87^{o}$ F

1381.   True or False: Florida's springs are renowned for their purity and clarity.
     True

1382.   What minerals are concentrated in Florida's springs? (Hint: Think of what minerals are in the rocks the springs move through.)
     calcium and magnesium carbonates

1383.   What Florida county has the most 1st magnitude springs?
     Wakulla County has four 1st magnitude springs.

1384.   Which of Florida's 1st magnitude springs are affected by ocean tides?
        • *Crystal River Springs*
        • *Spring Creek Springs*

1385.   True or False: If water pressure above a spring exceeds the pressure within the aquifer, the spring will reverse its flow and siphon into the aquifer.
        True

1386.   What factors make Florida the perfect region for spring formation?
        • *heavy rainfall*
        • *high humidity*
        • *porous soluble limestone thousands of feet thick*

1387.   True or False: Florida's springs are in danger of contamination.
        True

1388.   What is endangering Florida's springs?
        pollution in spring recharge areas

1389.   How does pollution threaten Florida's springs?
        • *Bank erosion can cause sedimentation and turbidity that affects water quality and aquatic ecosystems.*
        • *Chemical fertilizers and pesticides can soak through the soil and reach the groundwater that flows into springs.*
        • *Septic tanks can affect springs by contributing bacteria, pathogens, and nutrients to the groundwater.*

1390.   How are invasive aquatic plants threatening Florida's springs?
        Invasive aquatic plants can overwhelm the native plants and destabilize spring ecosystems.

1391.   How is Florida's population explosion threatening springs?
        Population needs have led to the over-pumping of groundwater in spring recharge areas, which depletes the supply of water flowing into springs.

1392.   What can you do to protect Florida's springs?
        • *Visit a spring and be careful not to erode or pollute the area.*
        • *Learn more about Florida's springs.*
        • *If you live in a spring recharge area:*
            •*use little or no fertilizer on your lawn.*
            •*conservatively water your lawn.*
            •*maintain your septic tank.*
            •*support storm water management and land use decisions that will protect the springs in your county.*

Sinkholes

1393.   How do sinkholes form?
        Acidic groundwater slowly dissolves underground limestone cavities. When a cavity enlarges, the ceiling weakens until the earth above sags or collapses into the cavity.

1394.   True or False: Florida has more sinkholes than any other state in the nation.
         True

1395.   How are Florida's sinkholes connected Florida's aquifer systems?
         Surface water drains into sinkholes and into the aquifers underlying Florida.

1396.   What are the three types of sinkholes that occur in Florida?
         • *collapse*
         • *solution*
         • *subsidence*

1397.   What types of sinkholes are characterized by a bowl-shaped depression?
         solution and subsidence

1398.   What type of sinkhole is the most common in Florida?
         collapse

1399.   True or False: Many of Florida's lakes and ponds are water-filled sinkholes.
         True

1400.   How many times in the twentieth century has Florida's Lake Jackson drained due
         to sinkhole collapse beneath the lake?
         5 times: 1907, 1933, 1957, 1982, and 1999

1401.   Why is it important to protect Florida's sinkholes from pollution?
         • *Since water drains into sinkholes and into Florida aquifers, any pollution
           entering the sinkhole could contaminate the aquifers.*
         • *Ninety-five percent of Florida's drinking water comes from Florida's
           aquifers.*

1402.   What material fills an alluvial sinkhole?
         soil and or sediments

1403.   What Florida parks could you visit to enjoy and investigate sinkholes?
         • *Devil's Millhopper Geological State Park*
         • *Falling Waters State Park*
         • *Manatee Springs State Park*
         • *O'Leno State Park*
         • *Paynes Prairie*
         • *Peacock Springs State Park*
         • *Silver River State Park*

1404.   What are the warning signs that a sinkhole may open up nearby?
         • *cracks on the ground, walls, floors, or pavement*
         • *sagging doors and windows that no longer close properly*
         • *slumping or leaning fence posts, telephone poles, or other structures*

1405.   True or False: In 1998 the digging of a well in Pasco County caused a massive
         sinkhole to open and shortly afterward 700 small sinkholes appeared in the sur-
         rounding area.
         True

1406.   What should you do if a sinkhole opens nearby?
> • *Fence or rope off the hole.*
> • *Keep children and animals away from the hole.*
> • *Notify the local Water Management District.*
> • *Protect the area from pollution.*
> • *If it is on or near your property, contact your property insurance company.*

Soils

1407.   What is the organic origin of Florida's soils?
> • *accumulated plant residues*
> • *weathered rock*

1408.   What soil types represent the majority of soils found in Florida?
> • *alfisols and ultisols (red loamy soils)*
> • *entisols and spodosols (sandy soils)*
> • *histosols (peaty soils)*

1409.   What flora (plant life) live in Florida's soils?
> • *algae*
> • *bacteria*
> • *fungi*
> • *plant roots*

1410.   What fauna (animal life) can be found in Florida's soils and what are their functions in the soil?
> • *Ants alter the density of soils.*
> • *Earthworms are responsible for large-scale soil mixing.*
> • *Millipedes are soil mixers.*
> • *Mites eat bacteria and fungi.*
> • *Mollusks deposit calcium and decompose matter.*
> • *Nematodes decompose organic matter in soils.*
> • *Springtails feed on plant material, feces, bacteria, and algae.*
> • *Termites are soil mixers.*

1411.   True or False: Soil is the least renewable physical component of the forest ecosystem.
> *True*

11
Geography of Florida

1412.   What is the total land and water area of Florida?
> *65,758 square miles*

1413.   What is the total land area of Florida?
> *52,997 square miles*

1414. What is Florida's total water area?
       11,767 square miles

1415. How many miles of tidal shoreline are in Florida?
       2,276 statute miles

1416. How many miles of beaches are in Florida?
       about 663 miles

1417. What is the largest of the Florida Keys?
       Key Largo

1418. How many miles separate Key West and Cuba?
       90 miles

1419. In what time zone is Florida?
       Most of Florida is in the Eastern time zone. The western Panhandle is in the Central time zone.

1420. What are the three land regions in Florida?
       • *Atlantic Coastal Plain*
       • *East Gulf Coastal Plain*
       • *Florida Uplands*

1421. In terms of total area, where does Florida rank among the states?
       22nd

1422. In terms of land area, where does Florida rank among the states?
       26th

1423. In terms of total water area, where does Florida rank among the states?
       3rd

1424. What is the length of Florida ?
       447 miles (St. Marys River to Key West)

1425. What is the width of Florida?
       361 miles (Atlantic Ocean to Perdido River)

1426. What is the geographic center of Florida?
       in Hernando County, 12 miles northwest of Brooksville

1427. How many of Florida's islands are greater than 10 acres in area?
       4,510

1428. What is the highest point in Florida?
       Britton Hill in Lakewood at 345 feet

1429. What is the lowest point in Florida?
       The lowest point in Florida is sea level where Florida meets the Atlantic Ocean and the Gulf of Mexico.

1430.   What is the average elevation in Florida?
> *98 feet or 30 meters*

1431.   What body of water borders the east coast of Florida?
> *the Atlantic Ocean*

1432.   What body of water borders the west coast of Florida?
> *the Gulf of Mexico*

1433.   What states border Florida?
> *Georgia and Alabama*

Bays and Barrier Islands

1434.   True or False: A bay is a partially enclosed body of water.
> *True*

1435.   True or False: Bays are fresh water.
> *False. Bay water is a mixture of sea water and fresh water. Bay waters are considered estuarine waters.*

1436.   True or False: All bays in Florida are shallow-water bays.
> *False. Florida has many deep-water bays.*

1437.   What bays are in Santa Rosa County?
> *• East Bay*
> *• Escambia Bay*
> *• Pensacola Bay*

1438.   Into what bay does the Yellow River empty?
> *East Bay*

1439.   What Florida counties border Choctawhatchee Bay?
> *• Okalossa County*
> *• Walton County*

1440.   Panama City sits at the mouth of what two Bay County bays?
> *East Bay and West Bay*

1441.   What body of water separates Cape San Blas from the mainland?
> *St. Joseph Bay*

1442.   Into what bay does the Caloosahatchee River flow?
> *San Carlos Bay on Florida's southwest coast*

1443.   Clearwater and Dunedin are located on what sound?
> *St. Joseph Sound*

1444. What bays border the city of Tampa?
- *Hillsboro Bay*
- *Old Tampa Bay*
- *Tampa Bay*

1445. On what barrier island is Pensacola Beach?
Santa Rosa Island

1446. True or False: Miami Beach is located on a barrier island.
True

1447. In what county is Placida Bayou?
Pinellas County

1448. What bodies of water border Sanibel Island?
- *Gulf of Mexico*
- *Pine Island Sound*
- *San Carlos Bay*

1449. Are there really 10,000 islands in the Ten Thousand Islands region of southwest Florida?
They are impossible to count, but there are a lot of magrove islands there!

1450. What bays border Apalachee Bay?
- *Dickenson Bay*
- *Ochlockonee Bay*

1451. What bays border Levy County?
- *Waccasassa Bay*
- *Withlacoochee Bay*

1452. What counties does Indian Bay border?
- *Hernando County*
- *Pasco County*

1453. What water body separates Hutchinson Island and the mainland?
Indian River Lagoon

1454. What water bodies border the Canaveral National Seashore?
- *Atlantic Ocean*
- *Mosquito Sound*

1455. What body of water separates Palm Beach from West Palm Beach?
The Intracoastal Waterway. In that area it is also known as Lake Worth.

1456. In what region of the state is Florida Bay?
southwest

1457. What is the name of the city that is situated on Biscayne Bay?
Miami

Cities, Towns, and Counties

1458.   What is the capital of Florida?
       Tallahassee

1459.   What is the largest city in the Panhandle?
       Pensacola

1460.   What is the largest city in south Florida?
       Miami

1461.   What is the largest city in Florida?
       Jacksonville

1462.   On which Florida coast is Tampa?
       the west coast, also known as the Gulf coast

1463.   On what Florida coast is Orlando?
       Orlando is in central Florida, and therefore not on either coast.

1464.   What body of water is off the coast of Fort Lauderdale?
       Atlantic Ocean

1465.   What major water body is off the coast of Pensacola?
       Gulf of Mexico

1466.   What Florida county has the most land area?
       Palm Beach County, which has 2,578 square miles

1467.   What Florida county has the least land area?
       Union County, which has 245 square miles

1468.   How many counties are in Florida?
       67

1469.   In what Florida County is the Space Coast?
       Brevard County

1470.   Why is the Space Coast so named?
       Brevard County is the home of Kennedy Space Center.

1471.   Punta Gorda is the county seat of what Florida county?
    Charlotte County

1472.   In what county is the town of Zephyrhills?
    Pasco County

1473.   What is the county seat of Baker County?
    Maclenny

1474.   What is the county seat of Bay County?
    Panama City

1475.   What is the county seat of Brevard County?
    Titusville

1476.   In what county is Lake City?
    Columbia County

1477.   What is the county seat of Collier County?
    Naples

1478.   In what county is Jacksonville?
    Duval County

1479.   What is the county seat of Duval County?
    Jacksonville

1480.   What is the county seat of Gadsden County?
    Quincy

1481.   In what county is Florida's capital city?
    Leon County

1482.   What is the county seat of Hillsborough County?
    Tampa

1483.   In what county is Orlando?
    Orange County

1484.   In what county is the town of Ocala?
    Marion County

1485.   What is the county seat of Pinellas County?
    Clearwater

1486.   What is the largest city in Pinellas County?
    St. Petersburg

1487.   What is the county seat of Miami-Dade County?
    Miami

1488.   What is the county seat of Broward County?
Fort Lauderdale

1489.   What is the county seat of Alachua County?
Gainesville

Lakes

1490.   True or False: Florida has more natural lakes than any other state in the southeast.
True

1491.   How were Florida's lakes formed?
Most of Florida's lakes were formed by erosion and collapse of karst limestone bedrock.

1492.   What is the largest freshwater lake in Florida and what is its area?
The largest freshwater lake in Florida is Lake Okeechobee; its area is 700 square miles or 448,000 surface acres.

1493.   What is the second largest freshwater lake in Florida and what is its area?
The second largest freshwater lake in Florida is Lake George; its area is 73 square miles or 46,000 surface acres.

1494.   True or False: Lake Okeechobee is the second largest freshwater lake contained entirely within the continental United States.
True. (Lake Michigan is the largest freshwater lake contained within the United States.)

1495.   What is the average depth of Lake Okeechobee?
9 feet

1496.   How many counties border Lake Okeechobee? Name them.
There are 5. They are
- *Glades County*
- *Hendry County*
- *Martin County*
- *Okeechobee County*
- *Palm Beach County*

1497.   What are the main sources of Lake Okeechobee's water?
rainfall and the Kissimmee River

1498.   What are Lake Okeechobee's major outflows?
- *agricultural canals (eastward and southward into the Everglades)*
- *Caloosahatchee River (westward)*
- *evaporation*
- *St. Lucie Canal (eastward)*

1499.   True or False: Invasive plants are not a problem in Florida's lakes.
False. Invasive plants are a big problem in Florida's lakes.

1500.   How many lakes greater than 5,000 acres are in Florida?
        31

1501.   How many lakes greater than 10 acres are in Florida?
        about 7,700

1502.   How many acres of lake surface are in Florida?
        about 3 million acres

Ports

1503.   What is the name of Fort Lauderdale's deep-water port?
        Port Everglades

1504.   Port Manatee is located at the mouth of what Florida Bay?
        Tampa Bay

1505.   What Florida ports had the highest rate of container movement in 2003?
        1. Port of Miami
        2. Port of Jacksonville
        3. Port Everglades

1506.   What Florida port had the most import and export tonnage in 2003?
        Port of Tampa

1507.   What Florida port had the most cruise ship traffic in 2003?
        Port Canaveral

1508.   What is Florida's northernmost seaport?
        Port of Fernandina

1509.   How many cruise ship passengers move through Florida's ports every year?
        over 13 million

1510.   How many cruise ship ports are in Florida?
        5

1511.   What is Florida's southernmost port?
        Port of Key West

1512.   What is Florida's westernmost port?
        Port of Pensacola

1513.   How many major sea ports are in Florida?
        20

1514.   How many international commercial sea ports are in Florida?
        14

1515. How many international commercial sea ports are located on Florida's Atlantic coast?

7

Rivers

1516. How many rivers are in Florida?

almost 1,700

1517. How many miles of rivers are in Florida?

about 10,000 miles

1518. What are the three classifications or types of Florida's rivers?
- *alluvial (sand and gravel bottom)*
- *blackwater (tea-colored water)*
- *spring-fed (spring water source)*

1519. True or False: Some of the rivers in Florida have multiple classifications.

True. For example a river can be both spring-fed and alluvial.

1520. Why do blackwater rivers have dark water?

Blackwater rivers are darkened by tannin in wood and decaying vegetation.

1521. What river originates at the Woodruff Dam in Chattahoochee?

Apalachicola River

1522. What river runs through Tampa?

Hillsborough River

1523. What type of river is the Hillsborough River?

blackwater

1524. How long is the Hillsborough River?

54 miles

1525. What is the longest river in Florida?

St. Johns River is 310 miles or 512 kilometers long.

1526. True or False: Most of Florida's 1,700 rivers and streams begin in northern Florida and travel southward.

True

1527. What Florida river has the highest average flow rate?

The Apalachicola River flows at the rate of 702.4 meters per second.

1528. What is unusual about the flow of the St. Johns River?

It flows from south to north.

1529. What river forms the eastern portion of the boundary between Florida and Georgia?

St. Marys River

1530.   What river was Florida's first federally designated National Wild and Scenic River?
Loxahatchee River

1531.   What Florida river has the greatest gradient or slope?
the Perdido River, which has a gradient of .8 meters per kilometer

1532.   What Florida river has the largest drainage basin?
The Apalachicola River drains 51,800 square kilometers of land.

1533.   True or False: Florida's rivers have identical chemical features.
False. There are many differences in the chemical features of Florida's water-ways.

1534.   What are the major chemical differences among Florida's rivers?
• *hardness*
• *nitrogen content*
• *phosphorous content*
• *specific conductance*

1535.   What is the longest river in northwest Florida?
Apalachicola River, which is 105 miles long

1536.   What type of river is the Apalachicola River?
alluvial

1537.   What river is 5.5 miles long, drains out of the Everglades, and runs through downtown Miami?
Miami River

1538.   What is the name of the river basin that supplies south Florida's fresh water?
Kissimmee River Basin

1539.   What type of river is the Kissimmee River?
blackwater

1540.   What famous Florida river begins in the Okefenokee Swamp and ends at the Gulf of Mexico?
Suwannee River

1541.   What type of river is the Suwannee River?
combination blackwater and spring-fed river

1542.   What fish species migrates from the Gulf of Mexico up the Suwannee River to spawn between February and May?
Gulf sturgeon

1543.   What river flows through Fort Lauderdale?
New River

1544.   What two rivers meet the Gulf of Mexico at Charlotte Harbor?
the Myakka River and the Peace River

1545.   Name some of the rivers in northern Florida.

- *Apalachicola River*
- *Aucilla River*
- *Blackwater River*
- *Chipola River*
- *Econfina River*
- *Fenholloway River*
- *Lower Suwannee River*
- *Ochlockonee River*
- *Perdido River*
- *Pinhook River*
- *Sopchoppy River*
- *St. Marks River*
- *Upper Suwannee River*
- *Wacissa River*
- *Wakulla River*
- *Withlachoochee River*
- *Yellow River*
- *Other answers are possible.*

12
History of Florida

Spanish conquistador

Archaeology

1546.   True or False: It is a third-degree felony to dig for artifacts on Florida state lands without a permit from the Division of Historical Resources.
> *True*

1547.   Who are the founding fathers of Florida archaeology?
- *Charles H. Fairbanks*
- *John W. Griffin*
- *Hale G. Smith*

Pre-Colonial Florida

1548.   What is the name of the archaeological site in south Florida that consists of a series of twenty-four large holes or basins cut into oolitic limestone bedrock?
> *the Miami Circle at Brickell Point*

1549.   What is the diameter of the Miami Circle?
> *approximately 38 feet*

1550.   What are the main features of the Crystal River State Archaeological Site?
- *burial mounds*
- *ceremonial complex*
- *ceremonial stones*
- *middens (mounds of ancient refuse, mostly shells)*

1551.   What archaeological site near Tallahassee contains a number of earthen mounds dating from 1300–1500 A.D.?

Lake Jackson Indian Mounds

1552.   What are the six archaeological culture periods in pre-colonial Florida?
- *Paleo-Indian 12000–6000 B.C.*
- *Early Archaic 6000–5000 B.C.*
- *Middle Archaic 5000–2000 B.C.*
- *Late Archaic 2000–1200 B.C.*
- *Woodland 1200 B.C.–1000 A.D.*
- *Mississippian 1000–1600 A.D.*

1553.   What are the cultural characteristics of the Paleo-Indian Period?
- *Sea level was about 100 feet lower than it is today.*
- *Semi-nomadic people hunted game with stone points and foraged for plants.*
- *The climate was dry.*

1554.   What are the cultural and environmental characteristics of the Early Archaic Period?
- *Communities began to settle.*
- *People fished, gathered, and hunted.*
- *Oak hardwoods covered most of Florida.*
- *Stone tools were developed.*

1555.   What are the main cultural and environmental characteristics of the Middle Archaic Period?
- *People began creating refined stone tools.*
- *Sea level stabilized.*

1556.   What are the cultural and environmental characteristics of the Late Archaic Period?
- *People made fiber-tempered pottery*
- *The climate was moister.*
- *Pine and mixed hardwood forests prevailed.*

1557.   What are the cultural characteristics of the Woodland Period?
- *People developed new pottery styles.*
- *People settled in communities.*
- *Complex religious and political systems evolved.*

1558.   What are the cultural characteristics of the Mississippian Period?
- *There were increasingly complex cultural developments.*
- *People lived in farming communities.*
- *New ideas infiltrated from other cultures.*

1559.   What were the hardest materials available to Florida's Native Americans?
Listed in descending order of hardness:
- *antler*
- *bone*
- *chert*
- *sharks' teeth*
- *shell*
- *wood*

1560.   What materials did the Native Americans use to make arrowheads?
> • *bone*
> • *chert*
> • *flint*
> • *ivory*

1561.   What material did the Native Americans use to make rope and cloth?
> *plant fibers*

1562.   What did early coastal peoples use to catch fish?
> • *nets*
> • *spears*
> • *traps*

1563.   True or False: A projectile point is a manufactured, sharp, penetrating tip which is used in conjunction with a spear, dart, or arrow.
> *True*

1564.   What materials from sea creatures did Native Americans use to make projectile points?
> • *catfish spines*
> • *garfish tails*
> • *horseshoe crab tails*
> • *sharks' teeth*
> • *stingray spines*

1565.   What materials from mammals did Native Americans use to make projectile points?
> • *bones*
> • *deer antlers*

1566.   What material did Florida's Native Americans use to make baskets?
> • *cattails*
> • *palm leaves*
> • *plant stems*
> • *vines*

1567.   How did Native Americans make their clay pots hard enough to use for cooking?
> *They baked their pots in fires for several hours.*

1568.   From what plant did Florida's Native Americans extract latex to use as a base for paint?
> *strangler fig*

1569.   What did Florida's Native Americans use to make white paint pigment?
> *finely powdered shell*

1570.   What did Florida's Native Americans use to make black paint pigment?
> *powdered charcoal*

1571.   What did Florida's Native Americans use to make red paint pigment?
> *powdered red clay*

1572.   What did Florida's Native Americans use to make violet paint pigment?
          juice from purple marl berries

1573.   What did Florida's Native Americans use to make blue paint pigment?
          They mixed juice from purple marl berries and a small amount of powdered shell.

1574.   What uses did Florida's Native Americans have for paint?
          • *body painting*
          • *mask making*
          • *pottery painting*

1575.   What did Florida's Native Americans use to boil water in?
          shells and clay pots

Colonial Florida

1576.   What is the name of the archaeological culture period of colonial Florida?
          Acculturative (1600–1710 A.D.)

1577.   What was the western capital of the colonial Spanish mission system in La Florida from 1656 to 1704? (Hint: It is near Tallahassee.)
          San Luis de Apalachee Mission

1578.   How many Apalachee Indians lived in or near the San Luis de Apalachee Mission?
          about 1400

1579.   What made the San Luis de Apalachee Mission one of Colonial Florida's prized provinces?
          fertile soils

1580.   Why the was the San Luis de Apalachee settlement abandoned?
          raids by the British and their Creek allies

1581.   What construction materials were used in the San Luis settlement buildings?
          Walls were made from wooden planks or wattle and daub, and the roofs were covered with thatch.

1582.   What were the most important buildings at the San Luis Mission?
          the church and the fort

1583.   True or False: The San Luis Mission military forces included some Spaniards and a majority of Apalachees.
          True

1584.   What types of structures were found in the San Luis Mission?
          • *chiefs' houses*   • *convent*
          • *church*   • *council houses*
          • *kitchen*   • *storage facilities*
          • *commoners' houses*

1585. What early Spanish friars and bishops wrote about colonial life in the San Luis Mission?
   - *Bishop Calderón*
   - *Fray Paiva*
   - *Fray Pareja*

Underwater Archaeology

1586. What is the name of the oldest shipwreck site in Florida?
   Emanuel Point Shipwreck, which is in Pensacola Bay

1587. How many sites in Florida contain archaeological remains of canoes?
   over 200

1588. How many historic shipwrecks lie along Florida's coasts?
   at least 2,000

1589. How many underwater archaeological preserves are in Florida?
   9, and more are planned

1590. What is the name of the sunken steamboat in the Suwannee River that is now an underwater archaeological site?
   City of Hawkinsville

1591. Where is the shipwreck of the *San Pedro*, a galleon of the 1733 Spanish Plate Fleet?
   in the Florida Keys, near Islamorada

Native Americans in Florida

1592. When did the first people live in Florida?
   about 12,000 years ago

1593. When the Spanish arrived, how many Native Americans lived in Florida?
   at least 250,000

1594. What Native American tribes lived in the southern regions of Florida when the Spanish first arrived?
   the Tequestas and Calusas

1595.   What Native American tribe lived in the Cape Canaveral area when Ponce de León arrived in Florida?
       Ais tribe

1596.   In what part of Florida did the Apalachees live when the Spanish first arrived?
       northern Florida

1597.   What region of Florida did the Tocobaga tribe inhabit when the Spanish arrived?
       the central Gulf coast

1598.   What Native American group lived in northeastern Florida when the Spanish arrived?
       the Timucuas

1599.   Where did the Seminole tribe live before they immigrated to Florida?
       They lived somewhere north of Florida, probably in Georgia or the Carolinas.

1600.   At the time Florida became a U.S. territory, how many Seminole settlements existed in Florida?
       about 34

1601.   When was the First Seminole War?
       1817–1818

1602.   What started the First Seminole War?
       Neamathla, a Seminole chief, warned U.S. troops not to trespass on tribal hunting grounds. About 250 soldiers responded to his warning by attacking a village.

1603.   When was the Second Seminole War?
       1835–1842

1604.   What started the Second Seminole War?
       Osceola incited rebellion against Seminole resettlement to the Indian territory out West by staging an ambush of American army troops led by Major Francis L. Dade.

1605.   When was the Third Seminole War?
       1855–1857

1606.   What started the Third Seminole War?
       Some white people destroyed Billy Bowlegs' banana stand in the Everglades.

1607.   True or False: At the time the United States acquired Florida, the Seminoles had only been in Florida about 120 years.
       True

1608.   What three famous Seminole leaders fought against the relocation of their tribes to Oklahoma during the Seminole Wars?
       • *Aripeka*
       • *Billy Bowlegs*
       • *Osceola*

1609.   Was Osceola a chief of the Seminoles?
>   *No. Although Osceola was neither an elected nor a hereditary chief, he was an important Seminole leader during the Second Seminole War.*

1610.   Who was the first woman to become an elected leader of the Seminoles?
>   *Betty Mae Tiger Jumper*

1611.   When and where was Betty Mae Tiger Jumper born?
>   *She was born in 1923 in Indiantown, which is east of Lake Okeechobee.*

1612.   Sam Jones was a famous Micosukee medicine man. What was his Indian name?
>   *Aripeka*

1613.   Billy Bowlegs traveled to Washington, D.C., twice to meet with which President?
>   *President Millard Fillmore*

1614.   Where did Osceola die?
>   *Fort Moultrie, South Carolina*

1615.   What famous Apache leader was sent to prison in Florida?
>   *Geronimo*

1616.   In what Florida fort was Geronimo imprisoned for one year?
>   *Fort Pickins near Pensacola, Florida*

1617.   How many Native American tribes have reservations in Florida today?
>   *2—the Seminole and Miccosukee tribes*

1618.   Name the Seminole and Miccosukee reservations in Florida.
>   Seminole reservations:
>   - *Big Cypress Reservation*
>   - *Brighton Reservation*
>   - *Fort Pierce Reservation*
>   - *Hollywood Reservation*
>   - *Immokalee Reservation*
>   - *Tampa Reservation*
>   Miccosukee reservations:
>   - *Alligator Alley Reservation*
>   - *Krome Avenue Reservation*
>   - *Tamiami Trail Reservation*

1619.   Today northern Florida is home to what Native American tribe?
>   *Northwest Florida is home to Creek Indians.*

1620.   How many sites are on the Florida Native American Heritage Trail?
>   *185*

1621.   Where are some of the Indian mounds you can visit in Florida?
>   In the Panhandle:
>   - *Fort Walton Indian Mound Museum and Park*
>   - *Lake Jackson Mounds State Archaeological Site*

In north Florida:
- *Shell Mound Archaeological Site*
- *Washington Oaks State Gardens*

In central Florida:
- *Crystal River State Archaeological Site*
- *Hontoon Island State Park*
- *Tomoka State Park*
- *Twin Mounds Archaeological District*

In east central Florida:
- *Horseshoe Beach Garden Patch Archaeological Site*
- *Mayacan Indian Mounds*

In west central Florida:
- *Historic Spanish Point*
- *Madeira Bickel Mound on Terra Ceia Island*
- *Philippe Park Temple Mound*
- *Tierra Verde Indian Mound*
- *Upper Tampa Archaeological District*

In south Florida:
- *Calusa Mounds*
- *Creek Mound Complex*
- *Mound Key State Archaeological Site*
- *Persimmons Mound*

Ponce de León

European Settlement through the Civil War

1622. Who was the leader of the first Spanish expedition to land in Florida and when did he arrive?
Juan Ponce de León in 1513

1623. When did Hernando de Soto first arrive in Florida?
May 30, 1539

1624. Where in Florida did de Soto land?
He landed in the area of present-day Tampa Bay.

1625. How many men and horses did de Soto bring with him?
600 men and 200 horses

1626.   What were the Spanish hoping to find in Florida?
             silver and gold

1627.   In 1763, Spain traded all of Florida to England in exchange for what?
             Florida was exchanged for Havana, Cuba, which England had captured.

1628.   What country sold Florida to the United States?
             Spain

1629.   What year did Florida become a U.S. territory?
             1821

1630.   What year did Florida become a state?
             1845

1631.   What Revolutionary War battles were fought in Florida?
             The Battle of Thomas Creek (May 17, 1777)
             Skirmish at Alligator Creek (June 30, 1778)
             The Battle of Pensacola (March 9–May 8 1781)

1632.   When did Spain cede Florida to the United States and what was the name of the
           treaty in which it did so?
             Spain ceded Florida to the United States in the Adams-Onis Treaty (also
             known as the US-Spanish Treaty of 1819), which was proclaimed in 1821.

1633.   Did Florida originally have two capitals?
             Yes. During British occupation (1763–1783) Florida was divided into two
             colonies—East Florida's capital was St. Augustine, and West Florida's capital
             was Pensacola. The two capitals were maintained during the second Spanish
             period (1783–1819) and into the American period from 1819–1824.

1634.   When was Tallahassee chosen as the capital of Florida?
             1824

1635.   Who was Florida's first governor before statehood?
             William P. DuVal was appointed by President James Monroe to be the first
             territorial governor of Florida in 1822.

1636.   Who was the first governor of the state of Florida?
             William Dunn Moseley was inaugurated governor on June 25, 1845.

1637.   How many states were admitted to the United States before Florida?
             26; Florida became the 27th state.

1638.   Did Florida side with the North or the South during the Civil War?
             Officially Florida sided with the Confederacy during the Civil War; however,
             there was strong Unionist sentiment in some parts of the state.

1639.   How many states seceded from the Union before Florida?
             2—South Carolina and Mississippi

1640.   When did Florida secede from the Union?
January 10, 1861

1641.   What was the largest battle fought in Florida during the Civil War?
The Battle of Olustee

1642.   When and where did the Battle of Olutsee take place?
near Lake City, on February 20, 1864

1643.   Who won the Battle of Olustee?
the Confederates

1644.   Was Florida's capital city captured during the Civil War?
no

1645.   True or False: Tallahassee was the only Confederate state capital east of the Mississippi River that was not captured by Union troops.
True

1646.   From what Florida port did most U.S. troops embark for Cuba during the Spanish-American War?
Tampa

1647.   Did enemy agents land in Florida during World War II?
Yes, on June 17, 1942, four German saboteurs paddled ashore at Ponte Vedra Beach in a rubber raft.

1648.   What medical doctor invented an ice machine to cool his patients in the hot Florida climate? (Hint: His discovery lead to air-conditioning and refrigeration.)
John Gorrie (1803–1855)

Mary McLeod Bethune

African-Americans in Florida

1649.   Who was the first African-American to hold a position in Florida's cabinet, and what position did he hold?
Jonathan C. Gibbs (1827–1874), who was Secretary of State from 1869 to 1872

1650.   What African-American man was elected to the Florida State House of Representatives in 1868, elected to the Florida Senate in 1869, and was also elected to the U.S. Congress?
Josiah Walls (1842–1905)

1651.   What African-American woman, born to former slaves in South Carolina in 1875, became a teacher, opened a school in Daytona, and became a leading Florida educator? (Hint: A Florida college bears her name.)
Mary McLeod Bethune (1875–1955)

1652.   What African-American established the African-American Episcopal Church in Florida?
Robert Meacham (1835–1902)

1653.   What African-American Floridian, born in 1856, became a famous newspaper writer for *The New York Globe*?
T. Thomas Fortune (1856–1928)

1654.   Who was the first president of Florida State Normal and Industrial School?
Thomas Tucker

1655.   What African-American woman from Green Cove Springs, Florida, became a distinguished sculptor?
Augusta Savage (1900–1962)

1656.   Who is Florida's most famous African-American nurse?
Clara Frye (1872–1937)

1657.   What African-American Floridian is known as the "Angel of Mercy"?
Earthe Mary Magdaline White (1876–1974)

1658.   Who was Florida's first African-American Supreme Court Justice?
Joseph W. Hatchett (1932–)

1659.   What African-American, born in Crescent City, Florida, in 1889, became a leader in the American Labor movement?
Phillip Randolph (1889–1979)

1660.   Name the first two African-American women who represented Florida in the U.S. Congress in Washington, D.C.
  • *Corrine Brown*
  • *Carrie Pittman Meek*

1661.   How many sites are on the Florida Black Heritage Trail?
141

Cuban-Americans in Florida

1662.   Why did thousands of Cubans flee to Key West in 1868?
The Ten Years War in Cuba

1663.   What industry did Cubans establish in Key West?
cigar manufacture

1664.   What pact ended the Ten Years War?
The Zanjon Pact in 1878

1665.   What Cuban, born in Havana and raised in St. Augustine, returned to Cuba as a priest and became an advocate of abolition and civil rights?
Felix Varela (1788–1853)

1666.   True or False: When Florida became a British colony the inhabitants of St. Augustine were evacuated to Cuba.
True

1667.   What Cuban leader founded the Cuban Revolutionary Party in 1892 at the historic San Carlos Institute of Key West?
José Martí

1668.   In addition to being an important Cuban patriot, for what is José Martí known?
He was a writer of international renown and his works are still studied today.

1669.   What Cuban Ybor City couple sheltered the exiled José Martí?
Ruperto and Pauline Pedroso. Their home eventually became the José Martí Shrine.

1670.   Who built the world's largest cigar factory?
Vincente Martinez y Bor

1671.   Who was the first Cuban elected to the Florida legislature?
Fernando Figueredo was elected in 1885.

1672.   What Cuban woman lived in Paris, Cuba, Madrid, and Miami, and was a famous artist, historian, and writer of folk tales?
Lydia Cabrera (1899–1991)

1673.   What year did thousands of Cubans begin fleeing to Miami in order to escape from Cuba's dictatorial regime?
1959

1674.   What is the name of the dictator who took control of Cuba in 1959?
Fidel Castro

1675.   Why is Miami's Freedom Tower also known as Miami's Ellis Island?
Freedom Tower, built in 1925, was leased by the federal government in 1962 for use as a Cuban Refugee Center.

1676.   What year did the CIA and a group of exiled Cubans invade Cuba in a futile attempt to overthrow Castro's government?
1961

1677. What is the name given to the unsuccessful 1961 invasion of Cuba?
the Bay of Pigs Invasion

1678. What percentage of Miami-Dade County's current population is Cuban?
about 40%

1679. How many sites are on the Florida Cuban Heritage Trail?
89

1680. What Miami shrine did Cuban refugees construct in 1966 to honor Cuba's patroness?
Our Lady of Charity Shrine, located at 3609 South Miami Avenue in Miami

Florida's Inventors, Promoters, and Politicians

1681. What famous inventor had a laboratory in Fort Myers?
Thomas Alva Edison

1682. What woman, born in Jacksonville, Illinois, in 1855, became Florida's first woman elected to the U.S. House of Representatives? (Hint: She was the daughter of William Jennings Bryan, a famous politician.)
Ruth Bryan Owen (1855–1954)

1683. What early Florida developer brought roads and railroads to southwest Florida and also set aside some of his own land for parks and preserves?
Barron G. Collier

1684. Who saved Florida from bankruptcy in 1881?
Hamilton Disston

1685. How many acres of Florida land did Hamilton Disston purchase?
4 million acres

1686. How much did Hamilton Disston pay for 4 million acres of Florida?
Hamilton Disston signed an IOU for $1 million.

1687. What was the one condition that Florida imposed on the sale of the land to Disston at 25 cents per acre?
The land had to be drained.

1688. When did Hamilton Disston pay off the IOU?
Disston never completely paid it off. He went broke in the panic-depression of 1893 and committed suicide in 1896.

1689. What transportation tycoon built the Tampa Bay Hotel?
Henry Plant

1690. What railroad tycoon helped found Standard Oil and used his fortune to develop Florida's east coast?
Henry M. Flagler

1691.   What was Henry Flagler's major contribution to Florida's development?
>*railroad development*

1692.   What part did Bion Barnett play in the development of Florida?
>*He created a huge banking empire.*

1693.   What lady tycoon helped to develop Sarasota?
>*Mrs. Potter Palmer*

1694.   What millionaire from Indiana created the Dixie Highway so he could sell real estate in Miami Beach?
>*Carl Fisher*

1695.   How did Carl Fisher create saleable real estate from mangrove swamps in Miami Beach?
>*He filled in the mangrove swamps with fill dirt pumped from the bottom of Biscayne Bay.*

1696.   What south Florida community was developed by George Merrick?
>*Coral Gables*

1697.   What Florida governor served the shortest term in office?
>*Wayne Mixson was governor for three days, from January 3 to January 6, 1987. Mixson was Bob Graham's lieutenant governor, so Mixson served the last days of the gubernatorial term for Graham, who resigned to begin his term in the U.S. Senate.*

Historic Places in Florida

1698.   Where was the first Spanish settlement in Florida?
>*Pensacola*

1699.   What Florida city is the oldest continuously inhabited European settlement in the United States?
>*St. Augustine*

1700.   What year was St. Augustine established?
>   *1565*

1701.   What country did St. Augustine's founders come from?
>   *Spain*

1702.   True or False: Castillo de San Marcos in St. Augustine is America's oldest masonry fort.
>   *True*

1703.   When was Castillo de San Marcos built?
>   *Work began on October 2, 1672, and took 20 years to complete.*

1704.   Who built Castillo de San Marcos?
>   *the Spanish, using Native American labor*

1705.   Name the Florida county that is home to the historic landmark Bok Tower Gardens.
>   *Polk County*

1706.   In what Florida county is Pelican Island National Wildlife Refuge?
>   *Indian River County*

1707.   What Florida city or county is home to the historic Ponce de Leon Inlet Lighthouse?
>   *Daytona Beach, Volusia County*

1708.   What is the name of the elaborate historic Italian-style villa in Miami-Dade County?
>   *Vizcaya*

1709.   What was the island garden at Vizcaya designed to look like?
>   *a barge*

1710.   What is the name of Henry M. Flagler's historic home in Palm Beach County?
>   *Whitehall*

1711.   What historic house in Key West was the home of a famous American writer and has been the home of several generations of polydactyl cats?
>   *the Ernest Hemingway Home and Museum*

1712.   In what Florida city and county is the historic Fort Walton Indian Mound?
>   *Fort Walton Beach, Okaloosa County*

1713.   How many of the bridges connecting the Florida Keys are on the National Register of Historic Places?
>   *3—the old Seven Mile Bridge, the Bahia Honda Bridge, and the Long Key Bridge*

1714.   What is the name of the historic schooner in St. Augustine harbor?
>   Governor Stone

1715.   How many buildings on the University of Florida's Gainesville campus are on the are listed on the National Register of Historic Places?
  21

1716.   What is the name of the historic plantation on Fort George Island?
  Kingsley Plantation

1717.   Where is the historic Okeechobee Battlefield?
  Okeechobee County

Lighthouses

1718.   How many historic lighthouses are in Florida?
  33

1719.   When was the first documented beacon established in Florida?
  1774

1720.   Who established the first beacon in Florida in 1774?
  the British

1721.   Where was the first beacon in Florida?
  Mosquito Inlet

1722.   Who was the first light keeper in Florida?
  Angelo Vackiere

1723.   How much was Angelo Vackiere paid to keep the first light in Florida?
  $24 per year

1724.   When did the first American lighthouse in Florida become operational?
  April 5, 1824

1725.   Where was the first American lighthouse in Florida?
  St. Augustine

1726.   Where was the first lighthouse on Florida's Gulf coast?
    Pensacola—it began operation in December 1859.

1727.   Where was the first lighthouse in the Florida Keys?
    Cape Florida—it began operation in December 1846.

1728.   How many lighthouses were operating in Florida before Florida became a state?
    13

1729.   Where is the oldest existing lighthouse in Florida?
    Amelia Island

1730.   What year was the Amelia Island Lighthouse built?
    1839

1731.   What famous Union General designed, built, or worked on seven of Florida's lighthouses in the 1850s?
    General George Gordon Meade

1732.   What is the name of the tallest lighthouse in Florida?
    Ponce de Leon Inlet Lighthouse

1733.   How tall is the Ponce de Leon Inlet Lighthouse?
    175 feet

1734.   What is the shortest lighthouse in Florida?
    the Cedar Keys Lighthouse

1735.   How tall is the Cedar Keys Lighthouse?
    23 feet

1736.   Where is the Cedar Keys Lighthouse?
    Seahorse Key

1737.   When was the last manned lighthouse built in Florida?
    1954. It was automated in 1964.

1738.   What historic lighthouse, dangerously destabilized in 1995 by Hurricane Opal, toppled into the sea in October 2005?
    Cape St. George Lighthouse, built in 1852

1739.   Where is the only Florida lighthouse on inland waters?
    Lake Dora

1740.   What lighthouse, built in 1838, has been moved twice, and is now known as Florida's "traveling lighthouse"?
    St. Joseph Point Lighthouse. After yellow fever decimated the population and a hurricane destroyed the town of Port St. Joe, the lighthouse was moved to St. Joseph Point in 1847. In 1960 the lighthouse was moved to Simmons Bayou, where it became a private residence.

1741. What lighthouse was originally built in Georgia and was later moved to Florida?
the Amelia Island Lighthouse

1742. True or False: Some of Florida's lighthouses are accessible only by boat.
True

1743. What lighthouse survived three separate earthquakes?
St Augustine Lighthouse survived earthquakes in 1879, 1886, and 1893.

1744. What famous author was shipwrecked off Florida's coast in 1897 and was guided to safety by the Ponce de Leon Inlet Lighthouse?
Stephen Crane

1745. What lighthouse survived 200 mph winds during the Labor Day hurricane in 1935?
Alligator Reef Lighthouse

1746. True or False: Florida's reef lighthouses are built in the water on top of coral reefs?
True

1747. How many reef lighthouses are in Florida waters?
13

Place Names

1748. What Florida city occupies the site of the first European settlement in the United States?
Pensacola

1749. What Florida county was named for citrus trees and the citrus industry?
Citrus County

1750. What was Brevard County called before it was renamed in 1855?
St. Lucie County

1751. What county was named for a common nickname for the South?
Dixie County

1752. What Florida county was named for Christopher Columbus?
Columbia County

1753. What two counties were named for the same famous Spanish explorer?
• *DeSoto County*
• *Hernando County*

1754. What county was named for Florida's first governor?
Duval County

1755. What Florida county was named for a famous railroad tycoon?
Flagler County

1756.   What Florida county was named after a famous early American scientist, printer, and author?
>   *Franklin County, which was named for Benjamin Franklin*

1757.   What Florida county was named after the Everglades?
>   *Glades County*

1758.   What Florida county was named for the Gulf of Mexico?
>   *Gulf County*

1759.   What county was named for the nearby St. Andrews Bay?
>   *Bay County*

1760.   What south Florida counties were at the center of a vote-counting controversy in the 2000 presidential election?
>   *Broward County and Palm Beach County*

1761.   What Florida county was named for first Secretary of the United States Treasury?
>   *Hamilton County, created in 1827, was named for Alexander Hamilton.*

1762.   What is the origin of the name Altamonte Springs, a town in Seminole county?
>   *Altamonte is Spanish for "high hill."*

1763.   Why was the settlement name St. Augustine chosen?
>   *The city of St. Augustine was named for the saint on whose feast day land was first sighted off the coast of Florida.*

1764.   How did Anna Maria Island in Manatee County get its name?
>   *Juan Ponce de León named the island for the queen of King Charles II, the sponsor of his expedition.*

1765.   Who is the town of Aripeka in Pasco County named after?
>   *Aripeka, a famous Miccosukee Indian*

1766.   How did Belle Glade in Palm Beach County get its name?
>   *Belle Glade was originally known as the Hillsborough Canal Settlement. When residents requested their own post office, they had to give the city a new name. A tourist had said the town was the "belle of the glades." So the citizens named their town Belle Glade.*

1767.   What town in Orange County, Florida, derives its name from the Muskogee word *pilo* (canoe)?
>   *Bithlo*

1768.   For whom is Blountstown in Calhoun County named?
>   *John Blount, a distinguished Seminole chief who occupied the reservation just east of the town*

1769.   What is the origin of the name Boca Raton?
>   *Boca ratón means "rat's mouth" in Spanish.*

1770.   For whom is the town Brooksville in Hernando County named?

Brooksville was named for Preston Brooks, a former congressman of South Carolina.

1771.   Why is Cape Canaveral so named?

Canaveral is the Spanish word for "a place of reeds or cane."

1772.   How did Clearwater get its name?

The town was first called Clear Water Harbor, because of a spring that bubbles up in the Gulf of Mexico close to shore, making the water in the vicinity clear.

1773.   How did Cross City get its name?

Cross City in Dixie County is located where two public roads cross.

1774.   How did Dade City get its name?

The city is named for Major Francis Langhorne Dade, a U.S. Army officer killed by Seminoles in the Second Seminole War.

1775.   Why is Daytona Beach so named?

Daytona Beach is named after its founder, Mathias Day.

1776.   For whom was Flagler Beach named?

Florida developer Henry M. Flagler

1777.   For whom was Fort Lauderdale named?

It was named for Major William Lauderdale, who—along with his men—built a fort at the edge of the Everglades to facilitate the removal of the Seminoles.

1778.   Who is Fort Pierce named after?

It's named after Lieutenant Colonel Benjamin Kendrick Pierce, the brother of U.S. President Franklin Pierce, who fought in Florida during the Seminole Wars.

1779.   How did Frostproof in Polk County get its name?

It was named by cowboys who brought cattle to the region during the winter months to escape frost.

1780.   Who is Gainesville named for?

General Edmund Pendleton Gaines, who is known for leading the capture of Aaron Burr

1781.   How did Groveland get its name?

Originally called Taylorville, the town was renamed Groveland due to the large number of citrus groves in the region.

1782.   How did Hollywood, Florida, get its name?

The town was named Hollywood-by-the-Sea by its founder, Joseph W. Young of California.

1783.   What does Hialeah mean?

Hialeah *means "pretty prairie" in Muskogee.*

1784.   What is the meaning of the name Islamorada?
        Isla morada means "purple island" in Spanish.

1785.   Why is Key West so called?
        It was originally known as Cayo Hueso, which is Spanish for "bone key." "Cayo Hueso" was eventually anglicized into "Key West."

1786.   For whom was Quincy, Florida, named?
        John Quincy Adams

1787.   What Florida town is named after the Temple orange?
        Temple Terrace in Hillsborough County

1788.   Why is Madeira Beach so named?
        Madeira Beach is named for the wine-producing island Madeira in Portugal.

1789.   What was Alachua County named after?
        The name was derived from a Seminole word meaning "sinkhole."

13
Florida Keys

1790.   In what county are the Florida Keys?
        Monroe County

1791.   What is the most populated Florida Key?
        Key West

1792.   What is the second most populated Florida Key?
        Key Largo

1793.   What is the least populated residential Florida Key?
        Layton Key

1794.   What nickname is given to people who were born in Key West?
        Conchs

1795.   How many islands are in the Florida Keys?
        over 800 islands and many more tiny mangrove islets

1796.   How many of the Florida Keys are inhabited?
        about 30

1797.   How high is the highest point above sea level in the Florida Keys?
        Part of Windley Key is 18 feet above sea level.

1798.   What year was the first railroad from the mainland to Key West completed?
         1912

1799.   How did people travel between the Florida Keys before the completion of the railroad between Homestead and Key West?
         They traveled by boat.

1800.   What year was the first railroad from the mainland to the Keys destroyed?
         It was destroyed in 1935 during the Labor Day hurricane.

1801.   How many bridges now connect the Florida Keys?
         42

1802.   How long is the longest bridge that connects the Florida Keys?
         7 miles long (the Seven Mile Bridge)

1803.   How many shipwrecks are in the waters off the Florida Keys?
         thousands

1804.   What early Key West industry depended on shipwrecks?
         Shipwreck salvage, which is also known as wrecking

14
Florida Law

Boating Laws

1805.   In Florida, vessels must be registered and numbered within how many days of purchase?
         30 days

1806.   What is the penalty for failing to register a vessel in Florida?
         $500 fine and a maximum of 30 days in jail

1807.   True or False: Florida does not require numbering on non-powered vessels.
         True

1808.   What is the legal minimum age for a powerboat operator in Florida?
         14 years

1809.   True or False: When a minor is operating a powerboat in Florida, the presence of an adult is required.
>   *True*

1810.   What is the legal minimum age of a personal watercraft operator in Florida?
>   *14 years. Legislation is under consideration to raise the legal minimum age of watercraft operators in Florida.*

1811.   True or False: To operate a powerboat in Florida a boat operator's license is mandatory.
>   *False. A boat operator's license is not required to operate powerboats in Florida.*

1812.   True or False: A passing exam score is required to obtain a Florida boat operator's license.
>   *True*

1813.   What is a personal watercraft?
>   *A personal watercraft is a vessel powered by an inboard motorized water jet pump, designed to be operated by someone sitting, standing, or kneeling on the vessel.*

1814.   During what hours is water skiing and personal watercraft use prohibited by law in Florida?
>   *from half an hour after sunset until half an hour before sunrise*

1815.   True or False: Florida law requires water skiers to wear a personal flotation device.
>   *True*

1816.   What is the penalty for illegal dumping of marine sanitation devices in Florida?
>   *$250*

1817.   True or False: Florida law allows random safety inspection of boats, including boarding.
>   *True*

1818.   By Florida law, what is a boat operator required to do if his or her vessel is involved in a boating accident where there is serious personal injury, death, or disappearance of any person under any circumstances?
>   *As quickly as possible, the boat operator must notify the Florida Fish and Wildlife Conservation Commission or the sheriff of the county in which the accident occurred.*

1819.   In Florida anyone who operates a vessel with willful disregard for the safety of persons or property can be cited for what?
>   *reckless operation (a first-degree misdemeanor)*

1820.   What does Florida law require of anyone convicted of a boating violation which resulted in a boating accident?
>   *Violators must attend and successfully complete a state-approved classroom boater education course.*

1821.   What vessel speed is allowed in a speed zone posted with "Idle Speed—No Wake" signs?

Vessel must operate at the minimum speed that will maintain steerageway.

1822.   What does "Slow Down—Minimum Wake" mean?

The vessel's wake must not be excessive nor create a hazard to other vessels.

1823.   True or False: It is a violation of Florida law to operate a vessel while impaired by alcohol or drugs.

True

1824.   True or False: A vessel operator suspected of boating under the influence must submit to sobriety tests and physical or chemical tests to determine blood or breath alcohol content.

True

1825.   In Florida, a vessel or vehicle operator is presumed to be under the influence if their blood or breath alcohol is at or above what level?

.08

1826.   True or False: Any person under 21 years of age who is found to have a breath alcohol level of .02 or higher while operating a vessel is in violation of Florida law.

True

Consumer Laws

1827.   What state office is responsible for investigating and prosecuting violations of Florida's consumer laws?

the Florida Attorney General's Office

1828.   After what event does Florida's emergency price gouging law make it unlawful for a merchant to increase prices?

after a declared emergency

1829.   Florida's emergency price gouging law makes it unlawful for a merchant to increase prices for what?

• *essential commodities*
• *rental units intended for living or storage*

1830.   What is the grace period allowed for canceling leases in Florida?

There is no grace period allowed for canceling leases in Florida.

1831.   What is the name of the law that holds car manufacturers responsible for replacing defective vehicles or refunding consumers' money?

the Lemon Law

1832.   What Florida legislative act was created to assist consumers with matters relating to motor vehicle repair shops?

Florida Motor Vehicle Repair Act

1833. True or False: By state law, car repair shops must return to the consumer replaced parts if initially requested.
> *True*

1834. True or False: If car repair work will cost over $100, a car repair shop must offer the consumer the option of a written estimate.
> *True*

1835. In Florida, car repair shops must get a consumer's approval if the car repair cost exceeds the car repair estimate by more than what amount?
> *$10 or 10 percent, whichever is greater*

1836. True or False: In Florida, consumers cannot cancel car repairs if they exceed the estimate.
> *False. Consumers can cancel car repairs if they exceed the estimate and the repair shop must reassemble the vehicle unless it is unsafe to drive.*

1837. True or False: In Florida, motor vehicle repair shops are required to register biennially with the Florida Department of Agriculture and Consumer Services.
> *True*

1838. True or False: In Florida motor vehicle repair shops are required to include their registration number in advertisements, or listings relating to motor vehicle repair in newspapers, magazines, and directories.
> *True*

1839. True or False: In Florida movers are not required to provide a consumer with a written cost estimate.
> *False. In Florida all movers are required to provide a consumer with a written estimate of the cost of their move.*

Driving Laws

1840. What two things must drivers carry while driving in Florida?
> • *a valid driver's license*
> • *vehicle registration*

1841. Which occupants of a motor vehicle are required by Florida law to wear safety belts?
> • *Drivers and front-seat passengers over age 18 must wear safety belts.*
> • *Passengers under the age of 18 must be belted in either the front or back seat.*

1842. True or False: Drivers are responsible for buckling passengers who are under the age of eighteen.
> *True*

1843. True or False: Passengers 18 years of age or older who are sitting in the front seat may be individually fined if they are not buckled up.
> *True*

1844. Under Florida law when must car headlights be turned on?
- *at night*
- *at dusk*
- *in the rain - headlights must be turned on day or night*

1845. True or False: In Florida it is permissible to make a right turn on red after stopping unless otherwise posted.
True

1846. What are the two motor vehicle insurance laws in Florida?
- *The financial responsibility law*
- *The no-fault law*

1847. What are the consequences if you are involved in a violation and you do not have insurance that is compliant with the financial responsibility law?
- *Your driver's license and/or license plates will be suspended for up to 3 years.*
- *You must pay a $15 reinstatement fee.*
- *You must show the DMV certified proof of full liability insurance for three years to get your driving privilege back.*
- *You may be required to pay for the damages before your driving privilege is reinstated.*

1848. What grace period does the Florida no-fault insurance law give to new residents before requiring that a vehicle owner purchase a Florida-law-compliant policy?
90 days

1849. What are the minimum coverage requirements under the no-fault insurance law?
- *$10,000 personal injury protection*
- *$10,000 property damage liability*

1850. True or False: You cannot buy a license plate or car registration for a four-wheeled vehicle in Florida without having insurance coverage issued in Florida.
True

1851. True or False: If your Florida driver's insurance is canceled or you fail to renew it, the insurance company is required to notify the Florida DMV.
True

1852. True or False: If you fail to provide the Florida DMV with proof of insurance, your driver's license and license plates could be suspended for up to three years.
True

1853. If your driver's license and license plates are suspended for not having insurance under the no-fault law, what must you do to get them back?
- *1st offense: $150 fine and proof of insurance*
- *2nd offense within three years: $250 fine and proof of insurance*
- *3rd offense within three years: $500 fine and proof of insurance*

1854. What does Florida law require bicycle riders under 16 years of age to wear?
helmets

1855.   After what age is a vision test required to renew a Florida drivers license?
        80

Environmental Laws

1856.   True or False: Unless authorized by law or permit, it is unlawful for any person to dump litter in any public area except in waste receptacles.
        True

1857.   True or False: According to Florida law, when litter is discarded from a motor vehicle, the operator or owner of the motor vehicle, or both, can be cited in violation of the litter law.
        True

1858.   What is the penalty for dumping non-commercial litter in Florida?
        $50

1859.   True or False: In Florida it is a third-degree felony to dump litter that is 500 pounds in weight or 100 cubic feet in volume.
        True

1860.   In Florida, any motor vehicle, vessel, aircraft, container, crane, winch, or machine used to dump litter that exceeds 500 pounds in weight or 100 cubic feet in volume is subject to what?
        forfeiture

1861.   What monetary damages can be awarded to a party injured by a felony litter law violator?
        • *attorney's fees*
        • *court costs*
        • *three times the actual damages or $200, whichever amount is greater*

1862.   How does littering harm the environment?
        • *Litter can become the home for disease-spreading insects such as flies and mosquitoes.*
        • *Materials such as plastic, glass, and aluminum can injure or kill animals.*

1863.   True or False: It is against the law to dump raw human waste from any vehicle or vessel on public or private lands or waters in the state of Florida.
        True

Fishing Regulations

1864.   True or False: Separate license fees are required for saltwater and freshwater fishing in Florida.
        True

1865.   Who is not required to have a fishing license in Florida?
        • *anyone fishing during Free Fishing Weekend*
        • *children under 16*
        • *Florida resident senior citizens 65 and older*

• Florida residents who are members of the armed forces and their dependents
• Florida residents who possess commercial fishing licenses
• Florida residents with permanent disabilities
• Florida residents fishing in the county of their residence with live bait and unreeled poles

1866.   True or False: Length and bag limits apply to many lakes and rivers in Florida.
   True

1867.   True or False: There is no bag limit on the Asian clam in Florida.
   True

1868.   What devices are not permitted in the taking of fish in Florida?
   • electricity
   • explosives
   • firearms
   • free floating or unattached devices
   • poison or other chemicals
   • spear guns

1869.   What must a fisherman do when he or she catches a fish that is under the size limit?
   immediately release it

1870.   True or False: The rules and regulations are the same for game and non-game fishing in Florida.
   False

1871.   What kinds of fish may not be used as bait in Florida?
   • black bass
   • live carp
   • live goldfish
   • peacock bass

1872.   True or False: Fishermen should check the fishing regulations for each body of water in which they plan to fish.
   True

1873.   True or False: Gasoline engines are not permitted on some lakes in Florida.
   True

1874.   True or False: Fishing is permitted in all of Florida's lakes.
   False. Fishing is prohibited in some of Florida's lakes.

Wildlife Protection Laws

1875.   What should you do if you suspect a wildlife law violation?
Report it to the Florida Wildlife Commission Wildlife Alert Reward Program (888-404-FWCC).

1876.   If you report a wildlife violation and the information leads to an arrest, how much reward are you eligible to receive?
up to $1,000

1877.   What actions violate Florida wildlife protection laws?
- *boating under the influence*
- *fishing by illegal methods*
- *harassment of wildlife*
- *illegal hunting, killing, or capturing of protected species*

1878.   What wildlife protection law violations are the least severe?
- *going over the bag limit of saltwater finfish, shellfish, or crustaceans*
- *going over the bag limit of small game*
- *having a gun in a wildlife management area*
- *taking game fish by use of a cast net*
- *taking protected wildlife species, closed season or area violations*

1879.   What wildlife law violations are category-two violations?
- *buying or selling saltwater species without a wholesale license*
- *taking of more than 3 over the bag limit of trout, snook, or redfish*
- *taking or attempting to take alligators*
- *taking saltwater fish with prohibited gear*

1880.   What wildlife law violations are category-three violations?
- *boating under the influence*
- *molesting threatened or endangered species, net violations, trap robbing*
- *sale or possession of game fish in commercial quantities*
- *taking, attempting to take, or possession of big game*

1881.   What category-four wildlife law violations carry the greatest penalties?
- *commercial trafficking of wildlife (except panfish)*
- *organized black-market taking and sale of protected species*
- *taking or killing of endangered species*

1882.   True or False: Of the four categories of violations Florida Fish and Wildlife Conservation Commission has defined, violations in categories three and four carry the most severe penalties.
True

15
Literary Florida

Zora Neale Hurston

1883. Who wrote a historical fiction series about Florida's cracker cowboys? (Hints: Titles in the Cracker Western series include *Riders of the Suwannee, Thunder on the St. Johns, Trail from St. Augustine, Ninety-Mile Prairie,* and *Ghosts of the Green Swamp.*)
> • *Lee Gramling wrote all of the titles listed above.*
> • *Rick Tonyan wrote* Guns of the Palmetto Plains.
> • *Jon Wilson wrote* Bridger's Run.

1884. Who wrote the song "Swanee River" (the true title of which is "Old Folks at Home")?
> *Stephen Foster*

1885. Who wrote the Florida historical novel *A Land Remembered?*
> *Patrick D. Smith*

1886. On what Florida-related subjects did author Patrick D. Smith base his historical fiction?
> • *Florida's migrant workers*
> • *Florida cattle industry*
> • *Florida crackers*
> • *Native Americans*

1887. What is the name of the autobiographical book that Marjory Stoneman Douglas co-authored with John Rothchild?
> *Marjory Stoneman Douglas: Voice of the River*

1888. What famous author lived in Key West from 1931 until 1961?
> *Ernest Hemingway*

1889. What books did Hemingway write while he lived in Key West?
> • *A Farewell to Arms*
> • *For Whom the Bell Tolls*
> • *The Snows of Kilimanjaro*

1890. What African-American woman author was born in Florida and is famous for collecting folklore and writing books that reflected Florida culture?
> *Zora Neale Hurston*

1891.   What Florida town was the birthplace of Zora Neale Hurston?
   Eatonville

1892.   What book written by Zora Neale Hurston was based on her hometown of Eatonville?
   Their Eyes Were Watching God

1893.   What African-American author and educator from Jacksonville wrote the lyrics to the official song of the NAACP (National Association for the Advancement of Colored People)?
   James Weldon Johnson

1894.   What Pulitzer Prize–winning author of historical novels such as *Hawaii, Mexico*, and *Colorado*, was associated with Eckerd College in St. Petersburg?
   James Michener

1895.   To what Florida town did author Harry Crews move after he was born and raised in Georgia?
   Gainesville

1896.   What are the best-known novels that Harry Crews wrote while he lived in Gainesville?
   • *A Feast of Snakes*
   • *All I Need of Hell*

1897.   What famous mystery author moved to Florida, where he developed a fictional character called Travis McGee?
   John D. MacDonald

1898.   Where did John D. MacDonald live?
   Sarasota

1899.   What was the occupation of John D. MacDonald's character Travis McGee?
   He was a detective.

1900.   What Pulitzer Prize–winning novel, authored by Marjorie Kinnan Rawlings, was set in Florida?
   The Yearling

1901.   Where in Florida did Marjorie Kinnan Rawlings live? (Hint: It was also the title of one of her best-known books.)
   Cross Creek

1902.   What is the name of the book written by Elie Wiesel, a European Jew who resettled in St. Petersburg, in which he details his narrow escape from a Nazi death camp?
   Night

1903.   In what Florida town did author Harriet Beecher Stowe live?
   Mandarin

1904.   What novel did Harriet Beecher Stowe write while living in Mandarin?
        Palmetto Leaves

1905.   What story did Stephen Crane write based on his shipwreck experience off the coast of Daytona Beach?
        The Open Boat

1906.   What author researched her book *The Edge of the Sea* in the Florida Keys?
        Rachel Carson

1907.   What nonfiction book about Florida was written by Gloria Jahoda?
        The Other Florida

1908.   What black American born in Jacksonville in 1871 wrote *Autobiography of an Ex-Colored Man?*
        James Weldon Johnson

1909.   Who wrote the book *A Seminole Legend: The Life of Betty Mae Tiger Jumper?*
        Bettie Mae Tiger Jumper and Patsy West

1910.   Who wrote the book *Death in the Everglades: The Murder of Guy Bradley, America's First Martyr to Environmentalism?*
        Stuart McIver

1911.   What early Florida travel book was written by Zane Grey in 1924?
        Tales of Southern Rivers

1912.   Who wrote the science fiction classic *From the Earth to the Moon,* which was set in Florida and published in 1865?
        Jules Verne

1913.   Who authored the memoir *Frost in Florida?*
        Helen Muir

1914.   Who wrote the Xanth series, which consists of more than twenty novels dealing with a fantasy recreation of Florida?
        Piers Anthony

1915.   Name a science fiction anthology set in Florida.
        Subtropical Speculations: Anthology of Florida Science Fiction

1916.   What book about the shipwrecking industry in the Florida Keys also became a film starring John Wayne?
        Reap the Wild Wind

16
Meteorology

Climate of Florida

1917. How many climate zones are in Florida?
> *3*

1918. What climate zones characterize Florida?
> • *Northern Florida—coolest climate zone in Florida; hot and humid from May to September*
> • *Central Florida—has about 1 month of temperatures and humidity below and 7 months above the human comfort range.*
> • *South Florida—has moderate temperatures most of the year; uncomfortable combination of high temperature and humidity from May through September.*

1919. What is winter like in northern and central Florida?
> *mild and wet*

1920. What is summer like in south Florida?
> *long, hot, and humid*

1921. In south Florida what is the rainy time of the year?
> *summer*

1922. True or False: During most of the year, the length of daylight in Florida does not differ greatly from northern states.
> *True*

1923. Why is it so much hotter in Florida than in the northern states? (Hint: When the sun's rays travel through the atmosphere, heat is transferred to the air.)
> *The sun reaches Florida at a higher angle than farther north. This means the sun's rays travel a shorter path through the atmosphere and therefore more heat is transferred to the land area.*

1924.   What are the chief factors that govern Florida's climate?
- *land and water distribution*
- *latitude*
- *ocean currents*
- *prevailing winds*
- *storms and pressure systems*

1925.   What is the highest temperature recorded in Florida?
109°F, recorded on June 29, 1931, at Monticello

1926.   What is the lowest temperature recorded in Florida?
-2°F, recorded on February 13, 1899, at Tallahassee

1927.   True or False: Because of the humid climate, before 1950 Florida had the smallest population of any southern state.
True—the development of air conditioning helped drive Florida's population growth.

1928.   Why was Florida a dangerous place to live before 1900?
Epidemics of yellow fever and malaria were common before 1900. After 1900 epidemics were less frequent due to efforts made to control mosquitoes and quarantine yellow fever victims.

Heat Waves

1929.   True or False: A heat wave is a period of abnormally hot weather.
True

1930.   How long does a heat wave last?
from one day to several weeks

1931.   What is the heat index?
The heat index is the apparent temperature that describes the combined effects of high air temperature and high humidity.

1932.   Why does a high heat index indicate a dangerous condition to humans?
The higher the heat index, the more difficult it is for the human body to cool itself.

1933.   Why is it important to wear sunglasses that block UV rays?
Protecting your eyes from UV rays reduces the risk of cataracts.

1934.   Why is it imperative that children and pets never be left in a closed car?
The temperature can rise to 135° F in under ten minutes, which can be fatal.

1935.   What should you do if you see a child or pet left unattended in a parked car?
- *Be prepared to give a location and description of the car.*
- *Call 911.*

1936. Who is at the greatest risk of heat-related illness?
- *elderly people*
- *infants and children up to four years of age*
- *people who are ill or on certain medications*
- *people who are overweight*
- *people who overexert themselves during work or exercise*

1937. What are the dangers of exposure to strong sun and heat?
- *cramping*
- *heat exhaustion*
- *heatstroke*
- *sunburn*
- *sunstroke*

1938. What are the symptoms and treatment of heat stress?
- ***Cramping*** *Occurs in legs and abdomen. Gentle massage may help. If symptoms persist, see a doctor.*
- ***Heat Exhaustion*** *Profuse sweating, weak pulse, and severe fatigue. Skin may appear pale and feel cold and clammy. In severe cases fainting and vomiting may occur. Move the person to a cool (preferably air-conditioned) location and apply cool compresses. Medical attention should be sought if symptoms persist.*
- ***Sunburn*** *Skin redness, swelling, pain, blisters, fever, and headaches. Ointments help mild cases. Severe sunburns should receive medical treatment.*
- ***Sunstroke*** *Very high (106°F) temperature, rapid and strong pulse, and hot, dry skin. Move victim immediately to cool location, apply cool, wet compresses, and seek medical help. Sunstroke can be fatal.*

1939. What can you do to avoid the dangers of heat-related illness?
- *Do not drink alcoholic beverages.*
- *Do not take salt tablets unless directed to do so by a physician.*
- *Don't get too much sun.*
- *Dress in lightweight, light-colored clothing that reflects heat and sunlight.*
- *Reduce or eliminate strenuous activities*
- *Spend time in air-conditioned places.*
- *Stay hydrated by drinking plenty of water.*

Hurricanes

1940. When is the official hurricane season?
June 1 to November 30

1941. When do most hurricanes usually form?
between July and October

1942. What wind speeds do tropical cyclones attain?
speeds greater than 74 mph (121 km/hr)

1943.   What are the two stages that a tropical cyclone passes through before reaching hurricane force?

> *tropical depression and tropical storm*

1944.   On average, how many tropical storms develop each year over the Atlantic Ocean, Caribbean Sea, and the Gulf of Mexico as of 1999?

> *10*

1945.   Out of the 10 tropical storms that develop each year over the Atlantic Ocean, Caribbean Sea, and the Gulf of Mexico, how many become hurricanes?

> *6*

1946.   In an average three-year period, how many hurricanes strike the United States every year?

> *5*

1947.   What shape is a hurricane?

> *A hurricane is usually circular.*

1948.   How large an area can hurricane winds cover?

> *up to 500 miles or 800 km*

1949.   What causes air to spiral inward toward the hurricane's eye?

> *extremely low central air pressure (around 28.35 in/72 cm of mercury)*

1950.   What is the eye of a hurricane?

> *a calm area in the center*

1951.   What is the diameter of a typical hurricane?

> *20 miles or 30 km*

1952.   From what do hurricanes get their energy?

> *warm tropical ocean water*

1953.   What causes hurricanes to weaken?

> • *moving over land*
> • *prolonged contact with colder northern ocean waters*

1954.   What kinds of weather do hurricanes cause?

> • *flooding*
> • *heavy rains*
> • *high winds*
> • *spin-off tornados*
> • *storm surges*

1955.   What is storm surge?

> *Storm surge is an abnormal rise in sea level accompanying a hurricane or other intense storm.*

1956.   How far inland can storm surges penetrate?
more than 12 miles

1957.   What three hurricane forces cause the most destruction?
• *flood or rain*
• *storm surge*
• *wind*

1958.   What is the most dangerous and damaging hurricane force?
storm surge

1959.   True or False: The strongest hurricanes can cause water levels 18 feet above normal high tide.
True

1960.   Who names hurricanes?
the U.S. National Weather Service

1961.   What year did the National Weather Service begin naming hurricanes?
1953

1962.   What scale is used to measure the strength of tropical storms?
Saffir-Simpson Scale

1963.   What is the least dangerous hurricane category on the Saffir-Simpson Scale?
1

1964.   What is the wind speed in a category 1 hurricane?
74–95 mph

1965.   What is the expected storm surge of a category 1 hurricane?
4–5 feet

1966.   What is the wind speed in a category 2 hurricane?
96–110 mph

1967.   What is the expected storm surge of a category 2 hurricane?
6–8 feet

1968.   What is the wind speed in a category 3 hurricane?
111–130 mph

1969.   What is the expected storm surge of a category 3 hurricane?
9–12 feet

1970.   What is the wind speed in a category 4 hurricane?
131–155 mph

1971.   What is the expected storm surge of a category 4 hurricane?
13–18 feet

1972.   What is the most dangerous hurricane category on the Saffir-Simpson Scale?
>   *5*

1973.   What is the wind speed in a category 5 hurricane?
>   *greater than 155 mph*

1974.   What is the expected storm surge of a category 5 hurricane?
>   *greater than 18 feet*

1975.   How do hurricanes play an important role in controlling the global temperature?
>   *They transport great quantities of heat energy into the heat-deficient higher latitude regions through evaporation of the ocean's water.*

1976.   What are the characteristics of a tropical disturbance?
>   *• distinct tropical weather system of organized convection*
>   *• origin in the tropics or subtropics*
>   *• storm diameter of 100–300 miles*
>   *• storm maintains identity for 24 hours or more*
>   *• tendency to wander*

1977.   What is the wind speed of a tropical depression?
>   *38 mph or less*

1978.   What are the characteristics of a tropical storm?
>   *• cyclonic storm with a distinct circular wind pattern*
>   *• sustained wind speeds ranging from 39–73 mph*

1979.   What year did four devastating hurricanes hit Florida within 2 months, and what were their names?
>   *2004—Charley, Frances, Ivan, and Jeanne*

1980.   What was Florida's most destructive and costly hurricane before the 2004 hurricane season?
>   *Hurricane Andrew, which hit south Florida in 1992*

1981.   True or False: Historically, forty percent of all hurricanes that have made landfall in the United States have hit Florida.
>   *True*

1982.   What items should be included in a hurricane survival kit?
>   Essentials:
>   *• battery-operated radio*
>   *• flashlight*
>   *• extra batteries*
>   *• Do not include candles—they cause more fires after a disaster than anything else.*
>   Water:
>   *• 1 gallon/person/day, minimum 3-day supply, in a food-grade plastic container*
>   *• at least 1 gallon of water per person per day for sanitation and food preparation (have at least a 3-day supply)*

Food: *Minimum 3-day supply of non-perishable food that requires no refrigeration, little to no preparation, and little or no water, such as the following:*
- *dry cereal*
- *peanut butter*
- *canned fruits*
- *canned vegetables*
- *canned juice*
- *ready-to-eat canned foods*
- *quick energy snacks*
- *graham crackers*

First-aid Kit (one for your home and one for each car):
- *scissors*
- *sunscreen*
- *thermometer*
- *tweezers*
- *needle*
- *cleansing agent/soap*
- *latex gloves (2 pairs)*
- *moistened towelettes*
- *assorted sizes of safety pins*
- *bandages*

Non-prescription Drugs:
- *laxative*
- *anti-diarrhea medication*
- *aspirin or non-aspirin pain reliever*
- *antacid (for stomach upset)*
- *activated charcoal (use if advised by the Poison Control Center)*
- *syrup of ipecac (use to induce vomiting if advised by the Poison Control Center)*

Tools and Supplies:
- *whistle*
- *aluminum foil*
- *crowbar*
- *compass*
- *paper*
- *pencil*
- *plastic sheeting*
- *medicine dropper*
- *needles*
- *thread*
- *signal flare*
- *matches in a waterproof container*
- *assorted nails and wood screws*
- *pliers*
- *screwdriver*
- *hammer*
- *plastic storage containers*
- *heavy cotton or hemp rope*
- *cash (try to have small bills and change available) or traveler's checks*
- *non-electric can opener*

- *utility knife*
- *mess kits, or paper cups, plates, and plastic utensils*
- *tape, duct and plumber's tape, or strap iron*
- *patch kit and can of seal-in-air for tires*
- *map of the area (for locating shelters)*
- *shut-off wrench to turn off household gas and water*

Sanitation:

- *disinfectant*
- *household chlorine bleach*
- *soap*
- *liquid detergent*
- *personal hygiene items*
- *plastic bucket with tight lid*
- *toilet paper, towelettes, and paper towels*
- *plastic garbage bags and ties (for personal sanitation uses)*

Clothing and Bedding:

- *sunglasses*
- *rain gear*
- *hat and gloves*
- *sturdy shoes or work boots*
- *blankets or sleeping bags*
- *at least one complete change of clothing and footwear per person*

Important Family Documents:

- *copies of will, insurance policies, contracts, deeds, stocks, and bonds*
- *copies of passports, social security cards, immunization records*
- *record of credit card account numbers and companies*
- *family records (birth, marriage, death certificates)*
- *record of bank account numbers*
- *inventory of valuable household goods*
- *important telephone numbers*

Family Medical Needs:

- *insulin*
- *prescription drugs*
- *denture needs*
- *extra eyeglasses*
- *contact lenses and supplies*
- *heart and blood pressure medication*

Entertainment:

- *games and books*

Lightning

1983.   What state is known as the lightning strike capital of the world?
Florida

1984.   What is peak lightning strike season in Florida?
summer (June through September)

1985.   How long are lightning bolts?
up to 60 miles or more

1986.   How far away from a storm can lightning strike?
> *10 miles or more*

1987.   How many lightning strikes occur in the U.S. every year?
> *over 40 million*

1988.   How many deaths due to lightning strikes occur in Florida every year?
> *about 10*

1989.   Rising and descending air within storm clouds causes the separation of what kind of electrical charges?
> *positive and negative charges*

1990.   What happens when the buildup of electrical energy between positively and negatively charged areas in a storm cloud discharges?
> *lightning*

1991.   True or False: A storm must be directly overhead in order to be dangerous.
> *False. Lightning can strike in clear blue skies.*

1992.   For how long could an average lightning flash illuminate a 100 watt light bulb?
> *3 months*

1993.   How hot is the air near a lightning strike?
> *50,000° F*

1994.   Rapid heating and cooling of the air near a lightning channel causes a shock wave that results in what?
> *thunder*

1995.   What is the diameter of an average bolt of lightning?
> *1 inch*

1996.   How many volts are in an average bolt of lightning?
> *about 100 million volts*

1997.   True or False: Lightning never strikes the same place twice.
> *False*

1998.   True or False: A cave is always a safe place in a thunderstorm.
> *False. If it is a shallow cave or old mine with metallic filings nearby, it can be a deadly location during a storm.*

1999.   True or False: An injured person who was struck by lightning carries an electrical charge.
> *False*

2000.   True or False: Rubber tires or a foam pad will insulate you from lightning.
> *False*

2001.   What environmental clues indicate a lightning storm may be approaching?
- *A.M. radio static*
- *darkening skies*
- *flashes of lightning*
- *increasing wind*
- *thunder*

2002.   How can you tell lightning is about to strike in your immediate vicinity?
- *hair stands on end*
- *skin tingles*

2003.   What defensive posture should you take if lightning is about to strike in your immediate vicinity?
- *Squat low to the ground on the balls of your feet.*
- *Put your head between your knees.*
- *Place your hands on your knees.*
- *Make yourself the smallest target possible.*
- *Minimize your contact with the ground.*

2004.   What should you do to protect yourself from lightning strikes?
- *Avoid being the tallest object.*
- *Avoid metal objects.*
- *Do not stand by open windows or doors during a thunderstorm.*
- *Do not stand under or near trees.*
- *Do not take a bath or shower during a storm.*
- *Do not use the telephone except for emergencies, and then use only cellular or cordless phones.*
- *Get out of boats and away from water.*
- *If lightning is occurring and a shelter is not available, get inside a hard-topped automobile and keep the windows up. The roof protects you, not the rubber tires.*
- *Suspend outdoor activities for thirty minutes after the last observed lightning strike.*
- *Unplug all unnecessary appliances before the storm.*
- *Watch for environmental clues.*
- *When outdoors, go inside a building when storms approach.*

Rain

2005.   On average, how many inches of rain fall in Florida every year?
50–55 inches

2006.   On average, how many gallons of rain fall in Florida every day?
150 billion gallons

2007.   What are the stages in the water cycle?
a. Heat from the sun causes water to evaporate and evapotranspirate.
b. Water vapor rises, expands, cools, and becomes visible as clouds.
c. Clouds grow, get heavy, and fall as rain.
d. Rain recharges aquifers, rivers, and lakes.

2008.   How much of the rain that falls in Florida every day returns to the atmosphere through evapotranspiration?
about 107 billion gallons

2009.   What parts of Florida get the most rain?
• *the Panhandle*
• *southeastern Florida*

2010.   True or False: El Niño and La Niña have no effect on Florida's weather.
False. El Niño and La Niña do affect Florida's weather.

2011.   What effects do El Niño and La Niña have on Florida's weather?
El Niño brings more rainfall and cooler temperatures to Florida in the winter. La Niña brings a warmer and drier winter and spring to Florida.

2012.   True or False: Jet stream patterns caused by both El Niño and La Niña actually suppress damaging freezes in Florida.
True

2013.   True or False: La Niña triggers drought in Florida.
True

Tornadoes

2014.   How many tornado seasons does Florida have?
2—spring (February–April) and summer (June–September)

2015.   Why are Florida's spring tornadoes more powerful than its summer tornadoes?
Because in the spring there are strong winds in the jet stream that produce fast and powerful storms.

2016.   What time are tornadoes likely to strike?
Tornadoes can strike at any time.

2017.   During what month have the most tornadoes occurred in Florida?
June

2018.   In what month do the deadliest tornadoes occur in Florida?
March

2019.   True or False: More tornadoes occur in Florida than any other state.
True

2020.   True or False: Florida tornadoes are much stronger in intensity than the tornadoes in the Great Plains.
False. Florida tornadoes are much weaker than tornados that occur in the Great Plains and the Midwest.

2021.   What is the difference between a water spout and a tornado?
A water spout is a whirlwind that travels over a body of water. A tornado is a whirlwind that travels over land.

2022.   True or False: Waterspouts may form their own clouds at the top.
   True

2023.   What scale is used to identify tornado damage?
   the Fujita Scale (also known as the Fujita-Pearson Scale)

2024.   On average, how many tornadoes occur in Florida every year?
   45

2025.   Under what weather conditions do tornadoes develop?
   • *in front of an advancing cold front*
   • *where masses of warm air converge*
   • *in isolated summer thunderstorms*
   • *in hurricane feeder bands*

2026.   What are the signs of a tornado?
   • *strong prolonged rotation in the cloud base*
   • *whirling dust or debris on the ground under a cloud base*
   • *hail or heavy rain followed by calm or a fast, intense wind shift*
   • *a loud, continuous roar or rumble, which doesn't fade after a few seconds like thunder*

2027.   What is the best thing to do during a tornado if you are in a house with a basement?
   • *Avoid windows.*
   • *Go to the basement.*
   • *Get under a heavy table or work bench, or cover yourself with a mattress or sleeping bag.*

2028.   What should you do during a tornado when you are in a house or apartment with no basement?
   • *Avoid windows.*
   • *Go to the lowest floor.*
   • *Stay in a small center room like a bathroom, a closet, under a stairway, or in an interior windowless hallway.*
   • *Crouch down, put your head between your knees, and cover the back of your head with your hands.*
   • *Cover yourself with thick padding such as a mattress or blankets to protect against falling debris.*

2029.   What should you do in an office building to protect yourself during a tornado?
   • *Avoid windows.*
   • *Go directly to an enclosed area in the center of the building. An interior stairwell is a good choice.*
   • *Crouch down, put your head between your knees, and cover the back of your head with your hands.*
   • *Stay off elevators.*

2030.   What should you do if you are at school and a tornado strikes?
> • *Follow the established tornado drill.*
> • *Stay away from windows.*
> • *Crouch down low, put your head down, and protect the back of your head with your arms.*

2031.   What should you do in the event of a tornado if you are in a car?
> • *If you can safely do so, drive out of the tornado's path by moving at right angles to the tornado.*
> • *If you cannot drive away from the tornado, park the car out of traffic lanes as quickly and safely as possible.*
> • *Get out and seek shelter in a sturdy building.*
> • *If there are no sturdy buildings around, run to low ground and lie flat with your face down. Protect the back of your head with your arms.*
> • *Do not seek shelter under bridges.*

2032.   What should you do if you are outside when a tornado strikes?
> *If you cannot get to a sturdy shelter, lie flat on low ground with your face down and protect the back of your head with your arms. If possible, use ground away from trees and cars, which could be blown on top of you.*

2033.   True or False: Opening windows to equalize air pressure will save a home from destruction by a tornado.
> *False. Opening windows could actually cause the house to blow up like a balloon.*

2034.   True or False: Tornadoes never strike big cities.
> *False. Several big cities, including Miami, have been hit by tornadoes.*

17
Oceans and Florida Coastline

Beaches

2035. How many miles of tidal shoreline are in Florida?
>*over 8,000 miles*

2036. True or False: Florida's white beach sand was washed down from the Appalachian Mountains over millions of years.
>*True*

2037. What is the source of the black/dark gray sand on beaches in the Venice area?
>*It is made of ground-up fossils from the heavy fossil deposits in the Venice area.*

2038. What makes the sand brown on some of Florida's beaches?
>*Florida's brown sand is made of ground-up shells.*

2039. True or False: Seawalls help prevent beach erosion.
>*False. Seawalls do not prevent beach erosion; in fact, they actually cause beach loss.*

2040. How do seawalls cause beach loss?
>• *The beaches and dunes naturally migrate inland but the seawalls block migration.*
>• *Seawalls narrow the beach by their placement.*
>• *Waves bounce off the seawall, then scour and erode the beach sediments in front of the wall.*

2041. How do Florida communities restore beaches when shorelines retreat?
>• *dredge sand and fill*
>• *scrape or bulldoze sand from low tide to upper beach areas*
>• *truck sand and fill*

2042. What Florida beach had the most dredge and fill operations from 1944–1994?
>*Lake Worth Inlet had 17 dredge and fill operations during that time, at a total cost of $31,614,438.*

2043.   How much did it cost to dredge and fill Florida's Atlantic coast beaches from 1944 to 1994?
   $550,176,055

2044.   True or False: Silver and gold treasures from sunken ships off Florida's coasts often wash up on Florida's beaches.
   True

Beach Water Quality

2045.   True or False: It is safe to swim in Florida's coastal waters most of the time.
   True

2046.   True or False: You cannot be sure that U.S. coastal beach water is safe to swim in unless it is tested, because water may contain disease-causing microorganisms.
   True

2047.   When was the Clean Water Act amended to include significant protections for beaches throughout the United States?
   On October 10, 2000, the Beach Environmental Assessment and Coastal Health Act (BEACH Act) was created.

2048.   What does the BEACH Act require the U.S. Environmental Protection Agency (EPA) to do?
   The EPA is required to conduct studies and develop better water quality criteria.

2049.   How does the BEACH Act work to ensure safe beaches?
   • mandates public access to beach pollution information
   • provides regular testing and monitoring of beach pollutants
   • requires that organizations work together to prevent, predict, and detect beach pollution quickly

2050.   Who is responsible for monitoring the water quality of the nation's beaches?
   state, tribal, and local health and environmental protection officials

2051.   What are the sources of disease-causing microorganisms in coastal waters?
   • boating wastes
   • malfunctioning septic systems
   • malfunctions at sewage treatment plants
   • polluted stormwater runoff
   • sewage overflows

2052.   When is beach pollution likely to be at the highest levels?
   during and immediately after rainstorms

2053.   Why is beach pollution most likely to occur during and immediately after rain storms?
   • Sewage treatment plants sometimes overflow onto beaches.
   • Pesticides, fertilizers, and animal wastes from lawns and farms are collected and concentrated rainwater runoff which flows into the sea.
   • Rainwater runoff carries trash and other pollutants into the sea.

2054.   What disease-causing microorganisms can be found in sewage?
  • *bacteria*
  • *protozoa*
  • *viruses*
  • *worms*

2055.   What common illnesses and symptoms could result from contact with bacteria-contaminated water?
  • *cholera*
  • *gastroenteritis*
  • *salmonellosis*

2056.   What common illnesses and symptoms could result from swimming in virus-contaminated water?
  • *common colds*
  • *diarrhea*
  • *fever*
  • *gastroenteritis*
  • *hepatitis*
  • *respiratory infections*
  • *sore throat*

2057.   What common illnesses and symptoms could result from swimming in water contaminated with protozoa?
  • *cryptosporidiosis*
  • *dysentery*
  • *gastroenteritis*
  • *giardiasis*

2058.   What common illnesses and symptoms could result from swimming in water contaminated with worms?
  • *chest pain*
  • *coughing*
  • *diarrhea*
  • *digestive disturbances*
  • *fever*
  • *restlessness*
  • *vomiting*

2059.   What should you do if you suspect beach water contamination?
  Contact your local health or environmental protection officials.

2060.   How can you find out about the quality of beach water?
  • *Ask your city, county, or other local health officials.*
  • *Local environmental protection offices can tell you if and when the water at your beach is monitored, who tests it, and where the results are posted.*

2061.   What can you do to avoid swimming in contaminated water?
  • *Avoid swimming after a heavy rain.*
  • *Do not swim near storm drains on the beach.*
  • *Do not swim if you see oil slicks or trash in the water.*

Beach Safety

2062. True or False: To swim safely at the beach, you should always swim within sight of a lifeguard.
        True

2063. What does it mean when a red flag is flying at the beach?
        Stay out of the water; strong undertow and riptides exist.

2064. What does it mean when a yellow flag is flying at the beach?
        Use caution in the water; undertow and riptides are possible.

2065. What does it mean when a blue flag is flying at the beach?
        Water is calm.

2066. What should you never do when swimming?
        • *Never swim alone.*
        • *Never take your eyes off your children.*

2067. What should you do if you are at the beach and a storm approaches?
        Seek shelter.

2068. What safety conditions should you watch for at the beach?
        • *approaching storms*
        • *large dangerous waves*
        • *lightning*
        • *rip currents*
        • *safety condition flags*

2069. What should you do if you are stung by a jellyfish?
        Seek first aid.

2070. True or False: A severe sunburn can result in death.
        True

2071. True or False: Avoiding sun exposure during the hours when the sun's rays are most intense will reduce the chances of sunburn.
        True

2072. During what hours are the sun's rays the most intense?
        from noon until about 3 P.M.

2073. True or False: You cannot get sunburned when it is cloudy.
        False. You can be burned by the sun when it is cloudy.

2074. How can you protect yourself from sunburn?
        • *Avoid exposure to the sun from 9 A.M. to 3 P.M., when UV rays are the most hazardous.*
        • *Stay hydrated by drinking plenty of water.*
        • *Wear a hat.*
        • *Wear sunscreen with at least SPF 15.*
        • *Wear sunglasses with UV protection.*

2075.   How can you prevent hot sand from burning your feet?
Wear shoes or sandals.

2076.   What should you do if you see lightning while you are at the beach?
Seek shelter.

2077.   What are the symptoms of sunburn?
Any or all of the following:
* *blisters*
* *fever*
* *headaches*
* *pain*
* *skin redness*
* *swelling*

Rip Currents

2078.   What causes rip currents?
Waves caused by strong offshore winds or distant storms move ashore and build up pressure on a sand bar until a narrow channel breaks through. Water rushes seaward thorough the narrow channel.

2079.   How wide are the narrow channels that rip currents make in sandbars?
usually 20 yards or less

2080.   True or False: Rip currents are also called rip tides.
True

2081.   What are the telltale signs of a rip current?
* *a brown plume in the surf*
* *a foam streak that extends seaward from breaking waves*

2082.   Why are rip currents a danger for swimmers?
Swimmers can be caught in rip currents and swept out to sea.

2083.   Can rip currents be forecast?
Yes. The National Weather Service is able to forecast rip currents more than 90 percent of the time.

2084.   What should swimmers do to avoid being caught in a rip current?
* *Know water conditions. Look for signs, flags, or status boards indicating hazardous situations.*
* *Know how to swim.*
* *Weak swimmers should avoid going into the surf above their knees on unguarded beaches and during times of strong onshore winds or high waves.*
* *Do not swim in dangerous areas such as inlets, or near piers and jetties where rip currents can be very strong.*
* *Know and watch for the telltale signs of rip currents.*

2085. How can a swimmer escape from a rip current?
> *There are two ways to escape from a rip current:*
> > • *Swim parallel to the shore until out of the rip current.*
> > • *Stay calm and let the rip current pull you away from shore until the current weakens—usually a distance of about 100 yards— then swim toward shore at an angle away from the rip current.*

2086. What is the best way to save someone who is caught in a rip current?
> *Throw a flotation device to them and get help from the beach patrol.*

Estuaries, Bays, and Lagoons

2087. What is an estuary?
> *An estuary is an area where salt water from the sea mixes with fresh water from the land.*

2088. What are the names of some bodies of water that are estuaries? (Hint: Think of places where fresh water meets salt water.)
> > • *bays*
> > • *lagoons*
> > • *river mouths*
> > • *salt marshes*

2089. What is a lagoon?
> *A lagoon is a broad, shallow estuarine system separated from the ocean by a barrier island.*

2090. What is a bay?
> *A bay is the part of a sea that indents the shoreline as the sea cuts into the land.*

2091. Why are estuaries important to Florida's coastline?
> *Estuarine plants help prevent erosion and stabilize shorelines.*

2092. What percentage of Florida's rare, endangered, and threatened species live in southwest Florida estuaries?
> *40%*

2093. Into what lagoon does the Loxahatchee River empty?
> *the Indian River Lagoon*

2094. True or False: Urban development is not threatening the diverse habitats in the Loxahatchee River watershed.
> *False. Urban development is threatening the diverse habitats in the Loxahatchee River watershed.*

2095. What problems are caused by urban development in the Loxahatchee River watershed?
> > • *Severed green pathways, habitat loss, and displaced wildlife result in insufficient resources to sustain wildlife.*

* *Man-made drainage canals and barriers in developed areas reduce water storage in some places, cause flooding, and degrade water quality in lakes and streams.*
* *Excessive pumping of groundwater for human use causes groundwater contamination by saltwater intrusion.*
* *Stormwater runoff carries contaminants from developments into bodies of water, causing degradation of water quality.*
* *Invasive non-native plants are crowding out native species.*

2096.   How are estuarine systems critical for the survival of many birds, mammals, fish, and other wildlife?

* *Estuarine ecosystems supply wildlife with the habitat they need for shelter, food, and reproduction.*
* *Migratory birds use estuaries to rest and forage.*
* *Shellfish require the protective environment of estuaries to spawn.*

2097.   True or False: The health of estuaries depends on the quantity, quality, and timing of freshwater input.

True

2098.   Why are Florida's bays and lagoons important to the state's economy?

* *Lagoons and bays provide jobs related to boating, water sports, shellfish harvesting, and commercial and recreational fishing.*
* *Tourists come to Florida to enjoy the lagoons and observe nature.*

2099.   What factors are threatening Florida's bays and lagoons?

* *agricultural pesticide and fertilizer runoff*
* *freshwater intrusion*
* *human negligence*
* *increased wastewater and storm water discharges*
* *increasing residential and commercial development*
* *industrial and municipal waste*
* *loss of marshlands*
* *pollution*
* *watershed expansion due to development*

2100.   On which coast is the Indian River Lagoon?

the east or Atlantic coast

2101.   How many miles long is the Indian River Lagoon?

The lagoon is 156 miles long and extends from Ponce de Leon Inlet to Jupiter Inlet.

2102.   How many animal species live in the Indian River Lagoon?

approximately 2,200

2103.   How many endangered species live in the Indian River Lagoon?

35

2104.   Where is Estero Bay?

Estero Bay is on Florida's Gulf coast.

2105.   What is a rookery?
        A rookery is a nesting area for birds.

2106.   How many rookeries and roosting islands are in Estero Bay?
        5

2107.   Name some of the birds that nest or roost in Estero Bay.
        • *brown pelicans*
        • *cormorants*
        • *egrets*
        • *frigatebirds*
        • *herons*
        • *ibis*

2108.   In what county is Lake Worth Lagoon?
        Palm Beach County

2109.   In what county is Apalachicola Bay?
        Franklin County

2110.   What rivers empty into Apalachicola Bay?
        • *Apalachicola River*
        • *New River*
        • *Ochlockonee River*
        • *Sopchoppy River*
        • *Wakulla River*

2111.   What three barrier islands in Florida's Panhandle are named for saints?
        • *St. Andrews Island*
        • *St. George Island*
        • *St. Vincent Island*

2112.   How many islands are in Apalachicola Bay?
        There are 4—St. George Island, Little St. George Island, St. Vincent Island,
        and Dog Island.

2113.   What island in Apalachicola Bay was cut in half in a government channel dredging
        operation?
        St. George Island

2114.   What island in Apalachicola Bay is a major spawning ground for blue crabs?
        Dog Island

2115.   What peninsula in the Panhandle used to be a barrier island?
        St. Joseph Peninsula

2116.   Where is Florida Bay?
        in the southwest corner of Florida

2117.   How many small islands are in Florida Bay?
        over 200

2118.   What are the indications that Florida Bay is in jeopardy?
> • *algal blooms*
> • *decline in fishing success*
> • *dying sea grasses*
> • *hypersalinity*

2119.   What is Florida's largest island?
> *Merritt Island*

2120.   In what county is Merritt Island?
> *Brevard County*

2121.   What is the area of Merritt Island?
> *40.5 square miles*

Coastal Preserves and Resources

2122.   Name the watershed ecosystems that contribute to the health of Florida's coastal environment.
> • *bays*
> • *estuaries*
> • *coastal creeks*
> • *coastal marshes and wetlands*
> • *coastal wetlands such as the Savannas Ecosystem, located in Martin and St. Lucie counties*
> • *lagoons*
> • *the Atlantic Coastal Ridge Ecosystem, which includes scrub, pine flatwoods, and forested sloughs*

2123.   How do coastal watersheds contribute to the health and condition of Florida's coastline?
> • *They improve water quality.*
> • *They control and prevent floods.*
> • *They protect shorelines.*
> • *They provide recreational and educational opportunities.*
> • *They provide habitat for endangered plants and animals.*

2124.   Where is the Atlantic Coastal Ridge Ecosystem located?
> *The Atlantic Coastal Ridge Ecosystem is on Florida's east coast in southern Martin County, between U.S. 1 and Interstate 95.*

2125.   True or False: Florida is purchasing and restoring environmentally sensitive lands in order to protect and create safe havens for endangered and threatened plants and animals.
> *True*

2126.   Names some of Florida's land acquisition programs.
> • *Florida Forever Program*
> • *Preservation 2000, also known as P-2000*

2127.　The Atlantic Coastal Ridge Ecosystem is a tributary to what rivers?
　　　　　• *north fork of the Loxahatchee River (Kitching Creek)*
　　　　　• *south fork of the St. Lucie River*

2128.　What county's aquifer is recharged by the Atlantic Coastal Ridge Ecosystem
　　　　　Martin County

2129.　How many acres are in the Savannas State Preserve?
　　　　　4600 acres in a 10-mile-long area extending from Fort Pierce to Jensen Beach

2130.　How does the freshwater aquifer underlying the Savannas State Preserve help prevent saltwater intrusion?
　　　　　The aquifer creates underground water pressure that holds back the Atlantic Ocean's underground saltwater wedge and prevents it from intruding into inland freshwater aquifers.

2131.　Where do the Florida Keys get their drinking water from?
　　　　　Florida Keys Aqueduct Authority, which has a well field near Florida City on the mainland

2132.　What is an archipelago?
　　　　　a group of islands

2133.　True or False: The Florida Keys watershed consists of a limestone island archipelago of some 1,700 islands.
　　　　　True

2134.　What shoreline and marine resources do the Florida Keys watershed include?
　　　　　• *coral reef formations*
　　　　　• *fish and wildlife*
　　　　　• *mangrove marshes*
　　　　　• *sea grass beds*
　　　　　• *wetlands*

Red Tide

2135.　What year did the first scientific documentation of red tide off Florida's coast occur?
　　　　　1946–1947

2136.　Where was the first scientifically documented occurrence of red tide in Florida?
　　　　　Venice

2137.　What are the signs of red tide?
　　　　　• *dead fish along the beaches*
　　　　　• *a stinging, choking hydrogen sulphide gas in the air*

2138.　What causes red tide?
　　　　　Red tide is caused by large masses of marine algae that produce toxic chemicals.

2139.   True or False: Red tide can cause severe respiratory irritation to humans at sea and along the shore.
          True

2140.   True or False: In Florida red tide occurs equally as often on both the Gulf coast and the Atlantic coast.
          False. Red tides occur most often in the Gulf of Mexico.

2141.   How far offshore do Florida red tide blooms typically begin?
          40–60 miles

2142.   What symptoms of exposure to toxic levels of red tide might humans experience?
          • *burning sensation of the eyes and nose*
          • *dry, choking cough*
          • *tingling lips and tongue*

2143.   True or False: When an algae bloom is severe, fish die rapidly from the neurotoxic effects of red tide, which enters their bloodstream through the gills.
          True

2144.   True or False: Fish exposed to sublethal concentrations of red tide may accumulate neurotoxins in their body.
          True

2145.   What happens to marine mammals that eat fish containing accumulated neurotoxins?
          They get sick and sometimes die.

2146.   True or False: Shellfish such as oysters, clams, mussels, mollusks, whelks, and coquinas can accumulate so much neurotoxin that they become toxic to humans.
          True

2147.   True or False: Red tide appears to be a natural phenomenon that has occurred more frequently in the twentieth and twenty-first centuries due to man-made pollution.
          True

2148.   What does an algae bloom look like on the surface of the water?
          Algae blooms are not always visible, but they may have a brownish-red sheen or a yellow-green color.

2149.   True or False: It is safe to eat shrimp, crab, scallops, and lobsters that are harvested in red tides since these shellfish do not accumulate the red tide toxin in the hard muscle tissue eaten by humans.
          True

Reefs

2150.   True or False: There are several types of reef ecosystems off Florida's coasts.
          True

2151.   How many coral species can be found in Florida's coral reefs?
          around 50

2152.   True or False: Florida is the only state in the continental United States that has extensive shallow coral reef formations near its coasts.
>   *True*

2153.   What type of coral sways in the current?
>   *soft coral*

2154.   Name some kinds of soft coral found in Florida waters.
>   • *sea fans*
>   • *sea plumes*
>   • *sea rods*
>   • *sea whips*

2155.   What type of coral forms rocklike structures?
>   *hard coral*

2156.   Name some kinds of hard coral found in Florida waters.
>   • *boulder coral*   • *lettuce coral*
>   • *brain coral*   • *mustard hill coral*
>   • *clubbed finger coral*   • *pillar coral*
>   • *elkhorn coral*   • *staghorn coral*
>   • *ivory bush coral*   • *star coral*

2157.   How does a coral reef grow?
>   *Coral reefs are built up over time by millions of tiny coral plants and animals. When corals die they are cemented together by sediments and growing coral.*

2158.   What is the name of the coral animal?
>   *polyp*

2159.   What is the name of the outer coral skeleton?
>   *coral*

2160.   True or False: Coral feed at night.
>   *True*

2161.   What do coral polyps do during the daytime?
>   *They stay inside their skeletons.*

2162.   True or False: Coral reefs grow quickly.
>   *False. Coral reefs grow slowly.*

2163.   How many feet do coral reefs grow in 1,000 years?
>   *Estimated growth rates range from 1 to 16 feet every 1,000 years.*

2164.   True or False: Some species of coral sting.
>   *True*

2165.   What kinds of plants and animals inhabit a coral reef?
>   • *algae*

- *anemones*
- *crabs*
- *lobster*
- *shrimp*
- *sponges*
- *various fish*

2166.   What do reef inhabitants do in a coral reef?
feed, breed, and sleep

2167.   True or False: Fish that dwell in coral reefs have developed special feeding mechanisms.
True

2168.   What special feeding mechanisms have evolved in coral-dwelling angelfish and butterflyfish?
Angelfish and butterflyfish have long snouts and strong teeth that enable them to reach into reef crevices for food.

2169.   What special feeding mechanisms have coral-dwelling parrotfish developed?
The teeth of the parrotfish are fused together like a beak to chip off pieces of coral, which they eat. The parrotfish's digestive system sorts out the food and they pass fine white sand.

2170.   How many states in the U.S. have coastal coral reefs? Name them.
There are 2—Florida and Hawaii.

2171.   What growth conditions do coral reefs require?
- *abundant sunshine*
- *good food supply*
- *plenty of oxygen*
- *warm water*

2172.   At what water depth do coral grow?
from mid-tide level to about 160 feet

2173.   What destroys and endangers coral reefs?
- *fresh water*
- *pollution*
- *silt*

2174.   True or False: Over the last several decades Florida reef habitats have been significantly reduced.
True

2175.   What is causing the reduction in reef habitat?
- *anchors dropped on or dragged through reefs*
- *careless divers*
- *coastal development*
- *fish, crab, and lobster traps destructively dropped into delicate reef communities*
- *polluted water*

2176.   What marine populations have been adversely affected by reef habitat loss?
> • *algae*   • *lobster*
> • *anemones*   • *shrimp*
> • *crabs*   • *sponges*
> • *fish*
> • *hard and soft coral*

2177.   What have humans done to create more marine habitat?
> *created artificial reefs*

2178.   What benefits do artificial reefs provide?
> • *alternate areas for scuba divers and fisherman, reducing the pressures on*
>   *natural reefs*
> • *food, shelter, and spawning areas for hundreds of marine species*

2179.   What is an artificial reef made of?
> *Artificial reefs are man-made habitats built from various materials that will*
> *stay anchored in heavy seas, including rocks, sunken ships, sunken bridges,*
> *and concrete.*

2180.   What are the two natural kinds of reefs off Florida's coast?
> • *coral reefs*
> • *limestone reefs*

2181.   How were limestone reefs formed?
> *Limestone bedrock was thrust up during the geologic upheaval that created*
> *Florida 35 million years ago.*

2182.   What type of reef is a Sabellariid worm reef?
> *coral*

2183.   How does a Sabellariid worm reef grow?
> *Each worm settles onto a hard, stable surface and constructs a protective tube*
> *out of sand. The worms attach their tubes to the tubes of neighboring worms,*
> *forming large colonies which grow into massive mounds.*

2184.   How do the Sabellariid worms protect themselves from drying out in the sun
at low tide?
> *They build sand hoods over their tubes.*

2185.   Why is it important to protect Florida's reefs?
> • *Coral reefs help prevent coastal erosion.*
> • *Reef habitat destruction affects the entire food chain, including humans.*
> • *We have a social responsibility to conserve natural resources for future*
>   *generations.*

2186.   How many mollusk species can be found in Florida Keys reefs?
> *1,200*

2187.   How many diseases affect Florida's coral reefs? Name them.
> *There are 3—black band disease, coral bleaching, and white band disease.*

2188.   Name some fish that inhabit Florida's rock reefs.

- *amberjack*
- *blue runner*
- *cobia*
- *gag grouper*
- *grunt*

- *mackerel*
- *sergeant major*
- *snapper*
- *spadefish*

The Gulf of Mexico

2189.   How many U.S. states border the Gulf of Mexico? Name them.
There are 5:

- *Alabama*
- *Florida*
- *Louisiana*
- *Mississippi*
- *Texas*

2190.   True or False: Pollution is not a problem in the Gulf of Mexico's ecosystems.
False

2191.   What percentage of the U.S. shrimp harvest comes from the Gulf of Mexico?
72%

2192.   True or False: The Gulf of Mexico is the sixth largest body of water in the world.
False. The Gulf of Mexico is the ninth largest body of water in the world.

2193.   What is the surface area of the Gulf of Mexico?
1.5 million square kilometers

2194.   How many estuaries are in the Gulf of Mexico?
over 200

2195.   How many acres of coastal wetlands are along the coast of the Gulf of Mexico?
about 5 million acres

2196.   How many major river systems empty into the Gulf of Mexico?
33

2197.   True or False: Parts of Canada are in the Gulf of Mexico's watershed.
True

2198.   What percentage of the continental U.S. drains into the Gulf of Mexico?
66%

2199.   True or False: Pollutants and debris dumped anywhere in the Gulf of Mexico's watershed eventually flow into the Gulf.
True

The Gulf Stream

2200.   What is the Gulf Stream?

The Gulf Stream is a stream of water current flows that through the Florida Straits south of Key West and moves steadily northward along the east coast.

2201.   What is the speed of the Gulf Stream?

about 5 knots

2202.   What is the Gulf Stream's nickname? (Hint: It is nicknamed for its color.)

Purple Majesty

2203.   How wide is the Gulf Stream?

25 to 40 miles

2204.   What is the temperature of the Gulf Stream near Florida?

Gulf Stream temperature varies from 86°F off Key West in summertime to 75°F off Jacksonville in winter.

2205.   Who was the first person to scientifically study and map the Gulf Stream?

Benjamin Franklin

2206.   Name some of the fish that live in the Gulf Stream.

- *billfish*
- *cobia*
- *dolphin*
- *grouper*
- *mackerel*
- *mullet*
- *snapper*
- *tarpon*
- *tuna*
- *wahoo*

Sand Dunes

2207.   What are the ecological functions of sand dunes?

- *Dunes are sand reserves for beaches.*
- *Dunes create a buffer between land and the high energy of the ocean.*
- *Dunes provide a barrier to salt intrusion from high tides and storm surges.*
- *Dunes protect the land behind them from erosion.*

2208.   How many zones are defined in Florida's dune systems? Name them.

There are 5. They are
- *pioneer dune zone*
- *fore dune zone*
- *dune field zone*
- *scrub dune zone*
- *hammock dune zone*

2209.   Where does the pioneer dune zone form?

The pioneer dune forms just above the highest tide level.

2210.   What are the features of the pioneer dune zone?

- *Windblown sand collects around obstructions such as fences, plants, and rocks.*

• *Low, tough herbs such as sea-rockets and seaside evening-primrose colonize the pioneer dune zone.*

2211.   What is the next dune stage in the evolution of a sand dune zone?
　　　As plants collect more sand and organic matter, the pioneer dune increases in height and becomes the fore dune.

2212.   What are the features of the fore dune?
　　　The fore dune is colonized by low, tough plants with extensive root systems that stabilize the dune.

2213.   How do fore dune zones become dune field zones?
　　　Older, stable fore dunes grow in height and organic content to become dune field zones.

2214.   How do dune field zones protect the land behind them?
　　　They absorb much of the energy from storm surges.

2215.   What is the next stage in the evolution of a sand dune?
　　　Dune field zones become scrub dune zones.

2216.   What features characterize scrub dune zones?
　　　• *Scrub dunes contain a lot of deposited organic material.*
　　　• *Woody plants such as the palmetto, wax myrtle, cabbage palm, and sea grapes colonize scrub dunes, creating a dense scrub zone.*

2217.   What are the characteristics of a hammock dune zone?
　　　• *Hammock dunes are farther inland than any other dune zone.*
　　　• *Hammock dunes are colonized by tall trees such as the live oak and slash pine.*

2218.   What dune zone is the oldest?
　　　hammock dune zone

2219.   What dune zone is the youngest?
　　　pioneer dune zone

2220.   Why must the plants in the pioneer and fore dune zones be particularly tough?
　　　• *They must grow in sandy, salty soils with little water or nutrients.*
　　　• *They must be able to withstand harsh conditions such as salt spray, burial, wind, heat, and drought.*

2221.   What adaptations have the plants in the fore dunes and pioneer dunes made to survive their harsh environment?
　　　• *Deep extensive root systems evolved to anchor plants and search for water.*
　　　• *Dune plants have evolved to conserve water and process salt.*
　　　• *Tough waxy leaves and stems resist tearing in the wind and waves.*

2222.   What methods do dune plants use to deal with high salt content of the soil?
　　　• *They limit salt penetration with thick, waxy cuticles.*
　　　• *They excrete salt or detoxify salt within their systems.*

2223.   How do the pioneer and fore dune zones keep the beach from eroding away?
> • *During periods of low wave activity, sand is deposited on the beach and blown into the dune system for storage.*
> • *When there is high wave activity the beach is eroded, and the pioneer and fore dunes erode also, thus giving up their sand to replenish the beach.*
> • *As sand is deposited on the beach the wind replenishes the dunes by blowing the sand into the pioneer and fore dunes.*

2224.   What man-made structures interfere with sand dune formation?
> • *buildings*
> • *jetties*
> • *seawalls*

Marine Species

2225.   What saltwater fish swims the fastest?
> *sailfish*

2226.   How fast can a sailfish swim?
> *up to 70 mph*

2227.   What kind of stinging marine animals can be found along Florida shores?
> • *catfish*
> • *jellyfish*
> • *Portuguese man-of-war*
> • *stingrays*

2228.   True or False: Jellyfish lack backbones, hearts, blood, brains, eyes, and gills.
> *True*

2229.   What percentage of the jellyfish is water?
> *95%*

2230.   How long are jellyfish tentacles?
> *from a few inches up to 120 feet long*

2231.   What color are jellyfish?
> *clear, or a color such as pale blue, orange, brown, white or pink*

2232.   True or False: Most jellyfish are at least partially transparent.
> *True*

2233.   What is the lifespan of a jellyfish?
> *5–7 years*

2234.   How long are the tentacles on a Portuguese man-of-war?
> *up to 60 feet*

2235.   True or False: The Portuguese man-of-war uses its tentacles to swim.

False. A Portuguese man-of-war moves through the water by inflating a pouch that is driven by the wind and current. They cannot steer.

2236.   True or False: The Portuguese man-of-war is a colony of many organisms.

True. Portuguese man-of-war is a jellyfish-like creature comprised of organisms called polyps.

2237.   How many sea horse species live off Florida's coasts?

3

2238.   True or False: Horseshoe crabs periodically shed their outer shell.

True

2239.   True or False: Horseshoe crabs can both bite and sting.

False. Horseshoe crabs cannot bite or sting.

2240.   What do horseshoe crabs use their tail for?

Horseshoe crabs use their tails for righting themselves when they are flipped onto their backs.

2241.   What is the lifespan of a horseshoe crab?

up to 20 years

2242.   True or False: The sea squirt is a saclike creature that eats by siphoning sea water to strain out food.

True

2243.   True or False: Needlefish swim on the surface of the water near the shore.

True

2244.   True or False: Sea hares are marine snails whose shells are small and internal.

True

2245.   What are sea hares most apt to do if they are disturbed?

When threatened sea hares emit a harmless purple ink.

2246.   Do sea slugs breathe through their gills, lungs, or skin?

skin

2247.   What is sea pork?

A sea pork is a large colony of tiny animals bound together within a sheet of rubbery gelatin.

2248.   What does a sea pork look like?

A sea pork resembles a yellow, orange, or purple blob of gelatin.

2249.   How does a sea pork eat?

It strains plankton from the water.

2250.   True or False: Purple sea snails make a raft of small bubbles to float on the surface of the ocean where they feed on Portuguese man-of-war.
True

2251.   True or False: Tube worms live under water and look like feather dusters when they are out of their tubes.
True

2252.   True or False: All tube worms can inflict painful stings.
False. Only some tube worms can sting.

2253.   True or False: Starfish, also called sea stars, are not related to fish.
True

2254.   What do starfish eat?
mollusks such as oysters, clams, and scallops

2255.   True or False: Starfish can regenerate lost limbs.
True

2256.   True or False: Brittle stars have flexible legs and can move faster than their sea star cousins.
True

2257.   True or False: Zooplankton are algae.
False. Zooplankton are animal plankton. Phytoplankton are algae.

2258.   True or False: There are many different species of phytoplankton.
True

2259.   What do phytoplankton eat?
Like all plants, phytoplankton use the energy of the sun to make their own food.

2260.   Are planktons closer to the bottom or the top of the food chain?
bottom

2261.   Zooplanktons are the larvae of what marine animals?
• barnacles
• crabs
• jellyfish
• worms

2262.   What is bioluminescence?
Bioluminescence is the chemical production of light by plants and animals.

2263.   True or False: Florida coastal waters contain bioluminescent organisms.
True

2264.   What organisms cause coastal surface waters to glow in the dark?
phytoplankton and zooplankton

2265.   When do plankton emit light?
         at night when the water is disturbed by movement

2266.   Why do plankton emit light?
         • *to attract mates*
         • *to attract prey*
         • *to find food in the deep, dark ocean*
         • *to protect themselves from predators*

2267.   What sea creatures are bioluminescent?
         • *crustaceans*
         • *jellyfish*
         • *parchment tube worms*
         • *some bacteria*
         • *some fish*
         • *some plankton*
         • *squid*

2268.   What colors are the bioluminescent lights emitted by sea creatures?
         • *blue*
         • *green*
         • *orange*
         • *red*
         • *violet*
         • *yellow*

2269.   How many sea turtles species live in Florida? Name them.
         There are 5. They are
         • *Atlantic hawksbill*
         • *Atlantic leatherback*
         • *green sea turtle*
         • *Kemp's ridley*
         • *loggerhead*

2270.   True or False: Sea turtles can breathe underwater through their gills.
         False. Sea turtles do not have gills. They breathe surface air through their nostrils.

2271.   How long can sea turtles remain under water before surfacing for air?
         about 40 minutes

2272.   What is the deepest ocean depth that sea turtles are known to dive?
         over 3,000 feet

2273.   True or False: Female sea turtles return to the beach where they were born to lay their eggs.
         True

2274. True or False: Some tagged sea turtles have been found 4,000 miles from their nesting beaches.
> *True*

2275. What time of year do sea turtles lay their eggs in Florida?
> *March–September*

2276. True or False: All of Florida's sea turtles nest on both the Atlantic coast and Gulf coast.
> *False. Only loggerhead turtles nest on both of Florida's coasts. Florida's other sea turtles species nest only on the Atlantic coast*

2277. How many eggs does a female sea turtle lay?
> *100 or more golf-ball-size eggs*

2278. True or False: Sea turtle eggs are hard like chicken eggs.
> *False. Sea turtle eggs are soft and leathery.*

2279. How long after they are laid do sea turtle eggs hatch?
> *about 2 months*

2280. What is the first thing sea turtle hatchlings do when they emerge from their eggs?
> *They try to get to the sea as quickly as they can.*

2281. Why is it important to protect sea turtle hatchlings from bright lights?
> *Bright lights disorient and confuse hatchlings and may cause them to go in the wrong direction away from the sea.*

2282. What are some of the predators that hatchling sea turtles face as they make their way from the nest to the sea?
> • *armadillos*
> • *birds*
> • *crabs*
> • *dogs*
> • *raccoons*

2283. How long does it take a sea turtle to reach maturity?
> *12–15 years*

2284. How many sea turtle hatchlings survive to adulthood?
> *It is estimated that only 1 in 10,000 sea turtle hatchlings survive to maturity.*

2285. True or False: Male sea turtle tracks can be found on Florida beaches.
> *False. Male sea turtles never leave the ocean.*

2286. True or False: Sea turtles excrete excess salt from their kidneys through a large gland at the rear corner of their eyes.
> *True*

2287.   Of the five sea turtle species found in Florida, how many have protected species status?
all 5

2288.   What are the penalties for crimes against sea turtles?
   • *civil penalties: fines up to $25,000*
   • *criminal penalties: fines up to $50,000 and up to 1-year imprisonment*

2289.   True or False: It is a violation of state and federal law to disturb a sea turtle nest.
True

2290.   True or False: Leatherback turtles have a very hard shell.
False. Leatherback turtles have a soft, leathery shell.

2291.   How many leatherback turtle species live in the world today?
1

2292.   What is the favorite food of the leatherback turtle?
jellyfish

2293.   What is the largest sea turtle species?
leatherback

2294.   What is the length of a mature leatherback turtle?
7 feet

2295.   How much does a mature leatherback turtle weigh?
   • *females weigh less than 1,000 pounds*
   • *males weigh up to 1,600 pounds*

2296.   What is endangering the world's sea turtle population?
   • *Capture of adult turtles for eggs, meat, leather, and tortoise shell has decreased breeding turtle populations.*
   • *Incidental capture of adult turtles in fishing nets and shrimp trawls have reduced the sea turtle population.*
   • *Over-developed coastal areas have reduced natural nesting habitats.*

2297.   True or False: Laws now require shrimp trawlers to use turtle exclusion devices (TEDS) on their nets.
True

2298.   What shark species are commonly found in Florida waters?
   • *Atlantic sharpnose shark*
   • *blacknose shark*
   • *blacktip shark*
   • *bonnethead shark*
   • *bull shark*
   • *great hammerhead shark*
   • *nurse shark*
   • *tiger shark*

2299.   True or False: Sharks are not found in fresh water.
         False. Several shark species are known to swim up coastal rivers.

2300.   True or False: Sharks can protrude their jaws to bite things in front of their snouts.
         True

2301.   Where does the Atlantic sharpnose shark migrate in the winter months?
         It migrates south of Florida and into deeper waters.

2302.   Where in Florida waters is the Atlantic sharpnose shark found?
         nearshore and offshore waters of the Gulf and Atlantic coasts

2303.   What does an Atlantic sharpnose shark eat?
         • *crabs*
         • *mollusks*
         • *segmented worms*
         • *shrimp*
         • *various fishes*

2304.   During what seasons is the blacknose shark most abundant off Florida's coasts?
         summer and fall

2305.   What does the blacknose shark eat?
         small fishes

2306.   What is the maximum length of a full-grown blacknose shark?
         about 55 inches

2307.   Which of Florida's sharks is a very fast swimmer and can often be seen at the surface of the water?
         blacktip shark

2308.   What sharks species are known to leap out of the water and spin around on their tails several times before dropping back into the sea?
         • *blacktip sharks*
         • *spinner sharks*

2309.   Where can the bonnethead shark be found?
         near shore in Florida waters and in shallow sand and mud flats

2310.   What does the bonnethead shark eat?
         • *crabs*
         • *mollusks*
         • *shrimp*
         • *small fishes*

2311.   True or False: The bull shark is one of the few shark species that can live in freshwater and they have been known to swim hundreds of miles inland up coastal rivers.
         True

2312.   Where can the bull shark be found?
- *estuarine waters*
- *in streams*
- *near shore and offshore waters of both the Gulf and Atlantic coasts of Florida*

2313.   What does a bull shark eat?
- *dolphins*
- *rays*
- *sea birds*
- *sea turtles*
- *sharks*
- *various fish and invertebrates*

2314.   How long are bull sharks?
up to 11 feet long

2315.   How many years can a bull shark live?
24 years or more

2316.   What is the most dangerous shark living in Florida waters?
bull shark

2317.   What is the second most dangerous shark living off Florida shores?
tiger shark

2318.   Where can the great hammerhead shark be found?
The great hammerhead shark swims in the open ocean and the shallow coastal waters of the Gulf and Atlantic coasts of Florida, including coral reefs, inlets, and bays.

2319.   What does the great hammerhead shark eat?
- *crabs*
- *sharks*
- *squid*
- *stingrays*
- *various bony fishes*

2320.   How long is a great hammerhead shark at birth?
about 2 feet long

2321.   How long is a mature great hammerhead shark?
about 18 feet long

2322.   Where in Florida waters can lemon sharks be found?
In estuaries and nearshore waters of the Gulf and Atlantic coasts of Florida and upstream in coastal fresh water

2323.   What does a lemon shark eat?
- *crustaceans*
- *mollusks*
- *rays*

> • *sea birds*
> • *small sharks*
> • *various bony fishes*

2324. What is the estimated lifespan of a lemon shark?
       27 years or more

2325. True or False: Lemon sharks have been involved in many attacks on humans.
       False

2326. What kind of shark is often seen lying motionless on the ocean floor?
       nurse shark

2327. Where do nurse sharks prefer to live?
       near reefs, rocks, and mangrove islands

2328. What do nurse sharks eat?
       They eat bottom-dwelling invertebrates such as spiny lobsters, shrimps, crabs, sea urchins, squid, octopi, marine mollusks, and some fish species.

2329. How many pups are in a nurse shark's litter?
       20–28

2330. Where can tiger sharks be found?
       • *all of Florida coastal waters*
       • *open ocean*
       • *river mouths*
       • *shallow bays*
       • *tropical waters worldwide*

2331. What does a tiger shark eat?
       • *almost anything*
       • *bony fish*
       • *conchs*
       • *crabs*
       • *garbage, for example, pieces of coal and wood, burlap bags, cans*
       • *marine birds*
       • *porpoises*
       • *rays*
       • *sea turtles*
       • *sharks*
       • *skates*

2332. What is the length of an adult tiger shark?
       about 18 feet

2333. How much does an adult tiger shark weigh?
       up to 2,000 pounds

2334. True or False: Tiger sharks rank second to the great white shark in the number of attacks on humans worldwide.
       True

2335.   True or False: It is extremely unlikely for a person to be bitten or attacked by a shark in Florida waters, and attacks are rarely life-threatening.
        True

2336.   During what hours are sharks most active?
        at night and during twilight hours

2337.   True or False: Sharks cannot regrow lost teeth.
        False. Sharks have multiple rows of teeth in their mouths; when they lose a tooth, the one behind it moves forward to take its place.

2338.   True or False: Sharks regenerate about 50,000 teeth in a lifetime.
        True

2339.   Sharks are keenly attracted to what smell?
        blood

2340.   What attracts the attention of sharks?
        • *bait*
        • *blood*
        • *excessive splashing*
        • *sheen of fish scales*
        • *shiny jewelry*

2341.   True or False: As top predator in most marine ecosystems, sharks fill an important role in maintaining balance within every ecosystem they inhabit.
        True

2342.   True or False: Humans are 10 times more likely to be struck by lightning in Florida than to be bitten by a shark.
        False. Humans are 30 times more likely to be struck by lightning in Florida than to be bitten by a shark

2343.   True or False: Humans are much more of a danger to sharks than sharks are to humans.
        True

2344.   How many sharks are killed by fisheries every year worldwide?
        estimated 100 million

2345.   How many people die from shark attacks every year worldwide?
        fewer than 10 people

2346.   What can swimmers do to reduce the chance of a shark attack?
        • *Avoid being in the water during darkness or twilight.*
        • *Avoid waters being used by sport or commercial fishermen, especially if they are fishing with bait or there are signs of feeding activity. The presence of diving seabirds may indicate the presence of feeding activity near the surface.*
        • *Beware in the areas between sandbars or near steep drop-offs because these are favorite hangouts for sharks.*

- *Do not allow pets in the water because they make movements that may attract sharks.*
- *Do not enter the water if bleeding.*
- *Do not enter the water if sharks have been sighted and evacuate the water if sharks are sighted while you are there.*
- *Do not harass a shark if you see one.*
- *Do not splash excessively.*
- *Do not wander far from shore.*
- *Do not wear shiny jewelry or shiny swimwear.*
- *Stay in groups since sharks are more likely to attack a lone individual.*
- *Swim only at beaches tended by lifeguards.*

2347.   True or False: Sightings of porpoises indicate the absence of sharks.
False. Sightings of porpoises do not indicate the absence of sharks as they often eat the same foods.

2348.   True or False: Shellfish do not live on dry sand.
True

2349.   True or False: Bivalves are shellfish that have two separate shells hinged together.
True

2350.   How many shells do snails have?
Snails are univalves, which means they have one shell.

2351.   True or False: Jingle shells anchor themselves to the sea floor with byssal threads that pass through a hole in the bottom half of their shells.
True

2352.   True or False: Jingle shells are very hard.
False. Jingle shells are soft and crush easily.

2353.   True or False: Moon snails are bivalves.
False. Moon snails are univalves.

2354.   True or False: Moon snails drill holes in bivalves and eat them.
True

2355.   How do moon snails drill holes in the hard shells of bivalves?
- *They rasp with file-like teeth*
- *A special gland produces an acid that helps them to dissolve the shell they are drilling through.*

2356.   True or False: Moon snails appear to have enormous feet because they inflate their feet with what?
water

2357.   What are common nicknames for the moon snail?
- *cat's eye*
- *shark's eye*

2358.   True or False: Many shellfish anchor themselves to the sea floor with byssal threads.
>   *True*

2359.   True or False: Some shellfish attach themselves to the shells of other shellfish.
>   *True*

2360.   What univalve family is known for their fancy frilly and spiny shells?
>   *Murex*

2361.   True or False: Sand dollars burrow into the sand by moving thousands of tiny spines on their shells.
>   *True*

2362.   How can you tell where a sand dollar is buried?
>   *The patterns of sand dollars are often visible on the surface of the sand.*

2363.   True or False: Mollusks obtain their oxygen from water.
>   *True*

2364.   How long can a mollusk live out of water?
>   *a few hours*

2365.   What spiny shellfish is known as the porcupine of the sea?
>   *sea urchin*

2366.   True or False: Sea beans are many different kinds of seeds that wash up on beaches.
>   *True*

2367.   What is the common nickname for mole crabs?
>   *sand fleas*

2368.   True or False: Mole crabs walk, swim, and dig backwards.
>   *True*

2369.   How many crab species live in Florida?
>   *At least 70, and there may be many more species not yet identified*

2370.   Name some crab species that are commonly found in Florida.

>   * *blue crab*
>   * *calico crab*
>   * *fiddler crab*
>   * *flame crab*
>   * *ghost crab*
>   * *hermit crab*
>   * *horseshoe crab*
>   * *mangrove crab*
>   * *stone crab*
>   * *Other answers are possible.*

2371.   How deep is a ghost crab burrow?
>   *3–4 feet*

2372.   True or False: Hermit crabs live in sponges and abandoned shells.
          True

2373.   True or False: The great land crab can climb trees.
          True

2374.   True or False: Barnacles attach themselves to surfaces using a waterproof glue.
          True

2375.   True or False: Abalone shells can be found on both Florida coasts.
          False. Abalone shells are not found anywhere in Florida.

2376.   Where can coquina shellfish be found in Florida?
          in the wet sand along the surf lines of Florida's beaches

2377.   Are clams, oysters, scallops, and mussels univalves or bivalves? (Hint: Univalves
          have one shell, bivalves have two.)
          bivalves

2378.   What echinoderms are native to Florida's coastal waters?
          • sea cucumbers
          • sea urchins
          • starfish (also called sea stars)

2379.   True or False: Sea sponges are plants.
          False. Sea sponges are animals.

2380.   True or False: Live sea sponges float on top of the water.
          False. Live sea sponges attach themselves to stones or coral.

2381.   How do sponges eat?
          Sponges feed by filtering microscopic food particles from the water.

2382.   How much water can a sea sponge pump in one day?
          10,000 times its own volume

2383.   True or False: Natural sponges used for cleaning are the skeletons of sea sponges.
          True

2384.   What types of sponge are most abundant in the Florida Keys sponge grounds?
          • About 59% are loggerhead sponges.
          • About 9.6% are vase sponges.

2385.   How many of Florida's sponge species are harvested commercially? Name them.
          There are 5. They are
                    • finger sponge
                    • glove sponge
                    • grass sponge
                    • sheepswool sponge
                    • yellow sponge

2386.   What are the tiny needle-like splinters in a sea sponge called?
            spicules

2387.   What organisms use the canals and chambers of sponges for habitat?
            small shrimplike and wormlike organisms

2388.   True or False: Live sponges are covered with skin.
            True

2389.   What color is the skin of a sheepswool sponge?
            black

2390.   How many pounds of sponges have been commercially harvested annually in
        Florida in recent years?
            60,000–70,000 pounds

2391.   What is Florida's legal minimum harvestable sponge size?
            5 inches

2392.   What bright red sponge can be seen on coastal rocks just below the high
        tide mark?
            red boring sponge

2393.   How does the red boring sponge bore into rocks?
            It secretes enzymes that dissolve the lime in rocks and concrete.

Marine Mammals

2394.   Name some marine mammals that live in the waters off Florida's coasts.
            • *dolphins*
            • *manatees*
            • *sea otters*
            • *whales*

2395.   What dolphin species can be found in Florida waters?
            • *Atlantic spotted dolphin*
            • *bottlenose dolphin*
            • *Risso's dolphin*
            • *rough-toothed dolphin*
            • *spinner dolphin*

2396.   Do dolphins breathe with their gills, lungs, or skin?
            Dolphins have lungs and they breathe through blowholes on the tops of their
            heads.

2397.   What whale species are found swimming in Florida's coastal waters?
            • *blue whale*   • *pygmy whale*
            • *dwarf sperm whale*   • *right whale*
            • *false killer whale*   • *sei whale*
            • *finback whale*   • *short-finned pilot whale*
            • *goosebeak whales*   • *sperm whale*
            • *humpback whale*

2398.   How many of Florida's marine mammals are endangered species? Name them.
> *6 or 7; they are:*
> - *Caribbean monk seal*
> - *finback whale*
> - *West Indian manatee (In 2006 the manatee's state status was changed to threatened. At this time its federal status is under review.)*
> - *humpback whale*
> - *right whale*
> - *sei whale*
> - *sperm whale*

2399.   Do whales breathe with gills, lungs, or skin?
> *Whales have lungs. They inhale and exhale through blowholes.*

2400.   What is the largest marine mammal listed as a species of special concern?
> *blue whale*

2401.   How much does a blue whale weigh?
> *up to 150 tons*

2402.   How long is a blue whale?
> *up to 100 feet*

2403.   How much does a mature blue whale eat daily?
> *around 8 tons*

2404.   What is the largest of all toothed whales?
> *sperm whale*

2405.   How much does a sperm whale weigh?
> *up to 53 tons*

2406.   How long is a sperm whale?
> *up to 55 feet*

2407.   How long can a sperm whale stay under water?
> *over an hour*

2408.   West Indian manatees are also known by what other names?
> - *Caribbean manatee*
> - *Florida manatee*
> - *sea cows*

2409.   How many manatees currently live in Florida?
> *around 2,000*

2410.   Where do manatees live during the summer?
> *in warm coastal waters*

2411.   Where do manatees live in winter?
>   *In winter manatees live where the water is warmer, usually inland in spring-fed waters, and in bays and estuaries.*

2412.   Are manatees carnivores, herbivores, or omnivores?
>   *herbivores*

2413.   How many manatee species exist in the world today?
>   *There are 4. They are*
>   • *Amazonian manatee*
>   • *Antillean manatee*
>   • *West African manatee*
>   • *West Indian manatee*

2414.   How many manatee species live in Florida?
>   *1, the West Indian manatee*

2415.   How long can manatees remain under water?
>   *Up to 20 minutes, but they usually surface to breathe every 3–5 minutes.*

2416.   What do manatees use their wide flat tails for?
>   *propulsion*

2417.   True or False: Manatees travel close to the bottom of the water.
>   *False. Manatees travel close to the surface of the water.*

2418.   True or False: Discarded fishing line, fishing hooks, plastic bags, six-pack holders, and other litter endanger the lives and health of manatees.
>   *True*

2419.   True or False: Manatees are fast swimmers.
>   *False. Manatees are slow swimmers.*

2420.   What animals prey upon manatees?
>   *Adult manatees have no predators except man. Manatee calves are preyed upon by alligators, crocodiles, and sharks.*

2421.   Why are recreational boats a threat to West Indian manatees?
>   *Boat propellers cause many manatee injuries and deaths.*

2422.   What color is an adult West Indian manatee?
>   *gray*

2423.   What color is a newborn West Indian manatee?
>   *pinkish*

2424.   How much do adult West Indian manatees weigh?
>   *600–2000 pounds*

2425.   What is the length of a mature West Indian manatee?
>   *8–14 feet*

2426. What is in the diet of a West Indian manatee?
   • *algae*
   • *grasses*
   • *mangroves*
   • *submerged and floating vegetation*

2427. How can you tell a manatee is under the water nearby?
   a series of small bubbles on the surface

2428. True or False: It is illegal to harass a West Indian manatee.
   True

2429. What should you do if you see a sick or injured manatee?
   Call the Florida Marine Patrol.

2430. True or False: Florida Fish and Wildlife Conservation Commission created manatee protection zones.
   True

2431. What is the boat speed limit in a manatee protection zone?
   25–30 mph in most manatee protection zones

2432. True or False: Water pollution is not a serious threat to manatees.
   False. Water pollution is a very serious threat to manatees.

2433. What Florida and Federal legislative acts currently protect the West Indian manatee?
   • *Federal Marine Mammal Protection Act of 1972*
   • *The Endangered Marine Species Act of 1973*
   • *The Florida Manatee Sanctuary Act of 1978*

2434. What is the penalty for violating Florida manatee protection laws?
   • *$1,000 fine and/or up to 60 days in jail*
   • *up to $25,000 civil penalty*

2435. What is the penalty for violating a federal manatee protection law?
   $100,000 fine and/or up to one year imprisonment

2436. What can you do to protect Florida's manatees?
   • *Do not pollute.*
   • *Join or visit a conservation organization.*
   • *Learn more about manatees.*
   • *Observe manatee protection laws.*

2437. What organizations are involved in Florida manatee protection?
   • *Defenders of Wildlife*
   • *Save the Manatee Club*
   • *Sierra Club*
   • *The Audubon Society*
   • *Other answers are possible.*

Seagrasses

2438.   What habitats form the base of the food web in Florida's lagoons and local coastal waters?
> • *mangrove swamps*
> • *seagrass beds*

2439.   True or False: Seagrasses are not actually grasses but are more closely related to the lily family.
> *True*

2440.   Do seagrasses require salt or fresh water?
> *salt water*

2441.   What kind of roots do seagrasses have?
> *strong, thick, fleshy roots*

2442.   True or False: Seagrasses are comprised of vertical shoots of three to five leaves connected by a horizontal stem-root beneath the sediment.
> *True*

2443.   What force does a horizontal stem-root help seagrass withstand?
> *wave action*

2444.   What shape are seagrass leaves?
> *There are many species of seagrass and the leaves have many different shapes: flat, round, or ribbon-shaped.*

2445.   What seagrass species live in south Florida's coastal waters?
> • *Johnson's seagrass*
> • *manatee grass*
> • *paddle grass*
> • *shoal grass*
> • *star grass*
> • *turtle grass*
> • *widgeon grass*

2446.   How do seagrasses help prevent erosion?
> • *Seagrass leaves absorb wave energy and allow sediments to settle out of the water column.*
> • *Seagrass roots and horizontal stems trap sediments and stabilize the sea bed.*

2447.   True or False: Seagrasses are an important habitat for algae and invertebrates.
> *True*

2448.   What do seagrasses do to improve water quality in shallow waters?
> *Seagrasses strip nutrients out of the water.*

2449.   True or False: Seagrass is a food source for many animals.
> *True*

2450.   True or False: Seagrasses provide habitat, shelter, and nurseries for many commercially and ecologically important species.

True

2451.   True or False: In the past fifty years Florida has lost a large fraction of seagrass beds.

True

2452.   What has caused the reduction in Florida's seagrass beds?
- *dredge and fill activities*
- *wastewater discharge*
- *pollution*
- *boat propeller scour (when seagrass gets caught in boat propellers and torn out)*

18

Parks in Florida

2453.   How many national forests are in Florida? Name them.

There are 3. They are
- *Apalachicola National Forest*
- *Ocala National Forest*
- *Osceola National Forest*

2454.   What is the largest national forest in Florida?

Apalachicola National Forest in northern Florida

2455.   How many acres are in Blackwater River State Forest?

about 190,000 acres

2456.   What Florida state park is named for a waterfall?

Falling Waters State Park

2457.   What is the height of the Falling Waters waterfall?

67 feet

2458.   What is unusual about the Falling Waters waterfall?

It plunges and disappears into a 100-foot-deep sinkhole.

2459.   What Florida state park is home to the only dry cavern in Florida that is open for tours?

Florida Caverns State Park

2460.   How many state parks are in Florida?

159. Visit the Florida state parks website (http://www.floridastateparks.org).

2461.   What is the Florida trail?

> *The Florida trail is a scenic hiking trail that is part of the national system of hiking paths.*

2462.   What was Florida's first state park?

> *Pine Log State Forest near Panama City*

2463.   What Florida national seashore includes within its boundaries several barrier islands, including Fort Pickins, Perdido Key, Fort Barrancas, Naval Oaks, and Okaloosa?

> *Gulf Islands National Seashore*

2464.   What national wildlife refuge is on Apalachee Bay?

> *St. Marks National Wildlife Refuge*

2465.   What Florida national wildlife refuge is accessible only by boat, canoe, or kayak?

> *St. Vincent National Wildlife Refuge*

2466.   What mammal did the U.S. Fish and Wildlife Service reestablish on Florida's St. Vincent Island?

> *red wolves*

2467.   How are the red wolves on St. Vincent Island helping the loggerhead turtle to make a comeback?

> *Red wolves prey on the predators of the loggerhead turtle.*

2468.   What is the namesake of Torreya State Park?

> *the torreya tree, which only grows in or near the park*

2469.   What Florida state park is home to the most productive spring in the world?

> *Wakulla Springs State Park*

2470.   How many islands are in the Cedar Keys National Wildlife Refuge?

> *12*

2471.   Which of Florida's national forests includes within its borders Alexander Springs, Salt Springs, Silver Glen Springs, Fern Hammock Springs, Juniper Springs, the Oklawaha River, and Lake Eaton Dry Sink?

> *Ocala National Forest*

2472.   What river disappears underground in O'Leno State Park and reemerges above ground in River Rise State Preserve?

> *the Santa Fe River*

2473.   What is the smallest of Florida's national forests?

> *Osceola National Forest*

2474.   What national forest is home to the Big Gum Swamp Wilderness?

> *Osceola National Forest*

2475.   What state preserve became a lake when the Alachua sinkhole became plugged
and then twenty years later became a prairie when the plug broke?
Paynes Prairie State Preserve

2476.   When the Alachua sinkhole plug broke how long did it take for the lake to drain?
3 days

2477.   How long did it take Paynes Prairie to form after the Alachua sinkhole plug broke?
2 years

2478.   Peacock Springs State Park is known for what features?
• *Bonnet Spring*
• *Peacock Spring*
• *underwater caves*

2479.   What state preserve in northern Florida is considered the most diverse hammock in
Florida?
San Felasco Hammock State Preserve

2480.   What national wildlife refuge and national seashore are sometimes closed as a
security precaution during and near space shuttle launches?
• *Canaveral National Seashore*
• *Merritt Island National Wildlife Refuge*

2481.   What Palm Beach County island is the home of Blowing Rocks State Preserve?
Jupiter Island

2482.   How and what do the blowing rocks blow at Blowing Rocks State Preserve?
At high tide the Atlantic Ocean surges through fissures and holes in the lime-
stone, creating water plumes as high as fifty feet.

2483.   What national wildlife refuge was established on Florida's central Gulf coast in 1943
as a winter preserve for migratory waterfowl?
Chassahowitzka National Wildlife Refuge

2484.   What Florida national wildlife refuge is the only federal preserve devoted to the
manatee?
Crystal River National Wildlife Refuge

2485.   How many national wildlife refuges are in Florida?
16

2486.   What conservation organization led the effort to establish Florida's Crystal River
National Wildlife Refuge?
The Nature Conservancy

2487.   What type of hammock is Highland Hammock State Park?
hardwood

2488.   What Florida state wildlife park has an underwater observatory in its main spring?
Hermosa Springs State Wildlife Park

2489.   What Florida state park is named after a Quaker merchant who, with his family, was captured by Indians in 1696 after a shipwreck off Jupiter Island?
    Jonathan Dickinson State Park; the story of their adventure is told in Jonathan Dickinson's Journal.

2490.   What is the name of the "living history" site in Lake Kissimmee State Park?
    Cow Camp

2491.   Most of what Volusia County national wildlife refuge is accessible only by boat?
    Lake Woodruff National Wildlife Refuge

2492.   What Florida state preserve has an Indian name meaning "chicken"?
    Tosohatchee State Preserve; even today the area is known for its wild turkey population.

2493.   The Archie Carr National Wildlife Refuge is the only national wildlife refuge devoted to what sea creature?
    sea turtles

2494.   What Atlantic coast national wildlife refuge is home to the largest sand dunes in Florida?
    Hobe Sound National Wildlife Refuge

2495.   How many acres are in the Big Cypress National Preserve?
    over 750,000 acres

2496.   What year did the U.S. Congress establish the Big Cypress National Preserve?
    1974

2497.   What southeast Florida national park is mostly under water and includes coral reefs and over forty small islands?
    Biscayne National Park

2498.   What southwest Florida aquatic preserve includes about ten thousand red mangrove islands?
    the Ten Thousand Islands Aquatic Preserve

2499.   In what southwest Florida state park could visitors observe crocodiles and alligators swimming side by side?
    Collier Seminole State Park

2500.   What river flows through the Loxahatchee National Wildlife Refuge?
    the Loxahatchee River

2501.   What Florida state park was the first underwater state park in the United States? (Hint: It is headquartered on Key Largo.)
    John Pennekamp Coral Reef State Park

2502.   What pristine Florida Key was saved from development by the Nature Conservancy and is named for a tree?
    Lignumvitae Key

2503.   What Florida state recreation area's name means "deep bay" in Spanish?
Bahia Honda State Recreation Area

2504.   What Florida key is home to the National Key Deer Refuge?
Big Pine Key

2505.   What historic fort is located in the Dry Tortugas National Park?
Fort Jefferson

19
Space Science
and Florida

2506.   What is the name of NASA's Florida space center?
Kennedy Space Center

2507.   In what town is the Kennedy Space Center located?
Cape Canaveral

2508.   What president established Cape Canaveral as a rocket test site?
President Harry S. Truman

2509.   When was Cape Canaveral established as a site for testing rocket systems?
October 1949

2510.   What president renamed the Launch Operations Center and the Cape Canaveral Auxiliary Air Force Station as the John F. Kennedy Space Center?
President Lyndon B. Johnson

2511.   When was the first rocket system tested at Cape Canaveral?
July 24, 1950

2512.   What was the name of the first rocket system tested at Cape Canaveral?
Bumper 8

2513. Why was Cape Canaveral an ideal location for testing missiles?

At the time the area was undeveloped, which made it a safe place to test, fuel, and launch missiles without endangering nearby communities. Another advantage was that the mild climate permitted year-round operations.

2514. What country launched the world's first artificial satellite?

Russia

2515. When did Russia launch the world's first artificial satellite?

October 4, 1957

2516. What was the name of the world's first artificial satellite?

Sputnik

2517. When was NASA established?

October 1, 1958

2518. Who was the first person to travel in space and when did the first manned space flight occur?

Russian cosmonaut Yuri Gagarin was the first person to travel in space. This occurred on April 12, 1961.

2519. What was the objective of NASA's Project Mercury?

to orbit and retrieve a manned Earth satellite

2520. When was Project Mercury initiated?

October 7, 1958, just 6 days after the founding of NASA

2521. Who was the first American astronaut in space, when did he go there, and what was the name of the launch vehicle?

Alan B. Shepard Jr. went up in Freedom 7 *on May 5, 1961.*

2522. What was the name of the NASA launch vehicle that first carried a chimpanzee into space?

Mercury-Atlas 5 *was the first two-orbit chimpanzee flight. The chimp, Enos, returned overheated but unharmed.*

2523. Who was the first American to orbit the Earth in space?

John H. Glenn Jr.

2524. What was the name of the first space vehicle that carried John Glenn into orbit?

Friendship 7

2525. When did John Glenn make his first orbit of the Earth?

February 20, 1962

2526. What were the reasons that the launch of the *Friendship 7* was delayed?

• *a broken hatch bolt*
• *a power failure at the Bermuda tracking station*
• *a slipped thermistor on Glenn's suit*
• *a stuck valve*

> • *bad weather*
> • *technical problems with the fuel tanks*
> • *too little propellant in the booster's tank*

2527.   True or False: After Project Mercury, the Gemini Program was the next major step toward landing on the moon.
>   *True*

2528.   How many passengers did the *Gemini* launch vehicle carry?
>   *2*

2529.   What were some of the accomplishments of the *Gemini* launch vehicle?
> • *the first rendezvous of one spacecraft with another*
> • *the first docking of a spacecraft to another propulsive stage*
> • *use of a propulsion stage to propel the spacecraft into a higher orbit*
> • *the first human travel into the Earth's radiation belts*

2530.   What capabilities necessary for landing on the moon did *Gemini* demonstrate?
> • *rendezvous and docking*
> • *duration of mission for up to two weeks*
> • *controlled landing*

2531.   What are other names for NASA launch pads?
>   *rocket stage or platform*

2532.   What is the name of the apparatus that provides support for the lines that carry fuel and power from ground sources into NASA rockets?
>   *umbilical mast or tower*

2533.   What is the name of the launch complex that was originally designed to accommodate Apollo-Saturn V space vehicles?
>   *Launch Complex 39*

2534.   True or False: Launch Complex 39 is the largest scientific building in the world.
>   *True*

2535.   What are the principal features of Launch Complex 39?
> • *a hangar big enough to enclose four Apollo-Saturn V space vehicles, each standing 363 feet (111 meters) tall and measuring up to 33 feet (10 meters) in diameter*
> • *movable launch platforms on which rockets are assembled and transported to the launch pad*
> • *a transport system for rockets and launchers, weighing 12 million pounds (5.44 million kilograms)*
> • *a movable service structure 45 stories tall*
> • *a control center*

2536.   How much did it cost to build the Cape Canaveral Launch Complex 39?
>   *$800 million*

2537.   Who was the first woman in space?
          Sally Ride

2538.   How did the *Apollo* space vehicles land on Earth?
          The Apollo *vehicles splashed down into the ocean.*

2539.   During the *Apollo 10* mission the astronauts flew to the moon in a separate the lunar module. What was this module called?
          Snoopy

2540.   The lunar module *Snoopy* descended to within 50,000 feet (15,240 meters) of the lunar surface, then rendezvoused and docked with the command ship. What was the name of the command ship?
          Charlie Brown

2541.   What Apollo mission put a man on the moon?
          Apollo 11

2542.   What was the name of the manned lunar landing vehicle used on the Apollo 11 mission?
          Eagle

2543.   When did the first manned vehicle land on the moon?
          July 20, 1969

2544.   Who piloted the lunar landing vehicle *Eagle* on the *Apollo 11* mission?
          Edwin E. Aldrin Jr. ("Buzz" Aldrin)

2545.   Who was the first man to walk on the moon?
          Neil Armstrong

2546.   What were the first words spoken on the moon?
          Neil Armstrong planted his left foot on the moon, and said, "That's one small step for man, one giant leap for mankind."

2547.   What was the name of the NASA program that sent men to the moon?
          Apollo

2548.   What did the launch vehicle *Voyager 1* discover about Jupiter?
          • *ice sheets that cover Ganymede and Europa, two of Jupiter's moons*
          • *Jupiter's rings*
          • *volcanoes on Jupiter's moon Io*

2549.   What planets did the launch vehicle *Voyager 2* investigate?
          Jupiter, Saturn, Uranus, Neptune, and their moons

2550.   Who was the commander of the *Apollo 13* mission?
          James A. Lovell Jr.

2551.   What was the major problem that *Apollo 13* encountered?
          Liquid oxygen tank 2 in the service module exploded and destroyed the fuel

cells that supplied life-sustaining oxygen and electrical power for the command and service modules, and the battery-powered backup electric supply in the spacecraft had a lifetime of only 10 hours.

2552.   How was the carbon dioxide problem solved on the *Apollo 13* mission?
Kennedy Space Center engineers built and tested a system that carried carbon dioxide–rich air from the lunar module through a hose into the command module's lithium hydroxide canisters. When the Apollo 13 *flight crew duplicated the procedure, carbon dioxide in the cabin returned to tolerable levels.*

20
Statistics

Boating

2553.   How many boats were registered in Florida in 2003?
978,225

2554.   What three states had the most boating accidents in 2002?
• *Florida (831)*
• *California (745)*
• *Michigan (226)*

2555.   True or False: Florida had more registered boats than any other state in 2002.
False. Michigan had the most registered boats in 2002 (1,000,337). Florida had 922,597.

2556.   What Florida county had the most boat accidents in 2003?
Monroe County (158)

2557.   How many boating fatalities occurred in Florida in 2003?
64

2558.   True or False: In 2003, most of the victims of fatal boating accidents were Florida residents.
True. 94% of Florida's 2003 boating fatality victims were Florida residents.

2559.   How many personal watercraft accidents occurred in Florida in 2003?
241

2560.   How many personal watercraft fatalities occurred in Florida in 2003?
10

2561.   What three Florida counties reported the most personal watercraft accidents in 2003?
• *Pinellas County (37)*
• *Monroe County (31)*
• *Palm Beach County (22)*

Crime

2562.   How many property crimes occurred in Florida in 2003?
757,379

2563.   How many motor vehicle thefts occurred in Florida in 2003?
81,536

2564.   What Florida county recorded the most arrests in 2004?
Miami-Dade County (143,721 arrests)

2565.   What Florida county recorded the second highest number of arrests in 2004?
Broward County (82,475 arrests)

2566.   What Florida county recorded the fewest arrests in 2004?
Lafayette County (116 total arrests)

2567.   In what three Florida counties did the most motor vehicle thefts occur in 2004?
• *Miami-Dade County (1,951)*
• *Hillsborough County (1,654)*
• *Broward County (810)*

2568.   In what Florida county were the most people arrested for DUI (Driving Under the Influence) in 2004?
Hillsborough County (6,412 DUI arrests)

2569.   What Florida county had the fewest DUI arrests in 2004?
Lafayette County (9 DUI arrests)

Miscellaneous

2570.   What was the median household income in Florida in 2003?
$38,985

2571.   What were the top three Florida counties with the highest median income in 1999?
• *St. Johns County ($48,732)*
• *Seminole County ($46,559)*
• *Clay County ($46,171)*

2572.   How many people under the age of 18 were living in poverty in Florida in 1999?
669,445

2573.   What three Florida counties have the most people under the age of 18 living in poverty in 1999?
• *Miami-Dade County (134,714 people)*
• *Broward County (59,44 people)*
• *Hillsborough County (46,334 people)*

2574.   How many homeless people lived in Florida during 2001–2002?
71,770

2575. True or False: More females than males graduated from high school in Florida every year from 2000–2003.
True

2576. True or False: Over 10,000 more females than males entered college in Florida every year from 1996–2000.
True

2577. What Florida county library spent the most per capita in the year 2000?
Alachua County Library District spent $3.55 per capita.

2578. What Florida county library spent the least per capita in the year 2000?
Clay County Public Library System spent $0.94 per capita.

2579. What Florida county library system had the largest collection of volumes in the year 2000?
The Miami-Dade Public Library System had 4,059,005 collection volumes.

2580. How many minority-owned businesses were listed in Florida the 1997 U.S. census?
286,885

2581. What were the sales receipts of Florida's minority-owned businesses as listed in the 1997 U.S. census?
$50,840,000

Motor Vehicle

2582. How many car accidents occur in Florida every year?
about 240,000

2583. What is the average number of car crashes that occur in Florida every day?
667

2584. How many alcohol-related car accidents occur in Florida every year?
around 22,000

2585. How many fatal car accidents occur in Florida every year?
around 3,000

2586. How many motorcycle accidents occur in Florida every year?
around 5,000

2587. How many bicycle accidents occur in Florida every year?
approximately 4,500

2588. How many pedestrians are hit by cars in Florida every year?
around 7,500

2589.   How many pedestrians are hit by cars and killed in Florida every year?
       around 500

Population

2590.   What was Florida's population in the year 2000?
       15,982,378

2591.   According to the 2000 census, what percentage of Florida's population is over 65 years of age?
       17.6%

2592.   According to the 2000 census, what percentage of Florida's population is under 18 years of age?
       22.8%

2593.   What are the three most populous counties in Florida?
       • *Miami-Dade County, population 2,253,362*
       • *Broward County, population 1,623,018*
       • *Palm Beach County, population 1,131,184*

2594.   According to the 2000 census, what is Florida's population density per square mile?
       Florida has 296.4 people per square mile.

2595.   What Florida county has the lowest population?
       Liberty County, population 7,021

2596.   What is the most densely populated county in Florida?
       Pinellas County, which has 3,292 people per square mile

2597.   What Florida county has the lowest population density per square mile?
       Liberty County, which has 8.4 people per square mile

2598.   What Florida county has the most surface water area?
       Monroe County, which has 2,740 square surface acres of water

2599.   What Florida county has the least surface water area?
       Hardee County, which has 1.03 square surface acres of water

2600.   According to the 2000 census, what is the average amount of time Floridians spend traveling to work?
       26.2 minutes

Weather

2601.   What causes the most weather-related deaths in Florida?
       lightning

2602.   What percentages of weather-related deaths in Florida from 1959–1993 were caused by weather hazards?
> • *lightning (53.1%)*
> • *drowning (16.1%)*
> • *tornadoes (12.9%)*
> • *hurricanes (8.7%)*
> • *wind (4.2%)*
> • *cold (3.5%)*

2603.   What was the average number of people killed by lightning in Florida each year from 1959 through 1994?
> *10*

2604.   What was the average number of people injured by lightning every year in Florida between 1959 and 1994?
> *33*

2605.   What three Florida counties had the most deaths due to lightning during the years 1959–1996?
> • *Brevard County (23 deaths)*
> • *Lake County (13 deaths)*
> • *Orange County (12 deaths)*

2606.   In what Florida county did the most injuries from lightning occur in the years 1959–1996?
> *Brevard (69 injuries)*

2607.   What is the total number of deaths that occurred in Florida due to lightning between 1959 and 1994?
> *1,524*

2608.   How many injuries occurred in Florida due to lightning between 1959 and 1994?
> *1,178*

2609.   In terms of damage due to lightning strikes, where does Florida rank among the 50 states during the years 1959–1994?
> *19th*

References and Further Reading

References and reading suggestions are listed under the index category which they factually support. In order to encourage research and reading, the References and Further Reading sections of this book may be legally copied by users of this book.

Agriculture of Florida

Florida Agricultural Statistics Brochure. 2004. http://www.florida-agriculture.com/pubs/pubform/pdf/Florida_Agriculture_Statistics_Brochure.pdf
Florida Department of Agriculture. Florida Agriculture Facts. Florida Agriculture Facts Brochure. Tallahassee, Florida, 2001.

Architecture in Florida

Daley, Sue, and Steven Gross. *Old Florida*. USA: Rizzoli International Publications, Inc., 2003.
Harvey, Karen. *America's First City: St Augustine's Historic Neighborhoods*. Lake Buena Vista, Florida: Tailored Tours Publications, Inc. 1992.
Nolan, David. *Houses of St. Augustine.* Sarasota: Pineapple Press, 1995.
Florida Gold Coast Publishing, Spanish Monastery. 2005 http://www.floridagoldcoast.com/attractions/spanishmonastery.htm. (20 Feb 2005).

Further Reading on Florida Architecture

Gordon, Elsbeth K. *Florida's Colonial Architectural Heritage*. Gainesville, Florida: University of Florida Press, 2002.
Haase, Ronald. *Classic Cracker: Florida's Wood-Frame Vernacular Architecture.* Sarasota: Pineapple Press, 1992.

Archaeology in Florida

Florida Department of State Office of Cultural and Historical Programs, Mission San Luis de Apalachee. 2005. http://dhr.dos.state.fl.us/archaeology/sanluis/. (20 Feb 2005).
Florida Department of State Office of Cultural and Historical Programs, The Spanish Village at Mission San Luis. 2005. http://dhr.dos.state.fl.us/archaeology/san-luis/facts/vol1.cfm. (20 Feb 2005).
Florida Department of State Office of Cultural and Historical Programs, The Church Complex at Mission San Luis. 2005. http://dhr.dos.state.fl.us/archaeology /sanluis/facts/vol2.cfm. (20 Feb 2005).Florida Department of State Office of Cultural and Historical Programs, The Fort and Garrison at Mission San Luis. 2005. http://dhr.dos.state.fl.us/archaeology /sanluis/facts/vol3.cfm. (20 Feb 2005).
Florida Department of State Office of Cultural and Historical Programs, The Apalachee at Mission San Luis. 2005. http://dhr.dos.state.fl.us/archaeology/sanluis/facts/vol4.cfm. (20 Feb 2005).

Florida Department of State Office of Cultural and Historical Programs, The Miami Circle Site Facts. 2005. http://dhr.dos.state.fl.us/archaeology/projects/ brickellpoint/facts.cfm. (20 Feb 2005).

Florida Department of State Office of Cultural and Historical Programs, Emanuel Point Shipwreck. 2005. http://dhr.dos.state.fl.us/archaeology/projects/shipwrecks /emanuelpoint/. (20 Feb 2005).

Florida Department of State Office of Cultural and Historical Programs, Prehistoric canoes in Florida. 2005. http://dhr.dos.state.fl.us/archaeology/underwater/canoes.cfm. (20 Feb 2005).

Singer, Steven D. *Shipwrecks of Florida*. Sarasota, Florida: Pineapple Press, Inc., 1998.

Art in Florida

Bardon, Doris, and Murry D. Laurie. *Florida's Museums and Cultural Attractions*. Sarasota, Florida: Pineapple Press, Inc. 1998.

Dreller, Aletta D., and Anne E. F. Jeffrey. *Art Lovers Guide to Florida*. Sarasota, Florida: Pineapple Press, Inc. 1998.

Mann, Maybelle. *Art in Florida: 1564–1945*. Sarasota, Florida: Pineapple Press, Inc., 1999.

Botanic Gardens in Florida

Ceo, Rocco J., and Joanna Lombard. *Historic Landscapes of Florida*. USA: The Deerling Foundation & The University of Miami School of Architecture, 2001.

Miami-Dade County Park and Recreation Department, Fruit and Spice Park. http://www.fruitandspicepark.org/. (20 Feb 2005).

Pinkas, Lilly. *Guide to the Gardens of Florida*. Sarasota, Florida: Pineapple Press, Inc., 1998.

Climate of Florida

Henry, James A., Kenneth M. Portier, and Jan Coyne. *Climate and Weather of Florida*. Sarasota, Florida: Pineapple Press, Inc., 1994.

Oklahoma State University Environmental Health and Safety, Heat Stress. http://www.pp.okstate.edu/ehs/training/heat.htm. (19 Feb 2005).

US Department of Commerce and National Oceanic Atmospheric Administration, Heat Wave A Major Summer Killer. http://www.nws.noaa.gov/om/brochures/ heatwave.pdf. (19 Feb 2005).

Winsberg, Mort. Climate of Florida. 2002. http://www.coaps.fsu.edu/climate_center/FLClimate.htm. (23 Nov 2004).

Economy of Florida

State of Florida.com, Florida Quick Facts. 2005. http://www.stateofflorida.com/Portal/DesktopDefault.aspx?tabid=95 (17 Feb 2005).

Ecosystems in Florida

Ewel, John J., and Ronald L. Myers, ed. *Ecosystems of Florida*. Orlando, Florida: University of Central Florida Press, 1990.

Means, D. Bruce, Anne Rudloe, and Ellie Whitney, Ph.D. *Priceless Florida*. Sarasota, Florida: Pineapple Press, Inc., 2004.

Florida Conservation Foundation. *Guide to Florida Environmental Issues and Information*. Winter Park, Florida: Florida Conservation Foundation, 1993.

Further Reading on Florida's Ecosystems

Douglas, Marjory Stoneman. *The Everglades: River of Grass*. Sarasota, Florida: Pineapple Press, Inc., 1997.

Valentine, James, and D. Bruce Means. *Florida Magnificent Wilderness*. Sarasota, Florida: Pineapple Press, Inc., 2006.

Environment

Broward County, Florida. Cleaner Cars Mean Cleaner Air. http://www.broward.org/environment/pub_air_2.pdf. (7 May 2006).

Broward County, Florida. Report Smoking Vehicles. http://www.broward.org/environment/pub_air_1.pdf. (7 May 2006).

Bureau of Solid and Hazardous Waste, Recycling and Litter Programs: Current Status and Potential Future Directions. 2001. http://www.dep.state.fl.us/waste/categories/recycling/pages/goals_main.htm. (12 Nov 2004).

Division of Waste Management Bureau of Solid and Hazardous Waste. *Solid Waste Management in Florida*. USA: 1999.

Florida Center For Solid And Hazardous Waste Management. Beneficial Utilization of Landfill Gas. 1994. http://www.floridacenter.org/publications/landfill_gas_reuse_options_94-7.pdf. (15 Feb 2005).

Florida Department of Environmental Protection. Pointless Personal Pollution. 2004. http://www.dep.state.fl.us/water/nonpoint/docs/nonpoint/ppp.pdf. (27 Nov 2004)

Florida Department of Environmental Protection. Solid Waste Management in Florida 2000. 2000. http://www.dep.state.fl.us/waste/categories/recycling/pages/00.htm. (11 Nov 2004).

Florida Department of Environmental Protection, Summary of Hazardous Waste Regulations. 1990. www.dep.state.fl.us/waste/categories/hazardous/pages/laws.htm. (12 Nov 2004).

Florida Department of Environmental Protection. Ultraviolet (UV) Disinfection for Domestic Wastewater. 2004. http://www.dep.state.fl.us/water/wastewater/dom/domuv.htm (14 Nov 2004).

Florida Department of Environmental Protection. Underground Injection Control. 2004. http://www.dep.state.fl.us/water/uic/index.htm (14 Nov 2004).

Florida Department of Environmental Protection Office of Water Policy. Florida Water Management Plan. 2004. http://www.dep.state.fl.us/water/waterpolicy/docs/FWP_Dec_2001.pdf. (18 Nov 2004).

Florida State University Institute of Science and Public Affairs, Water Resources Atlas of Florida. Tallahassee, FL: Institute of Science and Public Affairs, Florida State Univeristy. 1998.

Florida Organics Recyclers Association and Florida Center for Solid and Hazardous Waste, Recycling Yard Trash: Best Management Practices Manual For Florida. 1996.

http://www.dep.state.fl.us/waste/quick_topics/publications/documents/yard_trash.pdf. (12 Nov 2004).

Reuse Coordinating Committee and the Water Conservation Initiative Water Reuse Work Group, Water Reuse for Florida. 2003. http://sofia.usgs.gov/publications/reports/floridawaters/fw_chap5.pdf (12 Nov 2004).

University of Florida, Institute of Food and Agricultural Sciences, Energy Efficiency & Environmental News: Energy in Garbage. 1992. http://edis.ifas.ufl.edu/BODY_EH333. (15 Feb 2005).

University of Florida, Institue of Food and Agricultural Sciences. Florida Invaders: Exotic Pests. 2003. http://edis.ifas.ufl.edu/pdffiles/CR/CR00800.pdf. (12 June 2006).

US Environmental Protection Agency, Landfill Gas-to-Energy Opportunities: Landfill Profiles for the State of Florida. 1999. http://www.epa.gov/lmop/res/pdf/fl_jan.pdf (27 Nov 2004).

US Environmental Protection Agency, Landfill Methane Outreach Program. 2004. http://www.epa.gov/landfill/res/orange.htm. (15 Nov 2005).

Florida Flora and Fauna

"Alligator Deaths." *St. Petersburg Times.* (June 26, 2001).

Alsop, Fred J. III. *Smithsonian Handbooks Birds of Florida.* New York, New York: DK Publishing Inc., 2002.

Ashton, R. E. and P. S. Ashton. *Handbook of Reptiles and Amphibians of Florida: The Amphibians.* Miami, Florida: Windward Publishing, 1988.

Brown, Paul Martin. *Wild Orchids of Florida.* Gainesville, Florida: University Press of Florida, 2002.

Carmichael, Pete, and Winston Williams. *Florida Fabulous Reptiles and Amphibians.* Tampa, Florida: World Publications, 2001.

Department of the Interior US Fish and Wildlife Service. The Facts on Key Deer. 1997. http://www.fws.gov/southeast/pubs/nkdgen1.pdf. (28 May 2006).

Deyup, Mark. *Florida's Fabulous Insects.* Tampa, Florida: World Publications, 2000.

Emmel, Thomas C. *Florida's Fabulous Butterflies.* Tampa, Florida: World Publications, 1997.

Florida Department of Agriculture and Consumer Services Division of Plant Industry. Slugs of Florida. 1999 rev 2004. http://creatures.ifas.ufl.edu/misc/florida_slugs.htm. (16 Feb 2005).

Florida Fish and Wildlife Commission. Florida's Endangered Species, Threatened Species and Species of Special Concern. 2004. http://www.wildflorida.org/species/Endangered-Threatened-Special-Concern-2004.pdf (14 Nov 2004).

Florida Fish and Wildlife Conservation Commission - Fish and Wildlife Research Institute, Common Causes of Fish Kills in Florida. 2004. http://www.floridamarine.org/features/view_article.asp?id=19955. (16 Nov 2004).

Florida Fish and Wildlife Conservation Commission. The "Bear" Facts. 2005. http://wld.fwc.state.fl.us/bear/bearfacts.htm. (16 Mar 2005).

Florida Museum of Natural History. Checklist of Florida Amphibians and Reptiles. http://www.flmnh.ufl.edu/natsci/herpetology/fl-guide/flaherps.htm#TOP (9 June 2006.)

Florida Ornithological Society Records Committee. Official State List of the Birds of Florida. 2003. http://www.fosbirds.org/RecordCommittee/StateListJuly2003.htm (30 Nov 2004).

Florida Panther.net. The Florida Panther. http://www.panther.state.fl.us/handbook/threats/inbreeding.html. (Feb 24 2005).

Florida Panther Society, Inc. Panther Facts. http://www.panthersociety.org /moreinfo.html. (16 Mar 2005).

Mitch Waite Group. Field Guide to Birds of North America: Great Blue Heron. http://identify.whatbird.com/obj/31/_/Great_Blue_Heron.aspx. (1 Jan 2006).

Mitch Waite Group. Field Guide to Birds of North America: Great Egret. http://identify.whatbird.com/obj/30/_/Great_Egret.aspx. (1 Jan 2006).

Mitch Waite Group. Field Guide to Birds of North America: Reddish Egret. http://identify.whatbird.com/obj/47/_/Reddish_Egret.aspx. (1 Jan 2006).

Mitch Waite Group. Field Guide to Birds of North America: Snowy Egret. http://identify.whatbird.com/obj/48/_/Snowy_Egret.aspx. (1 Jan 2006).

North American Bear Center. Black Bear Facts. 2006. http://www.bear.org/Black/Black_Bear_Facts.html. (8 June 2006).

Price, Thomas. Poisonous Critters of Florida: Bees, Wasps and Hornets. 1998. http://wwwpediatrics.med.miami.edu/FPIC/critters/bees.html#hon (25 Nov 2004).

Price, Thomas. Poisonous Critters of Florida: Caterpillars. 1998. http://wwwpediatrics.med.miami.edu/FPIC/critters/caterpil.html (25 Nov 2004).

Price, Thomas. Poisonous Critters of Florida: Marine Life. 1998. http://wwwpediatrics.med.miami.edu/FPIC/critters/marine.html (25 Nov 2004).

Price, Thomas. Poisonous Critters of Florida: Snakes. 1998. http://wwwpediatrics.med.miami.edu/FPIC/critters/snakes.html (25 Nov 2004).

Price, Thomas. Poisonous Critters of Florida: Spiders. 1998. http://wwwpediatrics.med.miami.edu/FPIC/critters/bla (25 Nov 2004).

Price, Thomas. Poisonous Critters of Florida: Stinging Insects. 1998. http://wwwpediatrics.med.miami.edu/FPIC/critters/sting.html (25 Nov 2004).

Thorn, Nancy. Florida Insects. 2001. http://www.venture-learn.org/Florida_insects/ florida_insects_index.htm (26 Nov 2004).

Thorn, Nancy. Florida Insect Information Table. 2001. http://www.venture-learn.org/Florida_insects/FI_info_table.htm 26 Nov 2004).

Tomlinson, Denise R., Bat Facts. 2000. http://www.floridabats.org/BatsAre.htm (21 Nov 2004).

Tomlinson, Denise R. Big Brown Bat. 2000. http://www.floridabats.org/ BigBrown.htm (21 Nov 2004).

Tomlinson, Denise R. Hoary Bat. 2000. http://www.floridabats.org/Hoary.htm (21 Nov 2004).

Tomlinson, Denise R. Wagners Mastiff Bat. 2000. http://www.floridabats.org/ Wagners.htm. (21 Nov 2004).

University of Florida, Institute of Food and Agricultural Sciences. Dragonflies and Damselflies (Insecta: Odonata). 2005. http://edis.ifas.ufl.edu/IN632 (27 May 2006).

University of Florida, Institute of Food and Agricultural Sciences. Featured Creatures: Dragonflies and Damselflies. 2005. http://creatures.ifas.ufl.edu/misc/odonata/odonata.htm. (27 May 2006).

University of Florida, Institute of Food and Agricultural Sciences, Florida Ecosystems. http://www.sfrc.ufl.edu/4h/Ecosystems/ecosystems.html. (27 Nov 2004).

University of Florida, Institute of Food and Agricultural Sciences. Pillbugs, Sowbugs, Centipedes, Millipedes and Earwigs. http://edis.ifas.ufl.edu/IG093. (26 Nov 2004).

University of Florida, Institute of Food and Agricultural Sciences, Scrub. http://www.sfrc.ufl.edu/4h/Ecosystems/Scrub/scrub.html. (27 Nov 2004).

University of Florida, Institute of Food and Agricultural Sciences, Upland Hardwoods. http://www.sfrc.ufl.edu/4h/Ecosystems/Upland_Hardwoods/upland_hard woods.html. (27 Nov 2004).

University of Florida, Institute of Food and Agricultural Sciences, Bottomland Forests. http://www.sfrc.ufl.edu/4h/Ecosystems/Bottomland_Hardwoods/bottomland_ hardwoods.html. (27 Nov 2004).

University of Florida, Institute of Food and Agricultural Sciences. Cockroaches and Their Management. 1994. http://edis.ifas.ufl.edu/IG082. (18 Jan 2006)

University of Florida, Institute of Food and Agricultural Sciences, Sand Hills. http://www.sfrc.ufl.edu/4h/Ecosystems/Sandhills/sandhills.html. (27 Nov 2004).

US Fish and Wildlife Service. Key Deer Fact Sheet. http://apc.tamu.edu/keydeer /KDFacts.pdf. (5 Mar 2005).

US Fish and Wildlife Service, Southeast Region. http://www.fws.gov/southeast/news/2005/r05-018.html. (9 June 2006).

Williams, Winston. *Florida's Fabulous Seashells*. Tampa, Florida: World Publications, 1988.

Williams, Winston. *Florida's Fabulous Waterbirds*. Tampa, Florida: World Publications, 2003.

Further Reading on Florida's Flora and Fauna

Ashton, Ray E., and Patricia Sawyer Ashton. *The Gopher Tortoise*. Sarasota, Florida, Pineapple Press, Inc., 2004.

Becker, John E. *The Florida Panther*. USA: Kidhaven Press, 2003.

Carmichael, Pete, and Winston William. *Florida Fabulous Reptiles and Amphibians*. Tampa, Florida: World Publications, 2001.

Maehr, David S., Herbert W. Kale II, and Karl Karalus. *Florida's Birds, 2nd Ed.* Sarasota, Florida: Pineapple Press, Inc., 2005.

Nellis, David W. *Common Coastal Birds of Florida and the Caribbean*. Sarasota, Florida: Pineapple Press Inc., 2003.

Williams, Winston. *Florida's Fabulous Waterbirds*. Tampa, Florida: World Publications, 2003.

Florida State Facts

State of Florida, Florida Facts and History. 2005. http://dhr.dos.state.fl.us/facts/. (19 Feb 2005).

State of Florida, Florida Facts and History. 2003. http://dhr.dos.state.fl.us/ facts/stats/quick/. (19 Feb 2005).

Further Reading on Florida State Facts

Kleinberg, Eliot. *Florida Fun Facts, 2nd Edition.* Sarasota, Florida: Pineapple Press, Inc., 2005.

Philcox, Phil, and Beverly Boe. *Sunshine State Almanac.* Sarasota, Florida: Pineapple Press, Inc., 1999.

Ryan, Susan Jane. *Florida A to Z.* Sarasota, Florida: Pineapple Press, Inc., 2003.

Geology of Florida

Brown, Robin C. *Florida's Fossils.* Sarasota, Florida: Pineapple Press, Inc., 1988.

Cervone, Sarah. Plant Management in Florida Waters - Aquifers. 2004. http://aquat1.ifas.ufl.edu/guide/aquifers.html. (14 Nov 2004).

Cooperative Extension of the University of Wisconsin. A3588 Management of Wisconson Soils. 2005. http://cecommerce.uwex.edu/pdfs/A3588.PDF (23 Jan 2006).

Florida Department of Environmental Protection. Water Resource Management - Drinking Water Program. 2005. http://www.dep.state.fl.us/water/drinkingwater/. (16 Feb 2005).

Florida Geographic Alliance. The Floridan Aquifer System. 2000. http://fga.freac.fsu.edu/gaw/resources/waterpdf/floridan_aquifer_system.pdf (17 Feb 2005)

Florida Geological Survey. Special Publication 35 Florida's Geological History and Geological Resources. 1994. http://fulltext10.fcla.edu/cgi/t/text/text-idx?c=feol&idno=UF00000124&format=pdf. (15 Feb 2005).

Florida Geological Survey. Special Publication No. 52 Florida Spring Classification System And Spring Glossary. Tallahassee, Florida: Florida Geological Survey, 2003.

McSorley, Robert McSorley. University of Florida Department of Food and Agricultural Sciences. Publication number: EENY-12 Soil-inhabiting Nematodes Phylum Nematoda. 1997. http://creatures.ifas.ufl.edu/nematode/soil_nematode.htm#soil. (23 Jan 2006).

South Florida Water Management District, Lake Okeechobee Drainage Basin. 2001 http://www.sfwmd.gov/org/ema/ecu/pdfs/ecu_okee.pdf (14 Nov 2004).

Stamm, Doug. *The Springs of Florida.* Sarasota, Florida: Pineapple Press, Inc., 1994.

University of Florida and Florida Department of Environmental Protection. Florida Geological Survey. Florida Sinkholes … Your Guide. 2003. http://aquat1.ifas.ufl.edu/guide/sinkholes.html (11 Feb 2005).

University of Florida Institute of Food and Agricultural Sciences. Florida Forestry information: Introduction to Florida Soils. http://www.sfrc.ufl.edu/Extension/ffws/soils.htm (11 Nov 2004).

University of Florida, and the Bureau of Invasive Plant Management, Geology. 2003. http://aquat1.ifas.ufl.edu/guide/geology.html#geologichistory. (17 Feb 2005).

Further Reading on Florida Geology

Cutchins, Judy, and Ginny Johnston. *Ice Age Giants of the South.* Sarasota, Florida: Pineapple Press, Inc., 2000.

Lantz, Peggy Sias, and Wendy A. Hale. *The Florida Water Story.* Sarasota, Florida: Pineapple Press, Inc., 1998.

Geography of Florida

Cervone, Sarah. Plant Management in Florida Waters - Lakes. 2004. http://aquat1.ifas.ufl.edu/guide/lakes.html. (14 Nov 2004).

Cervone, Sarah. Plant Management in Florida Waters - Rivers. 2004. http://aquat1.ifas.ufl.edu/guide/rivers.html. (14 Nov 2003).

Florida Fish and Wildlife Conservation Commission. Florida Lakes. http://www.florida conservation.org/fishing/lakes.html. (6 Jan 2006).

Florida Ports Council. Florida Port Statistics. 2003. http://www.flaports.org/statistics.htm. (14 Nov 2004).

Great Lakes Information Network. Lake Michigan. http://www.great-lakes.net/lakes/michigan.html#overview. (6 Jan 2006).

Marth, Del, and Marty Marth. *The Rivers of Florida*. Sarasota, Florida: Pineapple Press, Inc., 1990.

Further Reading on the Geography of Florida

Fernald, Edward A., and Elizabeth D. Purdum, ed. *Atlas of Florida,* Revised Edition. Gainesville, Florida: University Press of Florida, 1992.

Morris, Allen. *Florida Place Names: Alachua to Zolfo Springs*. Sarasota, Florida: Pineapple Press, Inc., 1995.

History of Florida

Allen, Rodney F. *Fifty-Five Famous Floridians*. Marceline, Missouri: Walsworth Publishing Company, 1985.

Bicentennial Commission of Florida. *Born of the Sun*. The Bicentennial Commission of Florida, 1976.

Bicentennial Commission of Florida, *The Florida Bicentennial Trail: A Heritage Revisited*. The Bicentennial Commission of Florida, 1976.

Brown, Robin C. *Florida's First People*. Sarasota, Florida: Pineapple Press, Inc., 1994.

Florida Department of State. *Florida Cuban Heritage Trail*. Tallahassee, Florida: Florida Department of State, 1996.

Florida Society Sons of the American Revolution. Revolutionary War in Florida. http://www.flssar.org/flarevol.htm. (6 Jan 2006).

Harner, Charles E. *Florida Promoters: The Men Who Made it Big*. Tampa, Florida: Trend House, 1973.

Jones, Maxine D., and Kevin M. McCarthy. *African Americans in Florida*. Sarasota, Florida: Pineapple Press, Inc., 1993.

Kleinberg, Eliot. *Historical Travelers Guide to Florida, 2nd Ed.*. Sarasota, Florida: Pineapple Press, Inc., 2006.

McCarthy, Kevin M. *Native Americans in Florida*. Sarasota, Florida: Pineapple Press, Inc., 1999.

Miccosukee Tribe of Indians of Florida. Miccosukee Reservations. 2002. http://www.miccosukeeresort.com/reserve.html. (12 June 2006).

Office of Cultural and Historical Programs. City Name Origins. 2005. http://dhr.dos.state.fl.us/facts/reports/names/city2.cfm. (14 Feb 2005).

Office of Cultural and Historical Programs. City Name Origins. 2005. http://dhr.dos.state.fl.us/facts/reports/names/city3.cfm. (14 Feb 2005).

Office of Cultural and Historical Programs. Name Origins of Florida Places. 2005.
　　http://dhr.dos.state.fl.us/facts/reports/names/index.cfm. (14 Feb 2005).
Office of Cultural and Historical Programs. County Name Origins. 2005.
　　http://dhr.dos.state.fl.us/facts/reports/names/county.cfm#A2. (14 Feb 2005).
Office of Cultural and Historical Programs. County Name Origins. 2005.
　　http://dhr.dos.state.fl.us/facts/reports/names/county2.cfm#J2. (14 Feb 2005).
Office of Cultural and Historial Programs. Mission San Luis de Apalachee. 2006.
　　http://dhr.dos.state.fl.us/archaeology/sanluis/facts/vol2.cfm. (12 June 2006).
Seminole Tribe of Florida. Tourism/Enterprises. 2005.
　　http://www.seminoletribe.com/enterprises/. (12 June 2006).
Singer, Steven D. *Shipwrecks of Florida: A Comprehensive Listing,* Second Edition.
　　Sarasota, Florida: Pineapple Press, Inc., 1998.
State of Florida.com, Historic Places. 2005. www.stateofflorida.com/natregofhisp.html.
　　(19 Feb 2005).
Taylor, Thomas W. *The Florida Lighthouse Trail.* Sarasota, Florida: Pineapple Press, Inc.,
　　2001.
Waitley, Douglas. *Florida History from the Highways.* Sarasota, Florida: Pineapple
　　Press, Inc., 2005.
Wilkinson, Jerry, Florida Keys 2000 Census Summary. 2001.
　　http://www.keyshistory.org/Census-2000.html (20 Nov 2004).

Further Reading on the History of Florida

Clark, James C. *200 Quick Looks at Florida History.* Sarasota, Florida: Pineapple Press,
　　Inc., 2000.
Florida Department of State. *Florida Cuban Heritage Trail.* Tallahassee, Florida: Florida
　　Department of State, 1996.

Invasive Species in Florida

Florida Department of Environmental Protection. Florida DEP State Lands: FAQs. 2004.
　　http://www.dep.state.fl.us/lands/invaspec/2ndlevpgs/faq.htm. (12. Feb 2005).
Florida Exotic Pest Plant Council, List of Invasive Plant Species. 2003. http://www.
　　fleppc.org/Plantlist/03list.htm (14 Nov 2004).
Invasive Species Focus Team Gulf of Mexico Program, An Initial Survey of Aquatic
　　Invasive Species Issues in the Gulf of Mexico Region version 4.0. 2000.
　　http://nis.gsmfc.org/pubs/Initial%20Survey%20of%20Invasive%20Species.pdf.
　　(22 Feb 2005).
University of Florida, Institute of Food and Agricultural Sciences. 2002. Ecological
　　Consequences of Invasion by Melaleuca Quinquenervia in South Florida
　　Wetlands: Paradise Damaged, not Lost. http://edis.ifas.ufl.edu/UW123. (12 Feb
　　2005).
University of Florida, Institute of Food and Agricultural Sciences, Invasive Insects
　　(Adventive Pest Insects) in Florida. http://edis.ifas.ufl.edu/IN503 (27 Nov
　　2004).

Legal Florida

Department of Highway Safety and Motor Vehicles. *Florida Drivers Handbook.*
　　Tallahassee, Florida: HSMV 71902. 2003.

Florida Fish and Wildlife Conservation Commission. 2004–2005 Florida Freshwater Sport Fishing Regulations. 2004. http://www.floridaconservation.org /Fishing/pdf/regs03.pdf. (5 Mar 2005).

Keane, Gerald E. *Florida Law: A Layman's Guide*. Sarasota, Florida: Pineapple Press, Inc., 2003.

National Association of State Boating Law Administrators, Reference Guide to State Boating Laws, sixth edition. 2000. http://www.uscgboating.org/regulations /Nasbla_Ref_Guide_6.pdf. (22 Feb 2005).

State of Florida, Florida Litter Law. 2003. http://www.litterinfo.org/laws.htm. (22 Feb 2005).

University of Florida Institute of Food and Agricultural Sciences, Laws that Protect Florida's Wildlife. 1993 Rev 2002. http://edis.ifas.ufl.edu/BODY_UW076. (17 Nov 2004).

Literary Florida

McCarthy, Kevin M. *The Book Lover's Guide to Florida: Authors, Books and Literary Sites*. Sarasota, Florida: Pineapple Press, Inc., 1992.

Meteorology

Coyne, Jan, James A. Henry, and Kenneth M. Portier. *The Climate and Weather of Florida*. Sarasota, Florida: Pineapple Press, Inc., 1994.

Florida Waters. Elizabeth D. Purdum, Florida Water Management Districts. 2002. http://sofia.usgs.gov/publications/reports/floridawaters. (27 May 2006).

Florida Oceanographic Coastal Center. Hurricane Information. 2003. http://www. floridaoceanographic.org/hurricane.html. (12 June 2006).

National Oceanic Atmospheric Administraion. Hurricane Basics. 1999. http://hurricanes.noaa.gov/pdf/hurricanebook.pdf. (12 June 2006).

National Oceanic Atmospheric Administration and National Severe Storms Laboratory. Questions and Answers About Lightning. 2004. http://www.nssl.noaa.gov/edu/ltg/. (18 Feb 2005).

The National Hurricane Center. Frequently Asked Questions. 2004. http://www.aoml.noaa.gov/hrd/tcfaq/tcfaqA.html. (26 Feb 2005).

The Tornado Project. The Fujita Scale. 1999. http://www.tornadoproject.com/ fscale/fscale.htm. (26 Feb 2005).

The Tornado Project. Tornado Myths. 1999. http://www.tornadoproject.com/ myths/myths.htm. (26 Feb 2005).

The Tornado Project. Safety. 1999. http://www.tornadoproject.com/safety/safety.htm. (26 Feb 2005).

University of Florida of Food and Agricultural Sciences. Florida's Water: Supply, Use, and Public Policy. 2000. http://edis.ifas.ufl.edu/FE207. (7 Mar 2005).

Winsberg, Morton D. *Florida Weather,* Second Edition. Gainesville, Florida: University Press of Florida, 2003.

Oceans and Florida Coastline

Burgess, George H. Reducing the Risk of a Shark Encounter: Advice to Aquatic Recreationists. 2005. http://www.flmnh.ufl.edu/fish/sharks/Attacks/relaris kreduce.htm. (15 Feb 2005)

Florida Fish and Wildlife Commission. Fish Biology.
   http://www.floridaconservation.org/fishing/Fishes. (14 Nov 2004).
Florida Fish and Wildlife Commission, Fishes index.
   http://www.floridaconservation.org/fishing/Fishes/index. (10 Oct 2004).
Florida Fish and Wildlife Commission, Horseshoe Crabs. 2004. http://www.florida
   marine.org/support/view_faqs.asp. (15 Feb 2005).
Florida Fish and Wildlife Commission, Jellyfish. 2005. http://www.wildflorida.org
   /critters/jellyfish.asp. (15 Feb 2005).
Florida Fish and Wildlife Commission Fish and Wildlife Research Institute, The Sea
   Aglow. http://www.floridamarine.org/features/view_article.asp?id=2513. (30
   Mar 2005).
Gore, Robert H. *The Gulf of Mexico.* Sarasota, Florida: Pineapple Press, Inc., 1992.
Gulf of Mexico Alliance. 2006. http://dep.state.fl.us/gulf/. (12 June 2006).
An Initial Survey of Aquatic Invasive Species Issues in the Gulf of Mexico Region.
   2000.http://nis.gsmfc.org/pubs/Initial%20Survey%20of%20Invasive%20Species.pdf.
   (22 Feb 2005).
Neal, William J., and Orrin H. Pilkey, ed. *Living with Florida's Atlantic Beaches.*
   Durham, North Carolina: Duke University Press, 2004.
McCarthy, Kevin M. *Apalachicola Bay.* Sarasota, Florida: Pineapple Press, Inc., 2004.
Reynolds III, John E., and Randall S. Wells. *Dolphins, Whales, and Manatees of
   Florida: A Guide to Sharing their World.* Gainesville, Florida: University Press
   of Florida, 2003.
South Florida Water Management District. http://www.sfwmd.gov. (12 June 2006).
University of Florida, Institute of Food and Agricultural Sciences. The Biology and
   Fishery of Florida's Commercial Sponges. 2000. http://edis.ifas.ufl.edu/SG045.
   (29 May 2006).
US Environmental Protection Agency, *Before You Go to the Beach.* Washington, D.C.:
   U.S. Environmental Protection Agency Office of Water, 2002.
U.S. Fish & Wildlife Service. Seagrasses. http://www.fws.gov/southeast/vbpdfs/
   commun/sg.pdf. (12 June 2006).
Wilkinson, Jerry, History of the Gulf Stream. http://www.keyshistory.org
   /gulfstream.html. (22 Nov 2004).

Further Reading on Oceans and Florida Coastline

Williams, Winston. *Florida's Fabulous Seashells.* Tampa, Florida: World Publications,
   1988.
Gore, Robert H. *The Gulf of Mexico.* Sarasota, Florida: Pineapple Press, Inc., 1992.
McCarthy, Kevin M. *Thirty Florida Shipwrecks.* Sarasota, Florida: Pineapple Press, Inc.,
   1992.

Parks in Florida

George, Jean Craighead. *Everglades Wildlife Guide.* Washington, D.C.: Division of
   Publications National Park Services, 1988.
Lippold, Mary and William Lippold. *Florida State and National Parks.* St. Augustine,
   Florida: CWS Publications, 1994.
National Park Service, The Everglades Ecosystems - Habitats. 2003.
   http://www.nps.gov/ever/eco/habitats.htm. (18 Feb 2005)

Ohr, Tim. *Florida's Fabulous Natural Places*. Tampa, Florida: World Publications, 1999.
South Florida Water Management District. *Discover a Watershed: The Everglades*.
    Bozeman, Montana: The Watercourse, 1996.

Further Reading on Florida Parks

Douglas, Marjory Stoneman. *The Everglades: River of Grass*. Sarasota, Florida:
    Pineapple Press, Inc., 1997.
Grunwald, Michael. *The Swamp: The Everglades, Florida, and the Politics of Paradise*.
    New York: Simon & Schuster, 2006.

Space Science and Florida

NASA Public Affairs Staff. *The Kennedy Space Center Story*. Kennedy Space Center,
    Florida: Graphic House, 1991.

Statistics

Bureau of Economic and Business Research, *Florida Statistical Abstract 2000*. USA:
    2001.
Bureau of Economic and Business Research, *Florida Statistical Abstract 2001*. USA:
    2002.
Bureau of Economic and Business Research, *Florida Statistical Abstract 2002*. USA:
    2003.
Bureau of Economic and Business Research, *Florida Statistical Abstract 2003*. USA:
    2004.
Florida Department of Highway Safety and Motor Vehicles. Traffic Crash Statistics
    Report 2003. 2003. http://www.hsmv.state.fl.us/hsmvdocs/cf2003.pdf. (28 Nov
    2004)
Florida Fish and Wildlife Commission, Division of Law Enforcement. 2003 Boating
    Accident Statistical Report. 2004. http://www.floridaconservation.org/law/
    boating/2003stats/2003StatBook1.pdf. (4 Mar 2005).
Florida Statistical Analysis Center. Arrests by County 2004. 2005.
    http://www.fdle.state.fl.us/FSAC/Crime_Trends/download/pdf/arr0305.pdf. (3
    June 2006).
Florida Statistical Analysis Center. Total Property Crime in Florida, 1989-2003. 2003.
    http://www.fdle.state.fl.us/FSAC/Crime_Trends/property/index.asp#Total%
    20Property%20Crime. (3 Mar 2005).
National Association of State Boating Law Administrators, Reference Guide to State
    Boating Laws, sixth edition. 2000. http://www.uscgboating.org/regulations
    /Nasbla_Ref_Guide_6.pdf. (22 Feb 2005).
National Oceanic Atmospheric Administration, NOAA Technical Memorandum NWS
    SR-193 Lightning Fatalities, Injuries, And Damage Reports In The United
    States From 1959-1994. 1997.
    http://www.nssl.noaa.gov/papers/techmemos/NWS-SR-193/techmemo-sr193-
    3.html#section3a. (19 Feb 2005).
National Weather Service Southern Region, Florida Lightning Statistics.
    http://www.srh.noaa.gov/mlb/holtgstats.html. (18 Feb 2005).

State Library and Archives of Florida. 2002 Library Directory with Statistics Circulation and Borrowers Table. 2002.
   http://dlis.dos.state.fl.us/bld/Research_Office/2002LibraryDirectory/table8.pdf. (21 Nov 2004)
State Library and Archives of Florida. 2002 Library Directory with Statistics Collections Table. 2002.
   http://dlis.dos.state.fl.us/bld/Research_Office/2002LibraryDirectory/table7.pdf. (21 Nov 2004).
United States Department of Agriculture Economic Research Service. County-Level Unemployment and Median Household Income for Florida. 2006.
   http://www.ers.usda.gov/Data/Unemployment/RDList2.asp?ST=FL. (4 June 2006).
U.S. Census Bureau. Florida Quick Facts. 2004.
   http://quickfacts.census.gov/qfd/states/12000.html. (11 Oct 2004).
U.S. Census Bureau. GCT- PH1 Population, Housing Units, Area, and Density: 2000. 2000. http://factfinder.census.gov. (28 Nov 2005).
U.S. Census Bureau. 1997 Survey of Minority Owned Business Enterprises. 1997. http://www.census.gov/prod/ec97/e97cs-1.pdf. (29 Nov 2004).

Wetlands: Marshes and Swamps in Florida

Bransilver, Connie, and Larry W. Richardson. *Florida's Unsung Wilderness: The Swamps*. Englewood, Colorado: Westcliffe Publishers, 2000.
Larson, Ron. *Swamp Song: A Natural History of Florida's Swamps*. Gainesville, Florida: University Press of Florida, 1995.
National Audubon Society. Saving Wetlands: A Citizen's Guide for Action in Florida. 1991. http://www.audubonofflorida.org/main/wetlands/chp2.htm. (19 Feb 2005).
National Audubon Society. Saving Wetlands: A Citizen's Guide for Action in Florida. 1991. http://www.audubonofflorida.org/main/wetlands/chp3.htm. (19 Feb 2005).
University of Florida, Plant Management in Florida Waters - Swamps. 2003.
   http://aquat1.ifas.ufl.edu/guide/swamps.html#swamptypes. (18 Nov 2005).

Graphic References

National Oceanic Atmospheric Administration, Lightning Photo.
   http://www.photolib.noaa.gov/collections.html.
Social Change Media, Southern Sydney Waste Planning and Management Board.
   http://media.socialchange.net.au/recycling. Sydney, Australia.
State Library and Archives of Florida, http://ibistro.dos.state.fl.us
U.S. Department of Agriculture, ARS Image Gallery www.ars.usda.gov/is/graphics/photos/dec04/k11622-1.htm. U.S. Department of Agriculture, Washington, DC.
US Fish and Wildlife Service/Bob Savannah. http://www.fws.gov/pictures/lineart/bobsavannah U.S. Fish and Wildlife Service, Washington, DC.
US Fish and Wildlife Service/Bob Hines. http://www.fws.gov/pictures/lineart/bobhines U.S. Fish and Wildlife Service, Washington, DC 20242.

Sunshine State Standards Benchmark Index

The Sunshine State Standards may be found online at
http://www.firn.edu/doe/curric/prek12/index.html

Index

The numbers refer to the relevant questions.

Photo and illustration credits

Courtesy of the Florida State Archives: pages 4, 103, 121, 140, 142, 172, 211
By Julia Andrews: pages 1, 72, 85, 95
By Deanna Brennen: pages 134, 136
By Elizabeth Jurado: pages 14, 127, 131, 156
From U.S. Fish and Wildlife Service, Bob Hines: page 50
From U.S. Fish and Wildlife Service, Bob Savannah: pages 102, 189